Immanent Critiques

Also by Martin Jay

The Dialectical Imagination: A History of the Frankfurt School and the Institute of Social Research, 1923–1950 (1973 and 1996)

Marxism and Totality: The Adventures of a Concept from Lukács to Habermas (1984)

Adorno (1984)

Permanent Exiles: Essays on the Intellectual Migration from Germany to America (1985)

Fin de Siècle Socialism and Other Essays (1988)

Force Fields: Between Intellectual History and Cultural Critique (1993)

Downcast Eyes: The Denigration of Vision in Twentieth-Century French Thought (1993)

Cultural Semantics: Keywords of Our Time (1998)

Refractions of Violence (2003)

La Crisis de la experiencia en la era postsubjetiva, ed. Eduardo Sabrovsky (2003)

Songs of Experience: Modern American and European Variations on a Universal Theme (2005)

The Virtues of Mendacity: On Lying in Politics (2010)

Essays from the Edge: Parerga and Paralipomena (2011)

Kracauer l'exilé (2014)

Reason after Its Eclipse: On Late Critical Theory (2016)

Splinters in Your Eye: Frankfurt School Provocations (2020)

Trois Études sur Adorno (2021)

Genesis and Validity: The Theory and Practice of Intellectual History (2022)

Utopía y Dialéctica: Ensayos sobre Herbert Marcuse (2023)

Immanent Critiques
The Frankfurt School under Pressure

Martin Jay

VERSO
London • New York

First published by Verso 2023
© Martin Jay 2023
Author and publisher extend their gratitude to the publications where these essays originally appeared, details of which are provided in the acknowledgments.

1 3 5 7 9 10 8 6 4 2

Verso
UK: 6 Meard Street, London W1F 0EG
US: 388 Atlantic Avenue, Brooklyn, NY 11217
versobooks.com

Verso is the imprint of New Left Books

ISBN-13: 978-1-80429-252-5
ISBN-13: 978-1-80429-254-9 (UK EBK)
ISBN-13: 978-1-80429-253-2 (US EBK)

British Library Cataloguing in Publication Data
A catalogue record for this book is available from the British Library

Library of Congress Cataloging-in-Publication Data

Names: Jay, Martin, 1944– author.
Title: Immanent critiques : the Frankfurt School under pressure / Martin
  Jay.
Description: London ; New York : Verso, 2023. | Includes bibliographical
  references and index.
Identifiers: LCCN 2023019886 (print) | LCCN 2023019887 (ebook) | ISBN
  9781804292525 (paperback) | ISBN 9781804292532 (ebk)
Subjects: LCSH: Frankfurt School of sociology. | Critical theory.
Classification: LCC HM467 .J388 2023 (print) | LCC HM467 (ebook) | DDC
  301.01—dc23/eng/20230513
LC record available at https://lccn.loc.gov/2023019886
LC ebook record available at https://lccn.loc.gov/2023019887

Typeset in Minion by Hewer Text UK Ltd, Edinburgh
Printed and bound by CPI Group (UK) Ltd, Croydon CR0 4YY

For the Institut für Sozialforschung
on the centenary of its founding

Contents

Introduction

From its earliest efforts to distinguish "critical" from "traditional" theory, the Frankfurt School struggled to formulate a viable justification or ground for its normative judgments. No longer content to identify with the "standpoint" of the proletariat, whether empirical or ascribed, and wary of traditional Marxist claims of "scientific" objectivity, its members were also reluctant to wager on the putatively emancipatory course of "world history" as a plausible alternative.[1] They turned instead to a mélange of alternatives provided by metaphysics, art, the utopian imagination and occasionally even theology. But, as historical materialists, they were also wary of alleged norms that hovered above the world in an ideal sphere that transcended specific circumstances, in particular those of their own fraught era. The tradition of critique from Kant to Marx had, after all, rejected dogmatic assertions of eternal truths, demanding instead an exploration of the theoretical unconscious of allegedly "self-evident" ideas and universal values, as well as—at least in the case of Marxist ideology critique—their concrete historical preconditions.

---

1 At times, the difficulty of establishing a firm "ground" or "foundation" led the first generation to question the very need to seek one. See Martin Jay, "Ungrounded: Horkheimer and the Founding of the Frankfurt School," in *Splinters in Your Eye: Frankfurt School Provocations* (London: Verso, 2020). Later generations of the School, however, were dissatisfied with what seemed a weak version of crypto-normativity and once again sought positive justifications for critique.

Reducing ideas to nothing but reflections of those preconditions, however, risked robbing them of their critical force, turning them into little more than expressions of the particular interests or emotional needs of those who generated, adopted and defended them. From the very beginning, the Frankfurt School vigorously distinguished its position from the relentless relativism of the sociology of knowledge, which turned all norms into mere perspectival expressions of partial interests.[2] As Adorno cautioned in *Minima Moralia*,

> Meaning is never free from its genesis, and it would be easy to show the trace of injustice, sentimentality, and frustrated and therefore doubly poisonous interest in everything which overlays or mediates that which is material. Yet if one wished to act radically on this insight, one would uproot all that is true along with everything untrue, everything which, however powerlessly, dares to try to escape the demesne of universal praxis, indeed all the chimerical anticipations of a worthier state of affairs, and would thereby fall back into that barbarism which one reproaches culture for mediating.[3]

Ironically, the same warning was later directed to Adorno himself by Jürgen Habermas, who worried that critical leverage was inadvertently lost through the overly aggressive critique of rationality in *Dialectic of Enlightenment*.[4]

To avoid the Scylla of transcendent, ahistorical dogmatism and the Charybdis of reductive ideology critique, members of the Frankfurt

---

2 See Martin Jay, "The Frankfurt School's Critique of Karl Mannheim and the Sociology of Knowledge," in *Permanent Exiles: Essays on the Intellectual Migration from Germany to America* (New York: Columbia University Press, 1985).

3 Theodor W. Adorno, *Minima Moralia: Reflections from Damaged Life*, trans. E. F. N. Jephcott (London: NLB, 1974), pp. 43–4.

4 Jürgen Habermas, *The Philosophical Discourse of Modernity*, trans. Frederick Lawrence (Cambridge, MA: MIT Press, 1987), where he claims that "the suspicion of ideology becomes *total*, but without any change of direction. It is turned not only against the irrational function of bourgeois ideals but against the rational potential of bourgeois culture itself, and thus it reaches into the foundation of any ideology critique that proceeds immanently . . . Now reason itself is suspected of the baneful confusion of power and validity claims, but still with the intent of enlightenment" (p. 118). For an argument that reason should be understood as both immanent and transcendent, see Rainer Forst, *Normativity and Power: Analyzing Social Orders of Justification*, trans. Ciaran Cronin (Oxford: Oxford University Press, 2017), Introduction.

School often turned to what became known as the method of "immanent critique" to generate normative impetus from an examination of
the tension between the expressed ideals of a society and its actual
performance. By pitting the self-understandings of historical actors
against their practical actions, or, put more impersonally, the professed
values of a culture against the structural obstacles to their implementation, immanent critique provided some distance between the "is" of
empirical reality and the "ought" of a better alternative. Or, more
precisely, it did so through a dialectical interpretation of the contradictions of a historically specific totality rather than a stark opposition
between existing facts and eternal values.

The theory and practice of "immanent critique" has generated a
substantial commentary of its own, which has ranged from debating its
putative origins in Hegel's dialectics to its current status as a plausible
source of normative judgment.[5] Walter Benjamin's introduction of the
method in his 1919 dissertation, "The Concept of Criticism in German
Romanticism," has suggested for some its roots in pre-Hegelian aesthetic
theories of work immanence in which artworks were judged according
to the realization of their ideal generic essences.[6] Questions have also

---

5 For examples, see Andrew Buchwalter, "Hegel, Marx, and the Concept of
Immanent Critique," *Journal of the History of Philosophy* 29: 2 (1991); Robert J. Antonio,
"Immanent Critique as the Core of Critical Theory: Its Origins and Developments in
Hegel, Marx and Contemporary Thought," *British Journal of Sociology* 32: 3 (September
1981); Craig Browne, "The End of Immanent Critique," *Journal of European Social
Theory* 11: 1 (2008); Karin de Boer, "Hegel's Conception of Immanent Critique: Its
Sources, Extent and Limit," in *Conceptions of Critique in Modern and Contemporary
Philosophy*, ed. Ruth Sonderegger and Karin de Boer (Houndmills, UK: Palgrave,
Macmillan, 2012); Titus Stahl, *Immanente Kritik. Elemente einer Theorie sozialer
Praktiken* (Frankfurt: Campus, 2013); James Gordon Finlayson, "Hegel, Adorno and the
Origins of Immanent Criticism," *British Journal for the History of Philosophy* 22: 6 (2014);
Alexei Procyshyn, "The Conditions of Immanent Critique," *Critical Horizons*, 23: 1
(2019); Michael A. Becker, "On Immanent Critique in Hegel's Philosophy," *Hegel Bulletin*
41: 2 (2020); Sanford Diehl, "Why Immanent Critique?" *European Journal of Philosophy*
30: 2 (June 2022). It should also be noted that the priority of immanence to transcendence
has been a leitmotif of non-Hegelian philosophy from Spinoza to Deleuze, but Critical
Theory did not draw on this version of it.

6 Walter Benjamin, "The Concept of Criticism in German Romanticism," in
Selected Writings, vol. 1, 1913–1926, ed. Marcus Bullock and Michael W. Jennings
(Cambridge, MA: Harvard University Press, 1996), where he uses the term to oppose
criticism based both on the criterion of external rules and on subjective judgments: "Not
only did Schlegel's concept of criticism achieve freedom from heteronomous aesthetic
doctrines, but it made this freedom possible in the first place by setting up for artworks

been raised about the relationship between the idea of an objective social or economic contradiction, on which Marxism traditionally depended, and the contradiction between ideals and practices, which foregrounds more subjective factors. The viability of immanent critique in a society which has somehow occluded or even suspended contradictions of either kind—a state of affairs implied by Marcuse's notion of a "one-dimensional society" and Adorno's concept of a "totally administered world"—was also tacitly challenged by Adorno himself, implying the need for transcendent values.[7] And the practical impact of exposing whichever immanent contradictions might still be located has also been called into question, as exposure alone has rarely motivated the collective action that would fuel successful change.

And yet despite these qualms, "immanent critique" has remained a potent weapon in the search to find a normative foundation for a theory determined to be critical, largely because of the multiple ways it can be interpreted and applied. It might mean, as it did for Hegel, an appreciation of the gap between an object and its concept. Expressed in the somewhat different idiom that contrasts appearances and essences, it suggests that existing objects or phenomena, the factual "givens" of the

---

a criterion other than the rule—namely, the criterion of an immanent structure specific to the work itself" (p. 155). For an excellent discussion, see John McCole, *Walter Benjamin and the Antinomies of Tradition* (Ithaca, NY: Cornell University Press, 1993), chapter 2. The term "work immanence" was popular in postwar Germany as an antidote to the overly politicized aesthetics of the Nazi era, but it lacked the strong critical impulse that Benjamin had found in the Romantics. The distinction between the immanence and transcendence of an artwork was also posited by Gérard Genette, in *The Work of Art: Immanence and Transcendence*, trans. G. M. Goshgarian (Ithaca, NY: Cornell University Press, 1997), but with different meanings.

7   Perhaps the most frequently cited expression of a retreat from immanent critique comes in Adorno's remarks on the crisis of irony in *Minima Moralia*: "Irony's medium, the difference between ideology and reality, has disappeared. The former resigns itself to confirmation of reality by its mere duplication . . . There is not a crevice in the cliff of the established order into which the ironist might hook a fingernail" (p. 211). It has sometimes been argued that Habermas, tacitly recognizing this problem, sought ways to restore transcendent (or at least "quasi-transcendental") standards, be they the anthropological "interests" in knowledge, meaning and emancipation he posited in *Knowledge and Human Interests*, trans. Jeremy J. Shapiro (Boston: Beacon, 1971) or as the telos of rational communicative interaction in his later work. But the latter can also be seen as still inspired by immanent critique in the sense that the norm of rational consensus is implied pragmatically in communicative interaction. See Titus Stahl, "Habermas and the Project of Immanent Critique," *Constellations* 20: 4 (2013).

world as it is, do not exhaust their unrealized possibilities.[8] Actuality, we might say, is not yet what it might potentially become. Norms are thus not abstractions hovering above the world, but always already latent in it as determinate negations dialectically intertwined in a concrete, complexly mediated totality with their positive, but imperfect manifestations. The latter, we might say with a little anthropomorphic license, feel "self-dissatisfaction" with their unrealized potential.[9]

These formulations may, however, seem too beholden to an idealist relational holism or dependent on a questionable slippage of "contradiction" from a logical to an ontological category, even if the latter is understood in historical rather than universal terms. If so, "immanent critique" can also be understood as overlapping with what philosophers call "performative contradictions."[10] Here, the tension can be located within speech acts, between their "constative" and "performative" dimensions, the first stating facts about the world, the second seeking to change it. For example, if someone asserts that rational communication is inherently impossible, but does so by trying to persuade an opponent through reasoned arguments, there is a performative contradiction between what is being asserted and what is being performed (or at least is intended to be performed). Extended to include more general actions beyond those performed by utterances alone, it is possible to call inconsistencies between what one says and what one does in the world a variant of a performative contradiction, which can then be immanently criticized. Not only applicable to individual speech acts, it can be

---

8   See Herbert Marcuse, "The Concept of Essence," in *Negations: Essays in Critical Theory,* trans. Jeremy J. Shapiro (Boston: Beacon, 1968). He sometimes contrasts essence with existence as well as appearance and argues that, contrary to Platonic and phenomenological usages—Husserl in particular—essences are not timeless. They should be seen as future-oriented possibilities, as Aristotle understood when he tied them to potentiality.

9   See Robert Hullot-Kentor, *Things beyond Resemblance: Collected Essays on Theodor W. Adorno* (New York: Columbia University Press, 2006), p. 230.

10   For a discussion of its importance for Habermas in particular, see Martin Jay, "The Debate over Performative Contradiction: Habermas versus the Poststructuralists," in *Force Fields: Between Intellectual History and Cultural Critique* (New York: Routledge, 1993); and Martin Morris, "On the Logic of the Performative Contradiction: Habermas and the Radical Critique of Reason," *Review of Politics* 58: 4 (1996). For a more general consideration, see José Antonio Errázuriz, "The Performative Contradiction as an Argumentative Device: An Analysis of Its Reach and Scope," *Logique et Analyse* 57: 225 (2014).

extrapolated to the values or ideologies espoused by communities as well. Thus, if a country calls itself "democratic," but in fact is a one-party dictatorship, it is open to the charge of failing to perform in accord with what it claims to be. In simpler terms, hypocrisy is an inviting target of immanent critique, however much it may also be taxed for violating a transcendent principle that posits sincerity and honesty as inherent values in themselves.

In these usages, immanent critique contrasts a laudable goal with its imperfect realization, for instance, when the countries calling themselves the "free world" are shown to be still riven with palpable forms of servitude. But conversely, it can also suggest questioning a concept, essence or norm to determine whether or not it contains inherent contradictions in itself or in its usages over time and in multiple contexts. The critique reveals that it is a palimpsest of different, perhaps even conflicting meanings—"freedom," for example, as negative "freedom from" and positive "freedom to"[11]—or exposes its tensions with other normative goals within a social or cultural complex. Thus, to take one example of the latter, the norm of aesthetic autonomy, which has served ever since the nineteenth century to celebrate the liberation of artistic expression from its religious, political or social constraints, can also be open to critique when it justifies unfeeling indifference to ethical questions or the struggle for social justice. Or, to put it in somewhat more abstract terms, the benefits of the differentiation of a cultural sphere called the aesthetic from other spheres of human endeavor, such as the economic, the religious or the political, may need to be balanced against the costs of overly specialized institutions becoming increasingly alienated from the integrated experiences of everyday life.

And finally, immanent critique may mean pitting certain practices or institutions in a society against others, rather than just against the ideals they fail to realize, and showing that one may undermine the proper functioning of the other. Thus, to use Habermas's terminology, the "colonization" of one value sphere by another—say, the aesthetic by the economic logic of commodity exchange, or that of discursive

---

11   For a recent account of this distinction, see Annelien de Dijn, *Freedom: An Unruly History* (Cambridge, MA: Harvard University Press, 2020). For an immanent critique of the idea of freedom showing how its practical application was racially inflected, see Tyler Stovall, *White Freedom: The Racial History of an Idea* (Princeton, NJ: Princeton University Press, 2021).

deliberation in a democracy by the transactional values of strategic rationality in the market—may be challenged by contrasting it with the norm of a functional equilibrium of spheres. Here the critique is directed against the "pathological" hypertrophy of one value sphere in a differentiated society whose norm would be a healthy balance rather than the imperial triumph of one over the others. Of course, it is also possible to challenge that irenic goal when the norms of each sphere themselves cry out for critical reflection.

All of these versions of immanent critique have found their way at one time or another into the Frankfurt School's normative arsenal. But they have also often been qualified by one significant reservation.[12] The telos of perfect consistency between object and concept, appearance and essence, or constative and performative dimensions of speech acts, which is the implied normative standard of all versions of immanent critique, can itself be open to question based on a different norm. The variant of Critical Theory that Adorno called "negative dialectics" pursued this path by valuing "non-identity," which challenged the assumption that total reconciliation or the full actualization of potentiality was inherently emancipatory. "The task of dialectical cognition," Adorno insisted, "is not, as its adversaries like to charge, to construe contradictions from above and to progress by resolving them—although Hegel's logic, now and again, proceeds in this fashion. Instead, it is up to dialectical cognition to pursue the inadequacy of thought and thing, to experience it in the thing."[13] Or, to put it in somewhat different terms, the Hegelian logic of the self-actualization of the concept in a reconciled totality was itself no more than an allegorical displacement of what Marx had understood as the nefarious imperative of the capitalist value-form to permeate all corners of social reality, and as such should be vigorously resisted.

Preserving the integrity of the "non-conceptual" object (or the non-conceptual resources of language like metaphor) against the overly constitutive power of the conceptualizing subject—or the social subject that is "capital"—should thus itself be construed normatively for contesting the domination of otherness through epistemological subsumption

---

12 What follows builds on the argument in "Ungrounded," pp. 4–5.

13 Theodor W. Adorno, *Negative Dialectics*, trans. E. B. Ashton (New York: Continuum, 1973), p. 153.

or ontological sublation.[14] But because upholding that norm is derived from a transcendent intuition (Herbert Schnädelbach once called Adorno "a noetic of the non-identical"[15]) rather than from the values of a specific culture, the implication of honoring it is that "immanent critique," however necessary, can never be sufficient. In fact, carried to an extreme, it may lead to the inadvertent realization of what it purports to be resisting, for, as Adorno argued, "the limit of immanent critique is that the law of the immanent context is ultimately one with the delusion that has to be overcome."[16] Or, to put it differently, the negative dialectic of transcendent and immanent critique is inherently unreconcilable, with each compensating for the inadequacies of the other without the prospect of a full overcoming of their differences. Accordingly, despite all their debts to Hegel and for all their utopian yearnings, the Frankfurt School did not seek a positive dialectical sublation (*Aufhebung*) of all contradictions, which was the implicit aim of immanent critique taken to its logical end.

A great deal more can be said about the strengths and limitations of immanent critique, but I want now to pivot to its relevance in introducing the essays that follow. They are all to one degree or another concerned with the group of thinkers that has come to be called "the Frankfurt School," which has now extended over at least three generations and been developed in contexts well beyond the German and American locations of their original members.[17] Before trying to present its program and narrate its history, we have to pause to consider its own vulnerability to

---

14   For a discussion, see Martin Jay, "Adorno and Blumenberg: Nonconceptuality and the *Bilderverbot*," in *Splinters in Your Eye*.

15   Herbert Schnädelbach, "Dialektik als Vernunftkritik: Zur Konstruktion des Rationalen bei Adorno," in *Adorno-Konferenz 1983*, ed. Ludwig von Friedeburg and Jürgen Habermas (Frankfurt: Suhrkamp, 1983), p. 75. A similar critique of Horkheimer's embrace of non-identity as a "transhistorical absolute" is leveled by George W. Shea IV in "Postmetaphysical Conundrums: The Problematic Return to Metaphysics in Horkheimer's Critique of Instrumental Reason," *New German Critique*, no. 144 (November 2021), p. 26.

16   Adorno, *Negative Dialectics*, p. 182.

17   There has also been considerable discussion about the relationship between the Institut für Sozialforschung, which over its century-long history included members and pursued projects that were not always informed by Critical Theory, and "the Frankfurt School," as its leading figures came to be called only after they returned to Germany from their American exile. In addition, the precise relationship between the work of other intellectuals in its larger orbit—for example, Siegfried Kracauer, Karl Korsch and Ernst Bloch—and the School has also occasioned substantial commentary.

immanent critique. That is, we have to acknowledge that the very image of a unified "school," implying hierarchical discipline and a body of canonical teachings, may itself suggest a certain hypostatization warranting critical reflection. For commentators, myself included, who have sought to provide synoptic accounts of their legacy, it has indeed been difficult to avoid homogenizing their work into a more or less coherent system, emblematized by the shorthand brand name "Critical Theory." The pressure to present a systematic, even "orthodox" version of their ideas has exerted a centripetal force, which has even led some critics to lament the reification of the School into an overly unified monolith.[18]

But insofar as one of the targets of Critical Theory was itself reification,[19] its adherents were acutely aware of that very danger, and those who have commented on their legacy have often been as well. A contrary, centrifugal impulse has thus also been at play in the development and reception of their ideas, which is best captured by metaphors like Wittgenstein's "family resemblances," Walter Benjamin's "constellation" or Adorno's "force field" to characterize their dynamic interactions, including both their overlapping congruities and their manifest tensions. It has thus been possible to retain the label, as we will do here, while recognizing both the commonalities and differences among the figures who are commonly associated with it.

In addition, from the beginning the ambiguous meaning of the term "Critical Theory" has also been recognized.[20] It is generally assumed to

---

18 Thus, for example, Kurt Newman writes: "It was precisely the work of thinkers like Fredric Jameson, Martin Jay, Susan Buck-Morss, and others—all Epistemic Leftists, to my mind—that led to the reification, if I can be forgiven that turn of phrase, or even hypostatization of the 'Frankfurt School' that we today speak about." "The Putative Left: Immanent Critique and the Intellectual History of Theory," US Intellectual History Blog, September 28, 2106, s-usih.org.

19 Precisely what this term meant was itself a source of considerable debate. For an early attempt to distinguish its usage in Adorno from that of Hegelian Marxists like Lukács, see Gillian Rose, The Melancholy Science: An Introduction to the Thought of Theodor W. Adorno (New York: Columbia University Press, 1978). For a more recent attempt to redefine the concept, see Axel Honneth, Reification: A New Look at an Old Idea, with commentaries by Judith Butler, Raymond Geuss and Jonathan Lear, ed. Martin Jay (Oxford: Oxford University Press, 2008).

20 The first thematic use of the term can be found in Max Horkheimer's "Traditional and Critical Theory," which first appeared in the Institute's Zeitschrift für Sozialforschung 6: 2 (1937). Its English translation appeared in his collection Critical Theory: Selected Essays, trans. Matthew J. O'Connell (New York: Continuum, 1972).

have been introduced without the intention of designating a distinct method, but rather as an Aesopian euphemism for the Marxism that the Frankfurt School had been reluctant to trumpet in its precarious American exile from Nazi Germany.[21] Ironically, some critics on the left, disappointed that the Frankfurt School did not proclaim its Marxist credentials more forthrightly, and other detractors on the right, charging it with masking its sinister political agenda, have remained convinced that the new label still remains little more than a smokescreen for that original point of departure.

But for those acknowledging both the continuities and discontinuities between Critical Theory and traditional Marxism, and I would count myself in their number, the story of its development and dissemination has been narrated as one of increasing, if never completed, autonomy from its roots in historical materialism understood both as a self-sufficient theory and as the inspiration for radical practice. To be sure, efforts have been periodically made to demonstrate the abiding power of its origins,[22] whose effects can still be seen even in its most recent iterations.[23] But the Frankfurt School's eclectic openness to non-Marxist theoretical traditions has even more frequently been accounted a source of its continuing vitality. As a result, later generations of the tradition, exemplified by Habermas, Albrecht Wellmer, Axel Honneth, Seyla Benhabib, Christoph Menke and Rainer Forst, have usually escaped banishment for "betraying" the Marxist militancy of the first generation, but rather been included in a "broad church" definition of the tradition, which eschews attempts to distinguish between orthodox and heretical adherents. Others, like Oskar Negt, Alexander Kluge and Detlev Claussen, who continued the militant traditions of the student movement and were less willing to give up entirely on proletarian radicalism than Habermas and his progeny,

---

21   This caution, it should be acknowledged, was apparent even earlier in the choice of the innocuous title of the Institute over the more explicit "Institute of Marxism" that was considered at the time. This decision has been seized on with particular relish by right-wing critics of "cultural Marxism," who see the Frankfurt School as the origin of all that is nefarious in modern culture.

22   See, for example, Charles Andrew Prusik, *Adorno and Neoliberalism: The Critique of Exchange Society* (London: Bloomsbury, 2020), which stresses the essential role of the Marxist critique of commodity fetishism in Adorno's work.

23   See, for example, Axel Honneth, *The Idea of Socialism: Towards a Renewal*, trans. Joseph Ganahl (Cambridge: Polity, 2017).

have also remained respected voices in the ongoing debates over the future of Critical Theory.

The rationale behind such a capacious attitude, to come back to the question of immanent critique, is that, from the onset, the Frankfurt School's critical energies have been directed not only to the external world it hoped to change, but also to its own theoretical assumptions and methodological procedures. Empirical investigations to expand and test its theories, albeit with reservations about their positivist affinities, were initially intended to harmonize with them, but ultimately led to the modification of the initial model of integrated interdisciplinary research launched when Horkheimer became the Institute's director.[24] For all its debts to Hegelian dialectics, Critical Theory did not entirely scorn competing insights derived from Kant, Schelling, Schopenhauer and Nietzsche, as well as non-philosophers like Freud and Weber. Subsequent generations were even more willing to draw on a welter of different sources, ranging from linguistics, philosophical anthropology and pragmatist philosophy to systems theory and object-relations psychology. The result has been that "Critical Theory," which from the beginning developed through critiques of other philosophical systems rather than positing one of its own, has itself become a dense network of sometimes reinforcing, sometimes clashing, ideas, methods and normative investments that do not congeal into a self-sufficient, fully coherent body of thought. As such, it has cried out for the exercise of what might be called immanent *self*-critique, acknowledging its own fissures and uncertainties, confronting its own blind spots and internal conflicts.

In so doing, its members and their sympathetic commentators have wrestled with issues that go well beyond the righteous indignation expressed by some of their critics about the alleged contradiction between sympathy for the oppressed and a relatively comfortable lifestyle.[25] This reproach, often coming from intellectuals who accepted the

---

24   See Helmut Dubiel, *Theory and Politics: Studies in the Development of Critical Theory*, trans. Benjamin Gregg (Cambridge, MA: MIT Press, 1985); and Martin Jay, "Positive and Negative Totalities: Tensions in Critical Theory's Vision of Interdisciplinary Research," in *Permanent Exiles*.

25   The obvious point should be made that narrowly escaping into exile and watching with agony as the Holocaust turned them into lucky survivors (and, as the tragic end of Walter Benjamin shows, not always that) cannot be equated with living comfortably.

discipline of political parties, was typified by Lukács's now familiar accusation that the Frankfurt School lived in "the grand hotel abyss" and Brecht's excoriation of them as "tui-intellectuals" who benefited from the generosity of a wealthy man who was himself the problem they were seeking to remedy. Emanating from *engagé* militants, often proud Communists who thought they were grounded in a working-class movement that successfully combined theory and practice, this accusation lost much of its power when that movement's own contradictions became fully apparent. That is, the gap between ideals and reality which undermined "actually existing socialist regimes" meant that their defenders were themselves no less vulnerable to immanent critique understood in this reductive way.[26] In comparison, the Frankfurt School had the advantage of frankly acknowledging from the beginning the impossibility of living the right way in a wrong world.[27]

We might say, to put it somewhat differently, that its members acknowledged the necessity of applying immanent critique from within, rather than waiting for it to be imposed from the outside by their opponents, thus putting pressure on the premises and results of their own work as well as on the external objects of their critical gaze. The exercises included in this volume were directly or indirectly conceived in the spirit of that effort. They are written, it should be confessed, by a commentator who has long been associated with presenting and promoting the Frankfurt School legacy, a task first attempted over fifty years ago in the doctoral dissertation that became *The Dialectical Imagination*.[28] Graciously introduced by Max Horkheimer and benefiting from the cooperation of Friedrich Pollock, Leo Löwenthal, Erich

---

26 See, for example, Andrew Arato, "Immanent Critique and Authoritarian Socialism," *Canadian Journal of Political and Social Theory* 7: 1–2 (1983). Herbert Marcuse's *Soviet Marxism: A Critical Analysis* (New York: Columbia University Press, 1958) also drew on immanent critique to tax the Soviet Union with failing to realize its theoretical potential.

27 The locus classicus of this claim was the often repeated remark of Adorno in *Minima Moralia*: "Es gibt kein richtiges Leben im falschen" ("Wrong life cannot be lived rightly," in Jephcott's translation).

28 Martin Jay, *The Dialectical Imagination: A History of the Frankfurt School and the Institute of Social Research, 1923–50* (Boston: Little, Brown, 1973); a second edition appeared with an extensive new preface in 1996 with the University of California Press, which is still in print. It has been translated into Japanese, Spanish, French, German, Italian, Dutch, Chinese, Indonesian, Portuguese, Greek, Turkish, Korean, Serbo-Croatian and Persian.

Fromm, Felix Weil, Paul Lazarsfeld and other surviving figures involved with the Institute's history, it was an essentially sympathetic reconstruction of the period from 1923 to 1950. It was followed by attempts to flesh out its narrative through thicker contextualizations—situating the history of Horkheimer and his colleagues in that of the intellectual migration from Germany to America and in the larger story of Western Marxism—and more focused attention on the intellectual trajectories of specific figures.[29]

But intellectual historians, no matter how charitable they may feel towards the people whose legacies they seek to reconstruct, are not press secretaries. *The Dialectical Imagination* was in no way intended as an apologetic court history, and did not hesitate to express reservations about certain of the Frankfurt School's positions when they were warranted. In fact, at the 1969 Socialist Scholars Conference I had already voiced reservations about the "metapolitics of utopianism" in the work of Herbert Marcuse.[30] Although the book was generally taken as a sympathetic account, a few militant followers of Critical Theory faulted it for historicizing Critical Theory in an elegiac mood rather than directly attempting to apply it to current problems.[31] Over the years, when I returned to examine aspects of

29 Martin Jay, *Marxism and Totality: The Adventures of a Concept from Lukács to Habermas* (Berkeley: University of California Press, 1984); *Adorno* (London: Fontana, 1984); *Permanent Exiles*; and as editor, *An Unmastered Past: The Autobiographical Reflections of Leo Lowenthal* (Berkeley: University of California Press, 1987).

30 The talk was published as "Metapolitics of Utopianism," *Dissent* (July/August 1970); reprinted as "How Utopian Is Marcuse?" in *The Revival of American Socialism*, ed. George Fischer (New York: Oxford University Press, 1971), and in *Permanent Exiles*.

31 This charge was most notably made by Douglas Kellner, Russell Jacoby and Gillian Rose. For an account of the response to the book, see Robert Zwarg, *Die Kritische Theorie in Amerika: Das Nachleben einer Tradition* (Göttingen: Vandenhoeck and Ruprecht, 2017). It would be impossible to acknowledge all of the subsequent historical studies by an international cohort of scholars, who have drawn on many sources not available to me to enrich or modify my narrative and revise at least some of my conclusions, but let me list only a few: Susan Buck-Morss, Rolf Wiggershaus, Gérard Raulet, Alfons Söllner, Richard Wolin, Barry Katz, James Schmidt, David Kettler, Thomas Wheatland, David Jenemann, Detlev Claussen, Stefan Müller-Doohm, Wolfgang Bonß, John Abromeit, Peter-Erwin Jansen, Philipp Lenhard, Alex Demerović, Peter Gordon, Manfred Gangl, Lars Rensmann, Jeanette Erazo Heufelder, Stuart Jeffries, Jack Jacobs, Howard Eiland, Michael Jennings, Nicola Emery, Daniel Burston, Joan Braune, Lawrence Friedman, Rainer Funk and Hans-Peter Gruber.

the School's legacy, it was always with a least a modicum of critical distance.[32]

Consistent with this practice, the essays that follow can be broadly construed as inspired by the Frankfurt School's model of immanent self-critique. That is, they put pressure on aspects of its legacy, often by invoking others that are in tension with them.[33] They do so by drawing on lessons learned through almost a lifetime of reading and rereading works by members of the School, as well as a decent sampling of the now astonishingly voluminous literature that has accumulated around them. Rather than judging its arguments from an allegedly superior position outside of the tradition, I have assumed that there is enough ammunition within it to combat both theoretical dogmatism and relativist despair. And there is also sufficient warrant to hope that wrestling with its legacy will contribute, however indirectly and with whatever delay, to keeping the gathering darkness at bay.

---

32   See, for example, Martin Jay, *Reason after Its Eclipse: On Late Critical Theory* (Madison: University of Wisconsin Press, 2016), which expresses reservations about the first generation's attempt to formulate a viable concept of substantive reason.

33   The challenges of "inheriting a legacy," in particular in that of the Frankfurt School, have been addressed in *MLN* 133: 3 (April 2018), edited by Kristina Mendicino and Gerhard Richter.

1
1968 in an Expanded Field: The Frankfurt School and the Uneven Course of History

Despite the distinction it drew between traditional theories that validated the status quo and critical ones that sought to change it, the Frankfurt School has always struggled to bridge the gap between radical theory and transformative praxis. The difficulties were perhaps never as evident as when its leaders were challenged by the demands of militant students inspired by that theory to embrace their cause in the turbulent year 1968. Reflecting a half-century later on the popular historical narrative that has been fashioned from that fraught encounter—that Marcuse, true to the radical origins of Critical Theory, had more courage than Horkheimer and Adorno in siding with the students—this essay seeks to complicate it by drawing on alternative models of historical reconstruction.

Following Benjamin's lead (refracted through the art critic Rosalind Krauss's notion of an "expanded field"), it argues against narrating history as a unified, unidirectional story based on hinge moments in favor of reconstructing it as a dynamic constellation that brings past(s) and present together in unexpected ways. By putting 1968 in a tense relationship with 1967, the year of the Six-Day War in the Middle East, and 1945, when the Holocaust, which the Frankfurt School had narrowly escaped, finally ended, it seeks to illuminate the sources of their often lamented indifference to the emancipatory potential of anti-colonial struggles outside of Europe and America. Without ignoring the costs of that neglect, it concludes that their sensitivity to the dangers of an Israeli defeat in 1967 helped immunize them against some of the more dubious effects of roman-ticizing the Third World.[1]

In the early winter of 1971, Herbert Marcuse visited Jerusalem as a guest of the Van Leer Foundation, giving talks in Haifa and Beersheba as well.[2] In addition to his academic encounters, he requested and was granted a meeting with the Israeli defense minister, Moshe Dayan, on December 29.[3] They discussed, among other things, possible negotiations between Israel and Egypt in the aftermath of the Six-Day War, a two-state solution to the conflict based on an Israeli withdrawal from the occupied territories, and the chances of a new violent conflict unless Israel did so. Marcuse solicited from Dayan an admission that Israel had originally seized land that belonged to the Palestinians but admitted, in turn, that in the recent war Israel did "nothing wrong" in defending its existence. In passing, Marcuse expressed concern about the possible assassination of the Egyptian president Anwar Sadat, should there be only a partial withdrawal from the Sinai Peninsula, a prediction that, alas, soon came true. So, too, did his anxious warning of a new war, which broke out less than two years later.

I begin with this anecdote not to revisit the troubled history of the Middle East in the past half-century, or, at least, not primarily for that reason, but rather to foreground the highly symbolic nature of the unusual encounter between Marcuse, the iconic figure of the New Left who inspired as no one else did the student-led unrest of 1968, and Dayan, the military hero of the decisive Israeli victory in the war that had taken place only a year earlier. In so doing, I want to signal my belief that we need to expand our understanding of the meaning of 1968 to include the seemingly distinct events that transpired in the Middle East the previous year. In this way, we can also enrich our understanding of

---

1   Originally delivered as the keynote to the conference "Kritische Theorie nach '68," organized by Rainer Forst at the Excellence Cluster on "Normative Orders" at the Johann-Wolfgang Goethe University in Frankfurt; it was published in *Critical Horizons* 21: 2 (May 2020).

2   For an account of his visit, see Jack Jacobs, *The Frankfurt School, Jewish Lives, and Antisemitism* (Cambridge: Cambridge University Press, 2015), pp. 117–23.

3   For a record of their discussion, see "Protocol of the Conversation between Philosopher Herbert Marcuse and Minister of Defense Moshe Dayan, December 29, 1971," *Telos*, no. 158 (Spring 2012). For an analysis, see Zvi Tauber, "Herbert Marcuse on the Arab-Israeli Conflict: His Conversation with Moshe Dayan," *Telos*, no. 158 (Spring 2012).

the Critical Theorists' fraught relationship to the German New Left and their differing response to post-colonial struggles. Only by exploring the Frankfurt School's response to the Six-Day War and more generally to the Palestinian cause as a putative placeholder for Third World anti-imperialist struggles can we make sense of the meaning of 1968 a half-century later, and what now seems its relative importance in the drama of global history.

In a conventional sense, to be sure, 1968 has already been situated in temporally and spatially expanded contexts. Historians often argue that its starting point should be more or less put in 1960, when the left wing of the Socialist German Student Union (SDS) broke from the Social Democratic Party (SPD).[4] What is sometimes called "the long 1960s" are understood to have ended only in 1977 and the so-called German Autumn, which led to the turn away from violent struggle symbolized by the collapse of the Red Army Faction and the acceptance of electoral politics by the nascent Green Party. In spatial terms, the generational rebellion *cum* political rupture that has come to be identified with the year 1968 has been sighted in no fewer than thirty-nine countries around the world, with the other major outbreaks located in the United States, France, Italy, Japan and Mexico.[5] Unrest in the Soviet bloc, especially in Czechoslovakia and Poland, has also been understood as part of the larger story. Without situating the German case in the international context of what has been called "the global sixties," it has seemed impossible to understand how heavily influenced it was by cultural and political trends from the outside.

Both of these expansions, however, implicitly posit an essential coherence, either as a diachronic narrative or as a unified synchronic comparison. In the temporal expansion, the story of 1968 is told as a cumulative emergence of transgressive forces that reached a crisis in that year, but then lost its momentum and sputtered into relative impotence a decade

---

4   See, for example, Timothy Scott Brown, *West Germany and the Global Sixties: The Antiauthoritarian Revolt, 1962–1978* (Cambridge: Cambridge University Press, 2013); and Elliot Neaman, *Free Radicals: Agitators, Hippies Urban Guerillas, and Germany's Youth Revolt of the 1960s and 1970s* (Candor, NY: Telos, 2016).

5   See, for example, Philipp Gassert and Martin Klimke, eds., *1968: Memories and Legacies of a Global Revolt* (Washington, DC: German Historical Institute, 2009). See also "*AHR* Reflections: 1968" in several different contexts in *American Historical Review* 123: 3 (June 2018).

later after a paroxysm of futile violence in the German Autumn. Although the maximalist, at times defiantly utopian, goals of the student movement are acknowledged to have been thwarted, much was changed, it is argued, in the political cultures and social mores of the countries where it was most active. The New Left may never have come to power, but the Old Left was largely delegitimized while the rise of new social movements, such as feminism, gay rights, and ecological activism, was accelerated. Although abandoned well before it reached its ultimate goal, the long march through the institutions is credited with leaving important reforms in its wake. And as Tiananmen Square, the Occupy movement and the Arab Spring show, there were also later echoes of some of the mass protest tactics developed by the student movement, albeit in the last two instances with new features aided by the changed social media landscape of the twenty-first century.

In the case of the spatial expansion, the German 1968 has come to be understood as part of a worldwide phenomenon, produced in part by common stimuli, such as opposition to the Vietnam War and genera-tional discontent with outdated university constraints, but also spread by mimetic contagion. Although national variations are of course acknowledged, the common forms of struggle adopted in different countries and the emphasis on youthful, often utopian activism are understood to transcend boundaries. As with temporal expansion, here, too, a more or less unified, coherent account resulted, which stressed the fruitful exchanges and mutual reinforcement that occurred across national boundaries with figures like Daniel Cohn-Bendit serving as their individual embodiment. Perhaps only 1848, which saw unrest in many European countries without full success in any, has been seen as comparable in its international scope to 1968.

What the symbolic juxtaposition of Herbert Marcuse and Moshe Dayan suggests, however, is that another concept of an expanded field is possible now that a half-century has passed, one that is less coherent and harmonious than the ones just described. Positing the stereoscopic or parallax quality of our hindsight, it resists the urge to come into focus as a singular, three-dimensional vision. Although the familiar notion of a force field or constellation introduced by Benjamin and adopted by Adorno is one inspiration for this alternative, another is the celebrated essay "Sculpture in the Expanded Field" by the American art historian and critic Rosalind Krauss, first published in 1979 and included in her collection *The Originality of the Avant-Garde and Other Modernist Myths*.[6] Drawing on the site-specific work of Robert Smithson and Robert Morris, she challenges the traditional notion of a sculpture: "The logic of sculpture, it would seem, is inseparable from the logic of the monument. By virtue of this logic a sculpture is a commemorative representation. It sits in a particular place and speaks in a symbolical tongue about the meaning of that place."[7] Such traditional sculptures are normally figurative, vertical and separated from the surrounding site by the intervention of a pedestal, which functions, in the way a frame does around a painting, to set the object apart.

In the late nineteenth century, Krauss argues, the traditional notion of sculpture began to erode as the mediating function of the pedestal diminished and the object lost its representational character, no longer an inert monument but increasingly a self-referential abstraction. Rather than having positive content, it entered what she calls its "negative condition—a kind of sitelessness, or homelessness, an absolute loss of place."[8] If it could be defined at all, it was more in terms of what it was not, which was preeminently architecture and landscape, than by what it was. Through a series of inversions and combinations, Krauss argued that sculpture should be understood as one term in a dynamic constellation of its apparent opposites, which themselves can be inverted and combined in turn. The details of her argument, which draws on mathematical transformations into Klein groups and structuralist semiotics, need not detain us now. What is important to register are the implications of her expanding an apparently integral object into what she calls "a universe of terms that are felt to be in opposition within a cultural situation."[9]

What disrupts traditional notions of sculpture may also work for historical dates that have been turned into inert monuments. No longer capable of serving as a nodal point of a single coherent narrative or as a marker for parallel events across national borders, "1968" is best understood in a tense relation to "1967." Juxtaposed rather than reconciled, they can only be brought together in a dynamic field of conflicting forces

---

6   Rosalind E. Krauss, *The Originality of the Avant-Garde and Other Modernist Myths* (Cambridge, MA: MIT Press, 1985).

7   Ibid., p. 279.

8   Ibid., p. 280.

9   Ibid., p. 289.

still in play even after a half-century has passed. Reminiscent of Ernst Bloch's notion of non-contemporaneity (*Ungleichzeitigkeit*),[10] but without his faith in the ultimate reconciliation of temporal contradictions, such an approach alerts us to the relativization of what seems to be a punctual moment in a single historical space-time continuum. To understand the role of the Frankfurt School in the German "1968" is therefore also to situate its history in the expanded field that includes the very different events of "1967," which resist incorporation into a unified narrative. It is to register the importance of 1967 in generating its negative relationship to aspects of the German 1968, and in coloring its attitude towards post-colonial struggles and the discourse they have spawned. By expanding the field in this way, we will avoid turning 1968 into an isolated monument on a pedestal that masks its connection to the multiple historical contexts that can set it into motion and help us understand its importance today.

Before attempting to articulate what we mean by this expanded field, we have to acknowledge that the magnetic push and pull of 1967—understood broadly as turmoil in the Middle East—was not entirely lost on the protagonists of 1968. That is, we have to remember that on June 2, 1967, less than a week before the outbreak of the Six-Day War, Benno Ohnesorg was killed by a policeman, many years later revealed as an East German Stasi agent, at a demonstration protesting the visit of the Shah of Iran. The radicalization of the student movement accelerated and intensified by the outrage at this murder was thus intimately entangled with unfolding events in the Middle East, an entanglement that only increased with the bitterly divided response of the movement to the Israeli victory in the war. Prior to the Six-Day War, the West German left, as might be expected in the aftermath of the Holocaust, was hesitant to criticize Israel and its role as a refuge for persecuted Jews. But once the existential threat to Israel seemed over and the problematic occupation of Palestinian lands solidified, that taboo was lifted. The shift became explicit, it is sometimes argued, when a resolution proposed by Günter Grass at an SDS meeting to support the State of Israel's right to exist was defeated.[11] This was a very

---

10   Ernst Bloch, *Heritage of Our Times*, trans. Neville and Stephen Plaice (Cambridge: Polity, 1991).

11   Ulrich Enzensberger, *Die Jahre der Kommune I: 1967–1968* (Cologne: Kiepenheuer und Witsch, 2004), p. 157. The vexed relationship between the German New Left, anti-Zionism and anti-Semitism has been the subject of a substantial literature. See, for

different Günter Grass, it might be noted parenthetically, from the one who in 2012 was to compose the provocative anti-Israeli poem "Was gesagt werden muss" that stirred so much controversy. Although the degree of East German involvement in the process is still much debated, the anti-Zionist stance of the Soviet bloc seems to have had an impact in reinforcing anti-imperialist sentiments in the German left, which often embraced the Palestinian cause with special gusto.[12] What is not, alas, at issue is the troubling tendency of certain anti-imperialist, anti-American and anti-Zionist militants to draw on traditional anti-Semitic prejudices in their zeal to defend that cause. Perhaps the most blatant of these was Dieter Kunzelmann, who emerged from the German wing of the Situationists, the SPUR, to become a leading figure in the Kommune I in Berlin and an outspoken critic of what he called the philo-Semitic "*Judenknax*" (Jewish neurosis) that induced postwar Germany to pay reparations to Israel. Because the Israeli cause was supported by the Americans and the Springer Press in West Germany, it was easy for Kunzelmann and his ilk to see it as a pillar of the hated status quo.

At the fringes of what became known as the extra-parliamentary movement (APO) were groups that matched rhetoric with action, including in certain cases lethal violence. Among the most notorious of these was the West Berlin Tupamaros, named after the Uruguayan

example, Martin W. Kloke, *Israel und die deutsche Linke: Zur Geschichte eines schwierigen Verhältnisses* (Frankfurt: Haag und Herchen, 1990); Micha Brumlik et al., *Der Antisemitismus und die Linke* (Frankfurt: Haag und Herchen, 1991); Karlheinz Schneider and Nikolas Simon, eds., *Solidarität und deutsche Geschichte: Die Linke zwischen Antisemitismus und Israelkritik* (Berlin: Arnoldsheiner Texte, 1984); Hans Kundani, *Utopia or Auschwitz: Germany's 1968 Generation and the Holocaust* (London: Hurst, 2009); Holger J. Schmidt, *Antizionismus, Israelkritik und "Judenknax": Antisemitismus in der deutschen Linke nach 1945* (Bonn: Bouvier, 2010); and Wolfgang Kraushaar, *München 1970: über die antisemitischen Wurzeln des deutschen Terrorismus* (Reinbek bei Hamburg: Rowohlt, 2013). For a more recent account, see Assaf Moghadam and Michel Wyss, "Of Anti-Zionists and Antideutsche: The Post-War German Left and Its Relationship with Israel," *Democracy and Security* 15: 1 (2018).

12 For an account of the GDR's support for the Palestinian cause and its impact on West German leftists, see Jeffrey Herf, *Undeclared Wars with Israel: East Germany and the West German Far Left, 1967–1989* (Cambridge: Cambridge University Press, 2015). For an alternative argument that this support was not fully systematic, see Lutz Maeke, *DDR und PLO: Die Palästinapolitik des SED-Staates* (Berlin: De Gruyter Oldenbourg, 2017).

guerrillas, to which Kunzelmann belonged. After some of their members went to an Al-Fatah training camp for terrorists in Jordan, they attempted to bomb the West Berlin Jewish Community Center on November 9, 1969, the anniversary of Kristallnacht, and desecrated monuments to the victims of the Holocaust.[13] Although the bomb, which was given to them by the double agent Peter Urbach, failed to explode, the episode signaled the beginning of a long and destructive alliance, which culminated in the participation of two German radicals, Wilfried Böse, formerly a sociology student in Frankfurt, and Brigitte Kuhlmann, in the hijacking of the Air France flight that was forced to land in Entebbe, Uganda, in July 1976. They were killed in the Israeli raid that rescued the hostages, with Kuhlmann in particular gaining added notoriety for the vicious way she singled out Jewish passengers for special treatment. An even more explicit example of the radical German left's openness to the siren call of anti-Semitism was the lawyer and one-time Red Army Faction member Horst Mahler, who passed through a Maoist phase to become a member of the far-right National Democratic Party of Germany from 2000 to its dissolution in 2003. An outspoken Holocaust denier, he was ultimately convicted and served a lengthy prison sentence for *Volksverhetzung* (incitement of popular hatred).

Much more, of course, can said about the tangled relationship between the fringe elements of the German New Left, anti-Zionism and anti-Semitism, a relationship that haunted German politics for years to come. Even Joschka Fischer, who made a successful career as a mainstream politician, had to explain his embarrassing presence at a PLO conference in Algeria in 1969.[14] Another leading figure in the Green Party, Hans-Christian Ströbele, who remained to the left of Fischer, had to resign his position when his resistance to the first Gulf War in 1991 turned into a defense of Iraqi missile attacks on Israeli citizens.[15] And, of course, there have been more recent philo-Semitic attempts by

---

13 Wolfgang Kraushaar, *Die Bombe im Jüdischen Gemeindehaus* (Hamburg: Hamburger Edition, 2005).

14 Paul Hockenos, *Joschka Fischer and the Making of the Berlin Republic: An Alternative History of Postwar Germany* (Oxford: Oxford University Press, 2008), pp. 89–91.

15 For an account, see Andrei S. Markovits and Philip S. Gorski, *The German Left: Red, Green and Beyond* (Oxford: Oxford University Press, 1993), pp. 136–7.

anti-nationalist leftists in the Anti-Deutschen movement to defend Israel indiscriminately against any criticisms whatsoever.[16]

What, I now want to ask, was the role of the Frankfurt School in this tangled web? There were, it seems, echoes of Marcuse's ideas about sexual liberation, along with those of Wilhelm Reich, in Dieter Kunzelmann's thinking, and some readers of Horkheimer and Adorno's *Dialectic of Enlightenment* may have used it to exculpate the specific German responsibility for the Holocaust in the name of a broader critique of Western civilization.[17] But by and large, the direct impact of Critical Theory on the anti-authoritarian movement's problematic conflation of anti-Zionism and anti-Semitism was minimal. The most outspoken critic of Zionism in the first generation of members turns out to have been Erich Fromm, who had no use for nationalism of any kind.[18] Instead, he remained true to the ideal of a binational secular state advocated by Judah Magnes and the Brit Shalom movement in the interwar era. Fromm, of course, had long since severed his ties with his former colleagues in the Institute of Social Research, and his critique of Zionism played scarcely any role in the anti-authoritarian APO's struggle to operationalize Critical Theory. There are, for example, only one or two passing references to him in the three volumes Wolfgang Kraushaar edited on the Frankfurt School and the student movement.[19]

The other members of the School all shared Marcuse's post-Holocaust anxiety over the threat to a safe haven for Jews in a world that had so recently spurned them.[20] However much they may have criticized specific Israeli policies towards the Palestinians or bemoaned the blunting of the messianic potential of Judaism in the creation of a

---

16   For one account, see Patrick Hagen, "Die Antideutschen und die Debatte der Linke über Israel," scribd.com.

17   This latter argument is made, inter alia, by Jeffrey Herf in *Reactionary Modernism: Technology, Culture and Politics in the Weimar Republic and the Third Reich* (Cambridge: Cambridge University Press, 1986).

18   See Jacobs, *The Frankfurt School, Jewish Lives and Antisemitism*, pp. 123–32.

19   Wolfgang Kraushaar, *Frankfurter Schule und Studentenbewegung: Von der Flaschenpost zum Molotowcocktail 1946–1995* (Frankfurt: Rogner & Bernhard bei Zweitausendeins, 1998), vol. 1, p. 484 and vol. 3, p. 227.

20   For the details of their positions, see Jacobs, *The Frankfurt School, Jewish Lives, and Antisemitism*, chapter 3. See also the essays on their individual reactions to the Holocaust in the *Münchner Beiträge zur jüdischen Geschichte und Kultur*, ed. Philipp Lenhard, 16: 2 (2022).

normal modern state,[21] they had no qualms about defending its right to exist. In 1956 during the Suez Crisis, Horkheimer and Adorno had called the Egyptian leader Gamal Abdel Nasser a "fascist chieftain who conspires with Moscow" and added that the Arab states "have been on the lookout for years for an opportunity to fall upon Israel and to slaughter the Jews who have found refuge there."[22] As Jack Jacobs notes, "Horkheimer's continuing doubts about the Jewish state had nothing in common with 'anti-Zionism.' Horkheimer was well aware that purported anti-Zionism provided a (thin) screen both for neo-Nazis, such as those writing in the late 1960's for the *Deutsche National Zeitung*, and for Communists in Eastern Europe."[23] Likewise, Adorno expressed support for Israel during the Six-Day War, intermingling remarks on the death of Benno Ohnesorg in a lecture he gave on aesthetics with references to "the terrible threat to Israel, the refuge of countless Jews who have fled a horrifying fate."[24] He was in fact preparing to visit Israel at the invitation of his friend Gershom Scholem before his sudden death in 1969. Even Leo Löwenthal, who had explicitly rejected Zionism as early as the mid-1920s, had no hesitation in declaring Israel's right to exist after he made his first visit in 1985.[25] The same attitude continued into the second generation of the Frankfurt School, as demonstrated by Jürgen Habermas's frequent visits to Israel, beginning with a trip in 1977 to celebrate the eightieth birthday of Gershom Scholem.[26] His controversial denunciation of segments of the APO as "left-wing fascists" may in part have reflected his wariness over their enthusiasm for denouncing Israel.[27]

---

21 For an expression of this disappointment, see Max Horkheimer, "The State of Israel," in *Dawn and Decline: Notes 1926–1931 and 1950–1969*, trans. Michael Shaw (New York: Continuum, 1978). This aphorism was written in 1961–2.

22 Letter from Horkheimer and Adorno to Julius Ebbinghaus, cited in Stefan Müller-Doohm, *Adorno: A Biography*, trans. Rodney Livingstone (Malden, MA: Polity, 2005), p. 413.

23 Jacobs, *The Frankfurt School, Jewish Lives, and Antisemitism*, p. 140.

24 Cited in Müller-Doohm, *Adorno*, p. 452.

25 For a discussion of his repudiation of Zionism in the 1920s, see *An Unmastered Past: The Autobiographical Reflections of Leo Lowenthal*, ed. Martin Jay (Berkeley: University of California Press, 1987), p. 114. For his responses to the 1985 visit, see "Ich will den Traum von der Utopie nicht aufgeben," in *Die andere Erinnerungen: Gespräche mit jüdischen Wissenschaftlern im Exil*, ed. Hajo Funke (Frankfurt: Fischer, 1989).

26 See Stefan Müller-Doohm, *Habermas: A Biography*, trans. Daniel Steuer (Malden, MA: Polity, 2016), p. 193–4.

27 Ibid., pp. 148–9. The linkage is not suggested by Müller-Doohm, as there were many other provocations, but the fervor of their anti-Zionism cannot have helped the militants' cause in his eyes.

Thus, despite the German New Left's tilt towards the Palestinians and against Zionism, which sometimes opened the door to latent or even manifest expressions of anti-Semitism, there would seem little to justify expanding the field of "1968" to include "1967" in any account that stresses Critical Theory's role in its inspiration. If, however, we step back from the specific issues raised by the overlap or lack thereof between the German New Left's attitude towards Zionism and the Frankfurt School's fidelity to the idea of a safe haven for the world's Jews, there is much more to the symbolic meaning of the encounter between Marcuse and Dayan in wider terms that do, I would argue, justify expanding the field of "1968" to include "1967." For, as Rosalind Krauss has argued, expanded fields also include oppositions and negations as well as positive reinforcements. I am referring here to what might be seen as the Frankfurt School's relative indifference to events outside of the American and European contexts they had experienced at firsthand, or more precisely, their skepticism about the redemptive role often assigned anti-imperialist movements outside the West, such as the Palestinian cause.

To be sure, when the Institute of Social Research was founded in the 1920s, the inclusion of the Marxist Sinologist Karl August Wittfogel signaled an interest in that wider world. But in time Wittfogel, who had been a staunch Communist in the interwar years and became a right-wing anti-communist after the war, was increasingly marginalized. When his relationship with Horkheimer's circle was officially severed in the late 1940s, there was no one to take his place as an expert in Asian affairs. As for Latin America, although Felix Weil moved back and forth from Buenos Aires to New York during the Institute's exile, and in fact wrote a book called *Argentine Riddle* in 1944, it was not considered a product of the Institute's work and had no echo in their thinking.[28] Although traces of an interest in classical Chinese thought and literature have been discerned in Walter Benjamin's work, they were not matched by any serious inclusion of its current role in his analysis of the crisis of modern civilization.[29]

---

28 Felix J. Weil, *Argentine Riddle* (New York: John Day, 1944); for a discussion of its marginal status at the Institute, see Jeanette Erazo Heufelder, *Der argentinische Krösus: Kleine Wirtschaftgeschichte der Frankfurter Schule* (Berlin: Berenberg, 2017), pp. 155–62.

29 See Peter Fenves, "Benjamin, Studying, China: Toward a Universal 'Universism,'" *Positions Asia Critique* 26: 1 (February 2018).

The relative indifference of the Frankfurt School to events outside of their own orbit has often been lamented. In a recent book titled *Left-Wing Melancholia*, the Italian intellectual historian Enzo Traverso sees it exemplified in what he calls the "missed dialogue" and "failed encounter" between Adorno and the Afro-Caribbean cultural critic and novelist C. L. R. James. Perhaps best remembered for his pioneering study of the Haitian Revolution, *Black Jacobins*,[30] James, along with W. E. B. Du Bois, Eric Williams and Stuart Hall, was one of the leading figures in what has come to be called the tradition of Black Marxism. Although he and Adorno actually met for meals on several occasions when both were in exile in New York in the 1940s, neither seems to have taken much away from their time together.[31] James, at the time a Trotskyist aligned with Trotsky's former secretary Raya Dunayevskaya in the so-called Johnson-Forest Tendency of the Socialist Workers Party, was introduced to Adorno by Marcuse, who, along with Fromm, was to maintain an extended correspondence with Dunayevskaya in the following decades.[32] Insofar as James and Dunayevskaya shared with Friedrich Pollock the analysis of the Soviet Union as an example of "state capitalism" rather than genuine socialism, the chances for a real dialogue might have seemed auspicious.[33]

But according to Traverso, Adorno and James differed in two fundamental ways. First, whereas Adorno had given up on the proletariat as the vanguard of revolution and had no interest in the anti-colonial struggles then still largely on the horizon, James was enough of an optimist to believe that revolution led by the working class was still historically possible. Rather than seeing the dialectic of Enlightenment as a

30   C. L. R. James, *Black Jacobins: Toussaint L'Ouverture and the San Domingo Revolution* (London: Secker and Warburg, 1938).

31   Enzo Traverso, *Left-Wing Melancholia: Marxism, History and Memory* (New York: Columbia University Press, 2016), pp. 166–77.

32   Kevin B. Anderson and Russell Rockwell, eds., *The Dunayevskaya-Marcuse-Fromm Correspondence, 1954–1978: Dialogues on Hegel, Marx and Critical Theory* (Lanham, MD: Lexington, 2012). Marcuse even wrote an introduction to her *Marxism and Freedom* in 1958.

33   C. L. R. James, *State Capitalism and World Revolution* (Chicago: Charles H. Kerr, 1986). The first edition of the book, written in collaboration with Dunayevskaya and Grace Lee, appeared in 1950. Pollock's "State Capitalism: Its Possibilities and Limitations," *Philosophy and Social Science* 9: 2 (1941), was conspicuously absent from its pages.

dark story of domination and decline, he still held out hope for struggle and resistance. Second, James did not entirely share Adorno's disdain for the culture industry as inherently conformist. Having himself been a skilled player of cricket in his native Trinidad, James later wrote a celebrated study of the difference between the white version of the game played in places like the United Kingdom and Australia, and the very different one played in places like the Caribbean.[34] Whereas the former coldly applied instrumental rationality to the game, the latter, he claimed, played it with aesthetic and even moral intensity. In the years to come, James would be turned into a founding figure in subaltern and post-colonial studies, while the Frankfurt School played only a minor role in their development. "We might legitimately ask," Traverso concludes, "whether such a missed dialogue was not the symptom of a *colonial unconscious* of Critical Theory, at least in the early Frankfurt School."[35]

Although it perhaps might better be called their noncolonial consciousness, Traverso's general point is not without merit. The leaders of the Frankfurt School offered, for example, no serious response to earlier episodes in the decolonization process such as the Algerian War, which some historians have seen as crucial in inspiring the nascent New Left not only in France, but also in Germany.[36] But it is not clear exactly how taking on board C. L. R. James's approach would have done much to compensate for the alleged Eurocentrism of Critical Theory and their pessimism about the chances for radical change. Although it might have focused more attention on the issues raised by the ongoing struggle against colonial rule and its racist legacy, insofar as James remained a Leninist, it is hard to say that his belief in a vanguard workers' party would have helped them to overcome their often-lamented political deficit, the notorious gap between the theory and practice that Marxism insisted must be united.

---

34 C. L. R. James, *Beyond a Boundary* (Durham, NC: Duke University Press, 1993).

35 Traverso, *Left-Wing Melancholia*, p. 174.

36 Quinn Slobodian, *Foreign Front: Third World Politics in Sixties Germany* (Durham, NC: Duke University Press, 2012). He also points to the importance of such episodes as the assassination of Patrice Lumumba in the Congo in 1961 in sparking protest in Germany and elsewhere. One of the ironies of history is that Adorno's Corsican grandfather, Jean François Calvelli, was a soldier sent to subdue uprisings against French rule in the 1840s. See Müller-Doohm, *Adorno,* pp. 6–7.

Moreover, to the extent that James shared in the romanticization of Third World liberation struggles as viable alternatives to inadequate revolutionary activism in the First World, his political wager on redemption coming from the periphery rather than the center of the world system of global capitalism does not look, at least from our current vantage point, to have been realizable. However justifiable it certainly is to condemn the evils of European imperialism, and include the often disastrous interventions of the United States in that lament, it is not clear that liberation from colonial rule has produced models of political and economic emancipation that the rest of the world should hasten to follow.

Already in *Minima Moralia*, Adorno had sounded the tocsin. In an aphorism entitled "Savages Are Not More Noble," he insisted that "an uncompromising mind is the very opposite of primitivism, neophytism or the 'non-capitalist world.' It presupposes experience, a historical memory, a fastidious intellect and above all an ample measure of satiety." Because colonized people so often seek to catch up with the West and share the alleged fruits of modern society, their aspirations are more likely to affirm than negate its repressive features. "Instead of expecting miracles of the pre-capitalist peoples," Adorno warned that "older nations should be on their guard against their un-imaginative, indolent taste for everything proven, and for the successes of the West."[37] Although Adorno was surely on shaky ground in reducing the tastes of precapitalist peoples to nothing but crass envy, his skepticism about the inflated role assigned them by some on the left has not been refuted by subsequent history.

If we pause for a moment to consider the mixed legacy of the one prominent Black Marxist who was directly influenced by Critical Theory, the celebrated African American activist Angela Davis, the limits of placing too much hope in Traverso's "missed dialogue" are apparent. Davis had studied philosophy with Marcuse at Brandeis in the early 1960s and went to Frankfurt in 1966 to work with Adorno. Although she impressed him as an astute student of Kant—we have a copy of the warm letter of recommendation he wrote on her

---

37 Theodor W. Adorno, *Minima Moralia: Reflections from Damaged Life*, trans. E. F. N. Jephcott (London: NLB, 1974), pp. 52–3.

behalf[38]—they were politically at odds. She later recalled that Adorno "discouraged me from seeking to discover ways of linking my seemingly discrepant interests in philosophy and social activism" and "suggested that my desire to work directly in the radical movements of that period was akin to a media studies scholar deciding to become a radio technician."[39] Marcuse, in contrast, vigorously defended her decision to return to activism in the United States, where she joined the Black Panthers and the Che-Lumumba Club, an all-Black group within the Communist Party.[40] When she was fired from her position teaching philosophy at UCLA because of her membership in the Party and was then accused of supplying guns to Black Panthers who had murdered a prison guard in helping their comrades to escape Soledad Prison, Marcuse never abandoned her. Captured after going underground, when she had been put on the FBI's Ten Most Wanted List, and tried for conspiracy to kidnap and murder, Davis was ultimately acquitted in 1972. But before that outcome, an international campaign was mounted on her behalf. It was waged with special fervor in Frankfurt, where supporters like Oskar Negt, with whom she had studied during her year in Frankfurt, fashioned her into an example of the unfairness of American justice. A solidarity committee held mass rallies beginning November 1970, culminating in a congress held in June 1972 with Marcuse as one of the main speakers, which attracted some 10,000 participants.[41] Although Oskar Negt's use of the occasion to denounce the terrorist tactics of the Red Army Faction may ultimately have had the greater impact on the subsequent history of the German New Left, the outpouring of support for Davis demonstrated

---

38   It is dated December 20, 1966. See literaturarchiv1968.de/.

39   Angela Davis, "Marcuse's Legacies," in *Herbert Marcuse: A Critical Reader*, ed. John Abromeit and W. Mark Cobb (New York: Routledge, 2004), pp. 46–7.

40   See, for example, Marcuse's introduction of Davis at a demonstration on October 24, 1969, in Kraushaar, *Die Frankfurter Schule und die Studentenbewegung*, vol. 2, p. 688.

41   Oskar Negt, "Der Fall Angela Davis," in Kraushaar, *Frankfurterschule und Studentenbewegung*, vol. 2, which concludes that no American court would ever set her free and make the FBI and president look ridiculous (p. 733). Negt also supported her being given an honorary doctorate at the university. See his warm letter of recommendation: ethecon.org. The first committees in 1970 are discussed in Kraushaar, *Frankfurter Schule und Studentenbewegung*, vol. 1, pp. 501–2, and the congress on pp. 521–2. Marcuse was among the main speakers.

her potential role as a bridge between Critical Theory and the emerging post-colonial movement, as well as feminism and Black power.[42]

Unfortunately, her unwavering loyalty to the orthodox Communism to which she had been introduced by her mother as a child in Birmingham, Alabama, did little to enable that outcome. Shortly after her triumphant visit to Frankfurt, Davis went to East Berlin, where she was greeted no less warmly by Erich Honecker, who had recently replaced Walter Ulbricht as the party leader, and defended, as she had done before, the Soviet bloc invasion of Czechoslovakia in 1968.[43] Running on the American Communist Party ticket as vice presidential candidate alongside Gus Hall in 1980 and 1984, she remained a CP member until after the dissolution of the Soviet Union in 1991. Davis's reputation, to be sure, managed in most respects to survive her dogged loyalty to the Party, and she was able to emerge from her years in its thrall as an influential advocate for various progressive causes, most notably prison reform and Third World feminism, in later years. But lost by her extended allegiance to an Old Left that was leaving the historical stage was any serious possibility that she might contribute to an overcoming of the Frankfurt School's Eurocentric perspective, which would expand the field of 1968 to include the implications of 1967, understood from the perspective of Enzo Traverso as a validation of Third World struggles.

It is thus not surprising that for a long time post-colonial theory took little notice of the tradition of Critical Theory, finding more intellectual nourishment in the congeries of disparate ideas that came to be called post-structuralism.[44] Even Heidegger could be made a more effective

---

42   For a discussion of the importance of Negt's speech, see Karrin Hanshew, "'Sympathy for the Devil?' The West German Left and the Challenge of Terrorism," *Contemporary European History* 21: 4 (2012), pp. 511–12.

43   Kraushaar, *Frankfurter Schule und Studentenbewegung*, vol. 1, p. 525. For a poignant appeal to Davis to reverse her support, see the open letter sent by the Czech dissident Jiří Pelikán in the *New York Review of Books*, August 31, 1972. For an account of her continuing interaction with the DDR and the role she played in its ideological self-image, see Sophie Lorenz, "Heldin des anderen Amerikas: Die DDR-Solidaritätsbewegung für Angela Davis, 1970–1973," *Zeithistorische Forschungen* 1 (2013).

44   It should be noted that there was also little interest in Critical Theory in Israel, which never went through a student rebellion of its own. See Moshe Zuckermann, "Kritische Theorie in Israel—Analyse einer Nichtreception," in *Theodor W. Adorno: Philosoph des beschädigten Lebens*, ed. Moshe Zuckerman (Göttingen: Wallstein, 2004).

ally in the effort to "provincialize Europe," as the subaltern studies historian of India Dipesh Chakrabarty called it.[45] Espen Hammer echoed the conventional wisdom in his 2006 book on *Adorno and the Political* when he wrote:

> With some important exceptions, he seems to have been virtually oblivious to the concerns of postcolonialism, including race, discrimination, and imperialism. His blunt Eurocentrism, focused as it was on Germany and Austria in particular, predisposed him to reject, or at least view with suspicion, forms of cultural expression—notoriously jazz—that did not fit into his own framework. It also led him to stake most of his claims for the role of art as embodying an alternative form of rationality on forms of aesthetic high modernism that since the mid-1960s have largely lost their attraction and relevance.[46]

Despite these apparent blind spots in the early Frankfurt School, some efforts were made to enlist insights from its legacy in the service of less parochial ends. In 1995, a Canadian scholar of Indian descent, Asha Varadharajan, compared the work of Edward Said, Gayatri Spivak and Adorno in book called *Exotic Parodies*.[47] Noting Said's own powerful attraction to Adorno's ideas, she argued that negative dialectics provided a better theoretical support than deconstruction for subaltern studies. "Although Adorno was relatively silent on imperialism per se," she argued, "his attention to the hegemony of the exchange principle and his critique of identitarian politics, have, I believe, become indispensable to the affirmation of otherness, the resistance to global capitalism (the particularly virulent form that colonialism has assumed) and, crucially, to the discourse of modernity that arrogates to itself 'the regulative political concepts' . . . that encode the claims of nation within decolonized space."[48]

More recently, the American philosophers Thomas McCarthy and Amy Allen have drawn on different moments in the multigenerational tradition of Critical Theory to make similar arguments. McCarthy, an

---

45   Dipesh Chakrabarty, *Provincializing Europe: Postcolonial Thought and Historical Difference* (Princeton, NJ: Princeton University Press, 2007).

46   Espen Hammer, *Adorno and the Political* (London: Routledge, 2006), p. 5.

47   Asha Varadharajan, *Exotic Parodies: Subjectivity in Adorno, Said and Spivak* (Minneapolis: University of Minnesota Press, 1995).

48   Ibid., p. 137.

indefatigable translator and insightful interpreter of Habermas's work, published a wide-ranging study, *Race, Empire, and the Idea of Human Development*, in 2009.[49] In it, he condemns the ways in which traditional notions of modernization were tainted by racist and imperialist assumptions but holds out hope for a more enlightened version of development theory that would combine the best legacies of Eurocentric liberal universalism with the value of multicultural particularism. Allen, in contrast, is far less sanguine about the possibility of squaring that circle. In *The End of Progress*, published in 2016, she criticizes McCarthy, along with Habermas, Axel Honneth and Rainer Forst, for maintaining an unwarranted optimism about the ability of prior developmental theories to shed their problematic Eurocentric baggage.[50] Determined to rid Critical Theory of its normative foundation in Enlightenment rationalism and its implicit belief in progressive, cross-cultural development, Allen seeks to combine Foucault's notion of genealogy—which she sees as "problematizing" rather than vindicatory or subversive—with Adorno's stress on immanent critique. The goal is a more capacious notion of what she calls "metanormative contextualization," which can include the insights of post-colonial discourse. The only way the ideal of progress can be salvaged, Allen contends, is to uncouple it from the assumption that it was a past fact with universal implications, which tacitly privileged Western modernization, and to link it with the possibility—indeed the moral imperative—of future improvement measured according to culturally immanent norms.

Ironically, despite the limited inclusion of non-European or non-American viewpoints bemoaned by commentators such as Traverso and Hammer, the first generation of Critical Theorists—Adorno in particular—have been praised by Varadharajan and Allen for their sensitivity to the dark side of the dialectic of enlightenment, in particular its dubious model of universal progressive development.[51] Although one commentator has argued

---

49   Thomas McCarthy, *Race, Empire, and the Idea of Human Development* (Cambridge: Cambridge University Press, 2009).

50   Amy Allen, *The End of Progress: Decolonizing the Foundations of Critical Theory* (New York: Columbia University Press, 2016). For a skeptical response to aspects of her argument, see my review in *Critical Inquiry* 45: 2 (2018).

51   For a general account, see James D. Ingram, "Critical Theory and Postcolonialism," in *The Routledge Companion to the Frankfurt School*, ed. Peter Gordon, Espen Hammer and Axel Honneth (New York: Routledge, 2018).

that Habermas's recent "postsecular" interest in the enduring value of religious norms suggests that he too may be seeking a "postcolonial" re-evaluation of Critical Theory, it has seemed harder, McCarthy to the contrary notwithstanding, to mobilize the second and third generations' contributions for that purpose.[52] Their nuanced defense of the normative legacy of Western thought, however much it may have been betrayed by imperialist and racist practices, makes them still seem, at least for some critics, insufficiently liberated from their European origins and experiences in American exile.

Whichever strand of the tradition is picked as most likely to escape Eurocentric parochialism, there is, I want to argue, a potential problem with any attempt to enrich the Frankfurt School's legacy and compensate for its political deficit by infusing it with post-colonial discourse, however well intended. To understand what I mean will require our returning to the importance of situating 1968 in an expanded field that includes the events of 1967. They can of course be read in different ways. From one perspective, the Six-Day War has been seen as a chapter in the Western imperialist incursion into the non-European world, an outcome of orientalist ideology and the resistance to it on the part of its victims. Certainly, this was the interpretation that allowed the pro-Palestinian wing of the German New Left to denounce Zionism so fervently as continuous with the American war in Vietnam and other examples of Western imperialism. Because the Frankfurt School did not share this interpretation, the subsequent criticism that we have encountered of its Eurocentric bias and its need to assimilate insights from post-colonial discourse might appear to be warranted.

But even beyond the dangers in too quick and easy an identification of the Israelis with a colonial settler experiment—their often violent struggle to expel the British from Palestine suggests it was more complicated than that—it is difficult with the hindsight of the past half-century to assign the Palestinians—or for that matter, any other movement for colonial liberation—a redemptive role that would somehow simply make up for the deficiencies of Eurocentrism. This is not to say, I hasten to add, that colonial independence was anything but a laudable goal or

---

52   Dafydd Huw Rees, "Decolonizing Philosophy?: Habermas and the Axial Age," *Constellations* 24: 2 (June 2017). He argues, however, that because Habermas accepts Karl Jaspers's notion of an axial age in which several major faiths emerged, he remains implicitly wedded to a notion of religion that is still too exclusive.

that imperialism, whether direct through political control, or indirect through economic or cultural domination, is in any way defensible. Whatever successes the decolonization process enjoyed in the past half-century, it is clear that many residues still remain of a world system heavily weighted to favor the former colonial powers. And the struggle to redress the balance is by no means over. Nor is it the case that post-colonial discourse in its various guises has always blithely romanticized the victims.

But what is clear is that, once liberated from Western domination, such countries or others in what used to be called the Third World, and now often identified with the Global South, were unable to realize the emancipatory, even utopian, potential imputed to them by certain European activists. Sympathizing with the plight of the "wretched of the earth" was one thing; relying on them to redeem humankind was another. Mindless solidarity with something called "the global left" made it hard to avoid supporting regimes and movements that were anything but emancipatory. Perhaps the most telling example is the woefully misplaced investment in Chinese Maoism during the Cultural Revolution by a number of prominent French intellectuals, including Jean-Paul Sartre, Philippe Sollers, Julia Kristeva and Alain Badiou.[53] French Maoists were also fervent supporters of the Palestinian cause, or at least were until 1972 and the brutal attack by the terrorist group Black September on Israeli athletes at the Munich Olympics. Many of the leaders of the *Gauche prolétarienne*—Alain Geismar, André Glucksmann, Benny Lévy, Tiennot Grumbach, Tony Lévy and Daniel Linhardt—had been nonobservant Jews, and were shocked into losing their innocence about the purity of the anti-Zionist cause.[54] The response among radical Germans seems to have been more muted, perhaps because one of the demands of the terrorists had been the freeing of the Baader-Meinhof gang, then in prison. But by the end of the decade, Maoism had lost much of its luster there as well.

To return to the main point of this essay, the idea of an expanded field helps us avoid turning 1968 into a discrete, self-contained episode in

---

53   See Richard Wolin, *The Wind from the East: French Intellectuals, the Cultural Revolution, and the Legacy of the 1960s* (Princeton, NJ: Princeton University Press, 2010).

54   Ibid., p. 352.

history, open to being represented in heroic terms, put on a pedestal and available for simple commemoration. Putting it into play with the Six-Day War and its effects alerts us to the importance of competing historical narratives, which can decenter 1968 beyond the more conventional temporal and spatial expansions mentioned earlier. To be sure, it has been possible to interpret the narrative centered on 1967 as potentially compatible with the dominant image of 1968 as a hopeful moment in the history of human emancipation. The latter can be seen as unleashing forces for change that might have been enriched by their integration with the comparable forces in the former that go by the name of anti-imperialist decolonization. Here, the anti-Zionist voices in the German New Left, despite their sometimes deplorable mobilization of anti-Semitic prejudices, can be seen as part of a constellation that, despite its never really coming to fruition, held out possibilities for a more fundamental challenge to the status quo. In a larger sense, the exhortation of commentators such as Enzo Traverso and Amy Allen to correct the Eurocentric bias of Critical Theory with lessons learned from postcolonial discourse amplifies this interpretation, which sees Third World redemptive politics as a way to overcome the pessimism and political deficit of the Frankfurt School.

But this interpretation is called into question if we read 1967 against that grain, in the way the majority of the members of the Frankfurt School did at the time, as less a failed attempt at Third World resistance to Western imperialism than as a threat to the survival of the Jewish people only narrowly averted. Then a very different constellation emerges in an enlarged field, one in which the lingering residues of 1945—understood as the unfinished business of the fascist era—play a vital role. Germany, more than any other locus of New Left politics, it has often been remarked, was haunted by a still unmastered past. The outrage of the student movement was fueled by a sense that the sins of their fathers had not really been worked through, both in terms of the continuity of personnel in positions of power and as a full confrontation of the reasons for the rise of Nazism. And conversely, the establishment's deep anxiety over what they saw as the excesses of the APO expressed fears that the rule of law was being trampled by radicals willing to use violence to undermine the hard-earned achievements of the postwar West German political order, thus repeating the mistakes of their Weimar predecessors. In other words, the still smoldering embers of 1945 helped ignite the flames of the German version of 1968.

There was, however, another potential reading of the unfinished business of 1945, which was alarming in a different way. Despite their qualms about specific Israeli policies, most of the members of the Frankfurt School were deeply anxious about a renewal, had Israel lost the Six-Day War, of the annihilation of the Jewish people merely interrupted by the defeat of Nazism. As a result, they resisted the simplistic reading of the conflict as a black and white episode in the anti-imperialist struggle for global justice, a reading which seduced many on the left. For them, the destruction of the Jewish people was enough of a threat to outweigh their criticism of specific Israeli policies undermining the legitimate rights of the Palestinians. Acknowledging this fear helps us understand, and perhaps even sympathize, with their Eurocentric inability to invest much hope in the putatively redemptive mission of the Third World, and their hesitation before expressing unqualified solidarity with the global left. It allows us to see the failure of Adorno's lunches with C. L. R. James to create an alliance of Critical Theory and post-colonial discourse as not so lamentable, after all.

From the perspective of a half-century later, the issues raised by the Six-Day War and its aftermath are, of course, anything but resolved and both sides in the conflict seem hopelessly locked in a struggle without end. But one thing is clear: it is impossible to summon the confidence that once invested post-colonial discourse with its halo of political righteousness. The lingering hope that the stalled European revolution would somehow be jump-started by those hitherto oppressed peoples who were finally asserting their place on the historical stage seems, at least at this juncture, unrealized. There may have been Maoist enthusiasts of the Cultural Revolution who looked to the China of those years for answers, but the country that is now fast becoming the most powerful engine of global capitalism is anything but a beacon of emancipation. Similar appraisals might be made of the once shining future of the Latin American left, now in such a shambles, as well as the hopes placed in national liberation struggles in Indochina or Africa, not to mention the Arab Spring of only a few years ago.

In other words, to return to that encounter in Jerusalem with which we began, it now seems clear that the historical shadow cast by Herbert Marcuse, as the embodiment of the idealistic student movement, has been much shorter and less pervasive than that cast by Moshe Dayan, the master of nationalist *Realpolitik* and the art of war. Or, to stay with our master metaphor, the gravitational pull of 1968 in its expanded field has not had the power of other talismanic years in the historical calendar. These would not only include 1967 and 1945, whose unfinished business, understood in various ways, was especially potent in Germany, but also the current year. For any historical field must take into account the present as a moment that helps to define how we understand what came before, either as a possible future that was actually realized or as one that was ironically reversed.[55] And it now seems that the line of force that can be drawn from 1967 to today crackles with much more energy than that between 1968 and the present.

But before ending on too sour a note, it would also be prudent to remember that our own "present moment" will itself fade into the past as the untotalized field of history continues relentlessly to expand and new narratives, both complementary and contradictory, vie for supremacy. For all we know, the Frankfurt School's controversial "strategy of hibernation" may still prove prescient as its messages in bottles wash up on new shores, and the relative gravitational pull of 1967 over 1968 may be reversed by events yet unforeseen. It may be best, however, to wait until the centenary of '68 to assess such conjectures. What cannot be doubted, however, is that the ever-evolving tradition of Critical Theory will have much to chew on in the interim.

---

55   For an ironic reading of Marcuse's *One-Dimensional Man*, see Martin Jay, "Irony and Dialectics: *One-Dimensional Man* and 1968," in *Splinters in Your Eye.*

2

Adorno and the Role of Sublimation in Artistic Creativity and Cultural Redemption

Despite the audacious attempt of the Frankfurt School to "marry" Marx and Freud,[1] Adorno often challenged the ideological implications of psychoanalytic categories, perhaps nowhere as vigorously as in his critique of the alleged role of sublimation in artistic creativity. He worried that it was tacitly aligned with an affirmative rather than critical understanding of culture and that it spiritualized the material needs of the desiring body. But at the same time, he shared Marcuse's distrust of immediate libidinal satisfaction, which could become "repressive de-sublimation" and ultimately support the current order it ostensibly transgressed.

To move beyond this theoretical impasse, Adorno engaged in what might be called an immanent critique of the concept of sublimation itself. Uncoupling it from Freud's emphasis on the artist's channeling of libidinal desire, he relocated it in the aesthetic transfiguration of suffering, both human and natural, which nonetheless avoided functioning as anodyne consolation. Rather than merely an extension of its creator's interiority, the artwork unintentionally expressed the protest of nature against its human domination. In addition, Adorno defended what might be called the posterior sublimation of devotional or cultic objects and practices into aesthetic ones, arguing that they preserved the memory of an earlier mimetic

---

1   For my reading of this attempt, see " 'In Psychoanalysis Nothing Is True but the Exaggerations': Freud and the Frankfurt School," in *Splinters in Your Eye: Frankfurt School Provocations* (London: Verso, 2020).

impulse which might serve as a resource against the instrumentalization of reason in the modern world. Sublimation, in other words, contained both an affirmative and a critical potential, the former manifested in the cultural "elevation" of the artist's allegedly base instincts into respectable high art, the latter in a negative dialectic preserving memories of both pain and pleasure.[2]

"Artists do not sublimate," Adorno insisted in *Minima Moralia*, the idea "that they neither satisfy nor repress their desires, but translate them into socially desirable achievements, their works, is a psychoanalytic illusion . . . Their lot is rather a hysterically excessive lack of inhibition over every conceivable fear; narcissism taken to its paranoiac limit. To anything sublimated they oppose idiosyncrasies."[3] However much he may have embraced the Frankfurt School's hope that Marxism could be enriched through insights from psychoanalysis, Adorno vigorously resisted Freud's theory of sublimation to explain artistic creation.[4] And yet, in other significant ways, the term did play an important role in his thinking, a role often ignored in accounts of his aesthetic theory. In what follows, I hope to show how central it in fact was to his understanding of art in the service of human emancipation.

Although Freud never used "sublimation" with perfect consistency after introducing the term in his *Three Essays on the Theory of Sexuality* in 1905, one of his clearest definitions was "a process that concerns object-libido and consists in the instinct directing itself towards an aim other than, and removed from, that of sexual satisfaction."[5] Based on a

2   This essay was generated by an invitation from Peter Gordon to contribute to a symposium on the fiftieth anniversary of Adorno's *Aesthetic Theory*, and was first published in *New German Critique*, no. 143 (August 2021).

3   Theodor W. Adorno, *Minima Moralia: Reflections from Damaged Life*, trans. E. F. N. Jephcott (London: NLB, 1974), pp. 212–13. On the value of idiosyncrasy for Critical Theory, see Axel Honneth, "Idiosyncrasy as a Tool of Knowledge: Social Criticism in the Age of the Normalized Intellectual," in *Pathologies of Reason: On the Legacy of Critical Theory*, trans. James Ingram (New York: Columbia University Press, 2009). For a discussion of its contradictory implications as a concept that signifies resistance to conceptuality, see Jan Plug, "Idiosyncrasies: of Anti-Semitism," in *Language without Soil: Adorno and Late Philosophical Modernity*, ed. Gerhard Richter (New York: Fordham University Press, 2010).

4   See Jay, " 'In Psychoanalysis Nothing Is True but the Exaggerations' "; and Helmut Dahmer, "Adorno's View of Psychoanalysis," *Thesis Eleven* 111: 1 (2012).

5   Sigmund Freud, "On Narcissism," in *The Standard Edition of the Complete Psychological Works of Sigmund Freud*, 24 vols., ed. and trans. James Strachey (London:

hydraulic model of flow, pressure, blockage and release, and applied to innate, somatically generated instincts or drives, it assumed that at least the libido or erotic drive was plastic in terms of its object choice.[6] According to Jean Laplanche and Jean-Bertrand Pontalis, "sublimation" borrowed some of its meaning from the aesthetic term "sublime . . . to qualify works that are grand and uplifting," as well as the chemical process of causing a body to pass directly from solid to gaseous state, which implied the spiritualization of materiality.[7] Applied to artistic creation, it signaled the transformation of private emotion into cultural meaning, subjective desire into artworks with enduring public value.

Many critics of Freud's theory of aesthetic sublimation have been troubled by its elitism and misogyny.[8] Adorno, however, had three other complaints against its alleged role in artistic creation. First, he charged that by claiming that the artist's transgressive impulses can be successfully channeled into culturally admirable works of art in lieu of being directly expressed or ascetically repressed, the theory of sublimation tacitly endorses what the Frankfurt School had called since the 1930s the "affirmative character of culture."[9] Unfulfilled yearnings in a still unfree society are said to be transfigured through sublimation into an allegedly "higher" realm of beauty, a realm of disinterested transcendence beyond base needs. But in fact, such a transfiguration offers only weak consolation for the oppressive social conditions that thwart real emancipation, which would honor the

---

Hogarth, 1953–74), vol. 14, p. 94. For an account of the ambiguities of sublimation in Freud, see Eckart Goebel, *Beyond Discontent: "Sublimation" from Goethe to Lacan*, trans. James C. Wagner (New York: Bloomsbury, 2012), chapter 4.

6 The hydraulic model of the mind has been criticized as based on a nineteenth-century interpretation of fluid behavior, and Freud is sometimes said not to have always relied on it. See Robert C. Solomon, *True to Our Feelings: What Our Emotions Are Really Telling Us* (Oxford: Oxford University Press, 2008).

7 Jean Laplanche and Jean-Bertrand Pontalis, *The Language of Psychoanalysis*, trans. Donald Nicholson-Smith (New York: Norton, 1973), p. 432.

8 Freud's elitism is evident in his "'Civilized' Sexual Morality and Modern Nervousness," in *Standard Edition*, vol. 9, p. 193. His gender bias appears in *Civilization and Its Discontents*, trans. James Strachey (New York: Norton, 1961), p. 50; and in *New Introductory Lectures on Psychoanalysis*, trans. James Strachey (New York: Norton, 1965), p. 134.

9 See Herbert Marcuse, "The Affirmative Character of Culture," in *Negations: Essays in Critical Theory*, trans. Jeremy J. Shapiro (Boston: Beacon, 1968).

validity of those needs.[10] Negation is only negated in sublimation by premature, conformist positivity, and contradiction falsely overcome by ideological reconciliation. "If successful sublimation and integration are made the end-all and be-all of the artwork," Adorno argued, "it loses the force by which it exceeds the given, which it renounces by its mere existence."[11]

For all its alleged distinction from repression, sublimation is no less of a defense mechanism against the immediate realization of desire, and thus hard to distinguish from symptom formation as such.[12] There is in Freudian theory, Adorno charged, "a total lack of adequate criteria for distinguishing 'positive' from 'negative' ego-functions, above all, sublimation from repression."[13] Or, more precisely, if there is such a criterion, it is external to psychological processes and located entirely in the society outside. The model of psychological "health" or "normality" underlying the ideal of cultural sublimation is based on a conformist adaptability to society as it is. The logic of affirmative adaptation was even clearer, Adorno contended, in the work of so-called neo-revisionist analysts, such as Karen Horney and his erstwhile colleague Erich Fromm, who wrongly discarded Freud's libido theory as inherently biologistic.[14] If there can be no fully realized individual psychological health in a pathological society, there is concomitantly no aesthetic compensation for the discontents of at least this civilization.[15]

10   Adorno was not alone in lamenting the renunciation inherent in sublimation. In *Life against Death: The Psychoanalytic Meaning of History* (New York: Vintage, 1959), Norman O. Brown would charge that "sublimation is the search for lost life; it presupposes and perpetuates the loss of life and cannot be the mode in which life itself is lived. Sublimation is the mode of an organism which must discover life rather than live, must know rather than be" (p. 171).

11   Theodor W. Adorno, *Aesthetic Theory*, ed., Gretel Adorno and Rolf Tiedemann, trans. Robert Hullot-Kentor (Minneapolis: University of Minnesota Press, 1997), p. 12.

12   The inclusion of sublimation along with repression as a defense mechanism was made by Anna Freud in *The Ego and the Mechanisms of Defense* (London: Hogarth, 1936).

13   Theodor W. Adorno, "Sociology and Psychology," *New Left Review* 1: 48 (January/February 1968), p. 86.

14   Theodor W. Adorno, "Revisionist Psychoanalysis," introduced and translated by Nan-Nan Lee, *Philosophy and Social Criticism* 40: 3 (2014).

15   Adorno's hostility to the therapeutic function of psychoanalysis, evident throughout *Minima Moralia*, can be explained by its dependence on sublimation. As Philip Rieff noted, "The psychoanalytic resolutions of conflict are embodied in a dialectical therapy which is itself a kind of sublimation, a transferring of the patient's conflicts to 'higher levels.'" *Freud: The Mind of a Moralist* (Garden City, NY: Anchor, 1961), p. 69.

Second, according to Adorno, sublimation transfigures the corporeal desires unmet in the current world through spiritualization, producing an idealist pseudo-solution to the material injuries produced by capitalism. Sublimation may be seen to feed the inner soul, but it ignores the legitimate demands of the desiring body. To be sure, Freud registered the corporeal origins of art in a way that Kant, who was pitted against him in *Aesthetic Theory*, did not: "The psychoanalytic theory of art is superior to idealist aesthetics in that it brings to light what is internal to art and not itself artistic. It helps free art from the spell of absolute spirit . . . But psychoanalysis too," Adorno then added, "casts a spell related to idealism, that of an absolutely subjective sign system denoting individual instinctual impulses."[16] The alleged sublimation of baser desires into higher works of art parallels the dubious distinction often made between "culture" and "civilization"—the former understood as the realm of noble ideas and beautiful forms, the latter as the locus of technological improvements, superficial social interactions and political machinations—that was a standard trope of reactionary antimodernism. Rather than serving as an anticipatory placeholder for genuine happiness in the future, that *promesse du bonheur* the Frankfurt School so often evoked, art understood in terms of sublimation was reduced to a surrogate pleasure in the present, scarcely less ideological in function than the popular entertainment provided by the culture industry. In contrast, Adorno argued, "he alone who could situate utopia in blind somatic pleasure, which, satisfying the ultimate intention, is intentionless, has a stable and valid idea of truth. In Freud's work, however, the dual hostility towards mind and pleasure, whose common root psychoanalysis has given us the means for discovering, is unintentionally reproduced."[17]

Finally, the theory of sublimation fails, for Adorno, to take into account the crucial distinction between the artwork and the artist who created it. It hurries past the former, which it reduces to a mere document of displaced neurosis, to decode what it takes to be the deeper motives of the latter. As such, it repeats the errors of what has been damned for more than a century as "psychologism," reducing the validity of an idea or art work to its genesis, a fallacy which had been the

16   Adorno, *Aesthetic Theory*, pp. 8–9.
17   Adorno, *Minima Moralia*, p. 61.

bugaboo of the modernist aesthetics in which Adorno had been steeped since his musical training in the 1920s.[18] "Psychoanalysis treats artworks as nothing but facts," Adorno charged, "yet it neglects their own objectivity, their inner consistency, their level of form, their critical impulse, their relation to nonpsychical reality, and, finally, their idea of truth."[19] Stressing the subjective production of artworks as projective daydreaming rather than their integrity as such, it fails to register their resistance to the domination of the production principle and the elevation of labor over play,[20] as well as their refusal to reduce happiness to an effect of praxis alone. Instead of preserving the non-identity of the artwork and the artist, it collapses one into the other. Because of its dogged adherence to an anti-utopian understanding of the reality principle and validating the status quo, psychoanalysis reduces imagination to mere escapism and fails to appreciate its ability to envisage an alternate reality. "If art has psychoanalytic roots, then they are the roots of fantasy in the fantasy of omnipotence," Adorno argued. "This fantasy includes the wish to bring about a better world. This frees the total dialectic, whereas the view of art as a merely subjective language of the unconscious does not even touch it."[21] Paradoxically, it is only by reminding the subject of the object world's resistance to the narcissistic fantasy of omnipotence that artworks can foreshadow a better world in which subjective domination is overcome.

For all of these reasons, Adorno disdained theories of artistic creation that drew on a reductive notion of sublimated libidinal desire. And yet, as was typical of his relentlessly dialectical method, he also acknowledged the concept's critical potential. Thus, he was able to say, building on his analysis of the contradictory implications of the idea of "progress,"[22] that "the ambiguity of 'sublimation' is the psychological

---

18   For an account of the modernist critique of psychologism, see Martin Jay, "Modernism and the Specter of Psychologism," in *Cultural Semantics: Keywords of Our Time* (Amherst: University of Massachusetts Press, 1998).

19   Adorno, *Aesthetic Theory*, p. 9.

20   Although critical of the traditional Marxist heroization of labor and production, Adorno did not affirm play as the alternative, as his critical remarks on Schiller's *Aesthetic Education* and Huizinga's *Homo Ludens* make clear. See *Aesthetic Theory*, pp. 317–19.

21   Ibid., p. 9.

22   See Adorno, "Progress," *Philosophical Forum* 15: 1 (1983).

symbol of social progress."[23] Defenders of Freud's notion of sublimation against Adorno's criticisms, such as Joel Whitebook, have thus perhaps gone too far in identifying his attitude entirely with unalloyed disdain.[24] One indication of the complexity of his position appeared in Adorno's critique of its apparent opposite, de-sublimation, in the contemporary world. If he believed that sublimation could function affirmatively in an unfree society, providing spiritualized consolations for unfulfilled corporeal desires, Adorno nonetheless refused to identify a truly emancipatory alternative with their immediate, direct gratification under current social conditions. Herbert Marcuse's condemnation of "repressive de-sublimation" in *One-Dimensional Man*[25] was echoed in *Aesthetic Theory*, where Adorno argued that "the de-sublimation, the immediate and momentary gain of pleasure that is demanded of art, is inner-aesthetically beneath art; in real terms, however, that momentary pleasure is unable to grant what is expected of it."[26] Or, as he put it in *Minima Moralia*, "Ascetic ideals constitute today a more solid bulwark against the madness of the profit-economy than did the hedonistic life sixty years ago against liberal repression."[27]

Adorno's implied defense of a certain notion of sublimation went beyond, however, his distrust of its putative opposite in the current "administered world." For he also identified a certain non-repressive potential in sublimation itself, at least understood as more than just the channeling of the artist's transgressive libidinal desires. In a remarkable passage beginning the aphorism "Second Harvest" in *Minima Moralia*, Adorno allowed us a glimpse of what this might mean. "Talent," he conjectured, "is perhaps nothing other than successfully sublimated rage."[28] In his later essay "Resignation," in which he defended himself against the charge that he had retreated into pure theory and neglected radical praxis, Adorno similarly argued: "Whoever thinks is without anger in all criticism; thinking sublimates anger. Because the thinking

23 Theodor W. Adorno, *Prisms*, trans. Samuel and Shierry Weber (London: Neville, Spearman, 1967), p. 85.

24 Joel Whitebook, *Perversion and Utopia: A Study in Psychoanalysis and Critical Theory* (Cambridge: MA: MIT Press, 1995), pp. 258–62.

25 Herbert Marcuse, *One-Dimensional Man: Studies in the Ideology of Advanced Industrial Society* (Boston: Beacon, 1964), pp. 75–8.

26 Adorno, *Aesthetic Theory*, p. 319.

27 Adorno, *Minima Moralia*, p. 97.

28 Ibid., p. 109.

person does not have to inflict anger upon himself, he furthermore has no desire to inflict it upon others."[29]

By foregrounding the sublimation of rage and anger he identified in talent and thought, Adorno went beyond Freud's equation of the term with the cultural transcendence and spiritual channeling of libido. Although Freud sometimes acknowledged that aggressive instinctual behavior could also be sublimated, when it came to its aesthetic expression, as classically demonstrated in his 1910 study of Leonardo da Vinci, the sexual drive predominated.[30] In the passages just cited from *Minima Moralia* and "Resignation," however, what is sublimated, according to Adorno, is not libidinal desire, but anger and rage. The result is anything but the sublime elevation of base desires, to recall the words of Laplanche and Pontalis, into something "grand and uplifting."[31] For even in a more just and happier society than our own, Adorno soberly cautioned, art will remain the commemorative repository of past suffering, which can never be rendered beautiful, let alone redeemed or justified. *Aesthetic Theory* ends, in fact, with the defiant words: "It would be preferable that some fine day art vanish altogether than that it forget the suffering that is its expression and in which form has its substance . . . what would art be, as the writing of history, if it shook off the memory of accumulated suffering."[32]

From one perspective, the suffering that must be remembered in art is that endured by generations *of* humans in inhumane conditions. But from another, it can also be understood as the suffering inflicted *by* humans on the natural world in their quest for self-preservation at all costs. In the aphorism in *Minima Moralia* in which Adorno defined talent as "successfully sublimated rage," he defined the latter as "the capacity to convert energies once intensified beyond measure to destroy

---

29   Theodor W. Adorno, "Resignation," in *The Culture Industry*, ed. J. M. Bernstein (London: Routledge, 1996), p. 175.

30   Sigmund Freud, "Leonardo da Vinci and a Memory of His Childhood," *Standard Edition*, vol. 11. Nietzsche, however, included the sublimation of cruelty in his genealogy of morality. See Goebel, *Beyond Discontent*, chapter 3; and Ken Gemes, "A Better Self: Freud and Nietzsche on Sublimation," in Richard Gipps and Michael Lacewing, eds., *The Oxford Handbook of Philosophy and Psychoanalysis* (Oxford: Oxford University Press, 2019).

31   For a discussion of the links between sublimation and the sublime, see Albrecht Wellmer, "Adorno, Modernity and the Sublime," in *Endgames: The Irreconcilable Nature of Modernity*, trans. David Midgley (Cambridge, MA: MIT Press, 1998).

32   Adorno, *Aesthetic Theory*, pp. 260–1.

recalcitrant objects, into the concentration of patient observation, so keeping as tight a hold on the secret of things, as one had earlier when finding no peace until the quavering voice had been wrenched from the mutilated toy."[33] In other words, unsublimated, raw aggression, whether in the service of self-preservation or the death drive, can lead to the destruction of "recalcitrant objects," but successfully sublimated, it has a very different function. Now it can produce an unhurried openness to "the secret of things," which reveals itself like the voices still audible in toys that have been damaged. What the child can hear is both the pain of the mutilated toy and its vital resistance to complete obliteration.

In so arguing, Adorno was tacitly restating his insistence on the autonomous artwork as more than a symptomatic expression of the artist's desires, for it is precisely through its stubborn irreducibility, the block it provides to consoling idealist metaphysics, that the aesthetic object resists the total domination of the subject who created it. That is, the suffering it remembers is not only that of the damaged lives of humankind, but also of the natural environment. As a placeholder for the suffering of the material world resulting from the domination of nature, works of art expand the scope of sublimation itself. More than the sublimation of subjective libidinal desire, they can also be understood as expressing the sublimation of the suffering of nature, both within and outside the human being. And as such, they manage, to repeat the words from *Minima Moralia*, to "convert energies once intensified beyond measure to destroy recalcitrant objects, into the concentration of patient observation, so keeping a tight hold on the secret of things."[34]

There is an additional way to wrest an alternative, more sympathetic reading of sublimation from Adorno's critique of its conventional Freudian reduction. Instead of focusing on the creative artist, whose desires are channeled into culturally acceptable forms, or the thoughtful person of talent who does the same with his or her rage against suffering, it examines the collective aesthetic transfiguration of prior cultural expressions or objects that are in danger of losing their intended efficacy. Instead of interpreting the product of artistic creativity as the congealed intentionality of the artist, conscious or not, this version of

---

33 Adorno, *Minima Moralia*, p. 109.
34 Ibid., p. 72.

sublimation—call it posterior—draws on what can be seen as the intentionless quality of the work, following Benjamin's dictum in *The Origin of German Tragic Drama* that "truth is the death of intention."[35] Here the emphasis is not on production or creation, but rather on what is revealed in time through subsequent aesthetic experience, on the way in which sublimation can be a retrospective, rescuing operation, communal more than individual, in which no longer vital cultural phenomena can find new life in different discursive and institutional contexts. However much the original artist's "idiosyncrasies," his or her "hysterically excessive lack of inhibition over every conceivable fear; narcissism taken to its paranoiac limit" may have inspired the work, its afterlife in the cultural appropriation of posterity is even more important.

Freud had himself acknowledged a role for posterior sublimation in his account of aesthetic reception when he contended that "our actual enjoyment of an imaginative work proceeds from a liberation of tensions in our minds."[36] But for Adorno, this was a misguided way to conceptualize its meaning, as he explained in his critique of the role Aristotle assigned in his *Poetics* to cathartic release in tragic drama. Aristotle, Adorno argued, "entrusts art with the task of providing aesthetic semblance as a substitute satisfaction for the bodily satisfaction of the targeted public's instincts and needs."[37] Producing a surrogate, false resolution of conflict, this kind of posterior sublimation purges rather than validates these affects and is thus tacitly allied with renunciation and repression. "The doctrine of catharsis," he charged, "imputes to art the principle that ultimately the culture industry appropriates and administers. The index of its untruth is the well-founded doubt whether the salutary Aristotelian effect ever occurred; substitute gratification may well have spawned repressed instincts."[38] As such, catharsis depends on the logic of sacrifice, which was a powerful motor of the dialectic of enlightenment.

---

35 Walter Benjamin, *The Origin of German Tragic Drama*, trans. John Osborne (London: NLB, 1977), p. 36.

36 Sigmund Freud, "Creative Writers and Day-Dreaming," in *Standard Edition*, vol. 9, p. 153. See Eckart Goebel, "On Being Shaken: Theodor W. Adorno on Sublimation," *Cultural Critique* 70 (Fall 2008), p. 161.

37 Adorno, *Aesthetic Theory*, p. 238.

38 Ibid. Although his early collaborator Josef Breuer had endorsed the therapeutic value of catharsis, Freud was more ambivalent. See Rieff, *Freud*, pp. 381–3.

Against Aristotle, Adorno insisted with Hegel that certain posterior sublimations can still preserve what they transcend and cancel, thereby escaping the deadly logic of sacrificial exchange: "No sublimation succeeds that does not guard in itself what it sublimates."[39] Certain posterior sublimations can resist the logic of sacrifice and retain some of the displaced instinctual energy and rage at suffering whose traces they bear. They can take many forms, but two examples, in particular, from the history of art are significant for our argument. The first is the redescription of devotional religious art from within the Western tradition in aesthetic terms or as examples of cultural patrimony for the nation or humankind as a whole. The second is the redefinition of so-called primitive objects or practices, which once served cultic, magical or other purposes, as formally beautiful and capable of being appreciated as such when extracted from their functional context. In other words, it has been possible to rescue and revalorize objects that appeared to have outlived their devotional or cultic functions and turn them into embodiments of Kant's "purposiveness without purpose." Objects and practices that once had potent performative powers in liturgical or cultic practices could be resituated in the discourse of art history. Here sublimation is not of the artist's libidinal desires or rage at suffering, but of the prior works that may have once resulted from them.

Let us take each in turn. The iconoclastic smashing of what were considered dangerous idols has been a frequent practice of both intra-religious iconoclastic movements, such as that in the Byzantine church during the eighth and ninth centuries and the European Reformation in the sixteenth century, and self-proclaimed virtuous political movements, such as those arising during the French Revolution.[40] Taken as more than harmless symbolic representations or mimetic images, idols were understood by their foes as fetishistic embodiments of false gods, dubious intercessors between the human and the divine, and remnants of irrational superstition.[41] In addition to these problematic religious

---

39   Ibid., p. 94.
40   See Alain Besançon, *The Forbidden Image: An Intellectual History of Iconoclasm*, trans. Jean Marie Todd (Chicago: University of Chicago Press, 2000).
41   For an analysis of the Iconoclastic Controversy, see Emmanuel Alloa, "Visual Studies in Byzantium: A Pictorial Turn *avant la lettre*," *Journal of Visual Culture* 12: 1 (April 2013). He points out that Western Christianity, turning to Aristotelian considerations of the sign, overcame anxiety over idolatry: "If an image is in actuality a referential sign, then even depictions of heathen deities lose all magical peril" (p. 25).

functions, they could also be condemned for legitimating hierarchical political power. For the critics of the ancien régime who dreamed of a new republic of virtue, "the arts were a result of luxury and vice, that . . . flourished only in decadent, over-civilized societies and provided opiates for the subjects of tyrannical rulers."[42]

The impulse to smash idols and topple symbols of privilege led to the actual destruction of many objects whose performative potency was seen as either literally or symbolically nefarious. Attempts to save them thus had to disrupt their power to make something happen (or at least neutralize the belief that they had that power), and then redescribe them as objects of disinterested aesthetic contemplation. The needed change was more than merely taxonomic or categorical, as something of the aura that had informed their ability to enable devotional respect had to be retained to secure their new value. Here posterior cultural sublimation avoided the lamentable effects of repression or even the outright destruction of objects. Churches might be stripped of their excessive ornamentation, but altarpieces, statues and the like could find new sanctuaries on or within the walls of secular museums. In Europe, a crucial turning point in the visual arts came during the de-Christianizing fervor of the French Revolution. As Stanley Idzerda noted in his pioneering study of revolutionary iconoclasm:

> The sale of many church buildings to private individuals raised fears that the mosaics, stained-glass windows, statues, and paintings in these buildings would be either destroyed or dispersed. To avoid the danger of such an artistic loss to the nation, the Constituent Assembly in 1790 created a Monuments Commission composed of members of several royal academies. The chief duty of this group was to inventory and collect in various depots those works of art thought worthy of preservation by the state.[43]

The transformation of the Louvre in Paris from a royal residence in 1793 into a repository of the people's cultural patrimony was the capstone of their efforts. Although the iconoclastic impulse was slow to disappear,

---

42   Stanley Idzerda, "Iconoclasm in the French Revolution," *American Historical Review* 60: 1 (October 1954), p. 19.

43   Ibid., p. 14.

the effect of the transformation was ultimately profound. By disentangling the sacred or political function of works from their aesthetic value and distinguishing between corrupt luxury, the emblem of aristocratic privilege, and disinterested beauty available for appreciation by all, it was possible to allow them to earn a different kind of respect in the semi-sacred space of a public museum. By the 1820s, Hegel could confidently say that in front of formerly devotional images, "We bow the knee no longer."[44] To be sure, such treasures could now be called "ornaments of the State," and gain economic value in the more profane space of the capitalist art market.[45] But they were also able to serve as embodiments of aesthetic value in an immanent realm of art for its own sake, which had the potential, as we will see Adorno argue, to produce more than Freud's cathartic "liberation of tensions in our minds."

A comparable story, although one less marked by the threat of puritanical or revolutionary violence, can be told of the aesthetic transformation of sacred music. Here the canonical case is Johann Sebastian Bach's great oratorio *St. Matthew's Passion*, written in 1727 to present a musical version of the Passion of Christ for Good Friday vesper services in the St. Thomas Church in Leipzig. A little more than a century later, Felix Mendelssohn conducted a streamlined version of it at the Singakademie in Berlin, the first time it had been moved from the sacred space of a church to the secular confines of a concert hall. Here it no longer served liturgical purposes for a religious congregation but functioned instead for a general audience as an exemplar of what soon would be called "absolute music."[46]

Although other examples can be adduced of the aesthetic sublimation of Western religious material, such as the reading of the Bible as literature rather than as Holy Scripture, let me turn now to the displacing of so-called primitive artifacts from a cultic to an aesthetic frame, where they could be appreciated in formal terms or as exemplars of universal archetypes.[47] After first being grouped together under the

---

44   G. W. F. Hegel, *Aesthetics: Lectures on Fine Arts*, 2 vols., trans. T. M. Knox (Oxford: Oxford University Press, 1988), vol. 1, p. 103.

45   Cited in Idzerda, "Iconoclasm in the French Revolution," p. 23.

46   Cecilia Applegate, *Bach in Berlin: Nation and Culture in Mendelssohn's Revival of the St. Matthew Passion* (Ithaca, NY: Cornell University Press, 2005).

47   See David Norton, ed., *A History of the English Bible as Literature*, 2 vols. (Cambridge: Cambridge University Press, 2012).

generic category of "primitive," their performative functions as literal instruments of magic or objects of religious worship were then sublimated into the metaphorical magic of autotelic works of art commanding a different kind of devotion. In fact, the literal transfer of those artifacts from natural history or ethnographic museums, where they served as "documents" of exotic cultures, to art museums, where they became "artworks" in their own right, gathered momentum in the early twentieth century. Celebrating "noble savages" as the antidote to decadent Western civilization had, of course, already enjoyed a long history,[48] but modernist artists were more inspired by the formal properties of the objects they had produced, which had hitherto been of interest only to anthropologists or collectors of exotic curiosities.[49] Although anticipated by Gauguin's fascination with the South Seas, the canonical turning point is often said to be the inspiration of African masks at the Trocadéro Museum in Paris in the composition of Picasso's *Les Demoiselles d'Avignon* in 1907.

Much has been made by post-modernist and post-colonial theorists, and justly so, of the costs of this aesthetic recoding and displacement, whose entanglement with the European imperialist appropriation of the material wealth of "exotic cultures" has not gone unremarked.[50] Whereas the cloistering of sacred artifacts in the secular sanctuary of the Louvre could be understood as undermining elite power and granting the masses access to art, the Western appropriation of objects from colonized cultures revealed a very different power dynamic. Moreover, the elevation of so-called primitive objects with originally ritual, decorative, apotropaic or magical functions into works of high art could also lead to

48   See Arthur O. Lovejoy and George Boas, *Primitivism and Related Ideas in Antiquity* (Baltimore: Johns Hopkins University Press, 1935).

49   The classic account is Robert Goldwater, *Primitivism in Modern Art* (Cambridge, MA: Belknap, 1986); see also William Rubin, *"Primitivism" in Twentieth-Century Art: Affinity of the Tribal and the Modern*, 2 vols. (New York: MOMA, 1984); and Colin Rhodes, *Primitivism and Modern Art* (London: Thames and Hudson, 1994). In literature as well, primitivism had its lure. See, for example, David Pan, *Primitive Renaissance: Rethinking German Expressionism* (Lincoln: University of Nebraska Press, 2001); and Ben Etherington, *Literary Primitivism* (Stanford, CA: Stanford University Press, 2017).

50   See, for example, Hal Foster, "The Primitive Unconscious of Modern Art," *October* 34 (Autumn 1985); and James Clifford, *The Predicament of Culture: Twentieth-Century Ethnography, Literature and Art* (Cambridge, MA: Harvard University Press, 1988).

their insertion into the art market as commodities, a fate already suffered by aesthetically sublimated religious objects rescued from iconoclastic destruction. Ironically, in this way so-called primitive objects were stripped of one fetishistic function only to be endowed with another. In addition, when read as instances of species-wide mythic or psychological archetypes, their irreducible otherness was subsumed under a dubious notion of ahistorical universality or alleged common "affinity,"[51] which tacitly imposed Western values on them by turning them into fungible exemplars of a vapid humanism that effaced their cultural specificity. All of these costs were real. And yet, despite them, their newly honored status in the eyes of modernist aesthetics allowed such objects the same opportunity to serve as authentic works of art that had been enjoyed by Western religious artifacts saved from the hammers of the iconoclasts.

How, we now have to ask, does Adorno's dialectical critique of sublimation comport with the posterior aesthetic redemption of traditional religious or "primitive" objects, with all of its ambiguities? Would his hostility to the claim that artists sublimate their desires extend to sublimation understood in this very different sense of posterior cultural redemption? Could his more positive claim that talent and thought can be understood as sublimations of rage at suffering, both of humans and of nature, be translated into a more generous attitude towards the posterior aesthetic sublimation of religious or cultic objects in the modern world? Could it extend beyond the sublimation of subjective desires to the spiritual transfiguration of the material world, the world of a nature that is more than dominated or repressed in the name of human self-preservation?

There are few explicit answers to these questions, but hints of Adorno's likely position appear in several of his related arguments. Although rarely commenting on the visual arts, he did ponder the implications of the sequestration of artworks in museums in an essay he wrote pitting Valéry's stress on aesthetic objects against Proust's on subjective experience:

> Works of art can fully embody the *promesse du bonheur* only when they have been uprooted from their native soil and have set out along

---

51   See Clifford, *The Predicament of Culture*, p. 190.

the path to their own destruction . . . The procedure which today rele-
gates every work of art to the museum, even Picasso's most recent
sculpture, is irreversible. It is not solely reprehensible, however, for it
presages a situation in which art, having completed its estrangement
from human ends, returns, in Novalis' words, to life.[52]

That is, the rescuing of endangered objects by their placement in museums—what we have been calling posterior cultural sublimation—is a
necessary stage in the preservation of their power to change our lives in
the future, when the happiness they promise may be achieved.

A similar argument informed Adorno's defense in 1951 of Bach
against his contemporary devotees, who wanted to find in him the
Pietist believer, musically expressing the revelation "of time-honored
bounds of tradition, of the spirit of medieval polyphony, of the theologically vaulted cosmos."[53] Those who insisted on playing Bach's music
only with original instruments and in sacred settings, hoping to restore
its "authenticity," were betraying, so Adorno charged, his compositional
innovations, which still resonate today: "They have made him into a
composer for organ festivals in well-preserved Baroque towns, into
ideology."[54] Despite their historicist pretentions, they are more like
purveyors of an allegedly timeless ontology, who fail to acknowledge the
movement of history, which compels form to develop with variations
rather than remain static. "No matter how it is done in the Church of St.
Thomas, a performance of the *St. Matthew Passion*, for instance, done
with meagre means sounds pale and indecisive to the present-day ear . . .
such a performance thereby contradicts the intrinsic essence of Bach's
music. The only adequate interpretation of the dynamic objectively
embedded in his work is one which realizes it."[55] To be true to Bach's
genius, Adorno concluded, is to recognize the inspiration he provides to

52   Adorno, "Valéry Proust Museum," in *Prisms*, p. 185. See also James Gordon
Finlayson, "The Artwork and the *Promesse du Bonheur* in Adorno," *European Journal of
Philosophy* 23: 3 (2015).

53   Theodor W. Adorno, "Bach Defended Against His Devotees," in *Prisms*, p. 135.
For discussions of his attitude towards Bach, see Max Paddison, *Adorno's Aesthetics of
Music* (Cambridge: Cambridge University Press, 1997), pp. 225–32; and Mark Berry,
"Romantic Modernism: Bach, Furtwängler, and Adorno," *New German Critique*, no. 104
(Summer 2008).

54   Ibid., p. 136.

55   Ibid., p. 144.

modern music: "Justice is done Bach ... solely through the most advanced composition, which in turn converges with the level of Bach's continually unfolding work ... his heritage has passed on to composition, which is loyal to him in being disloyal; it calls his music by name in producing it anew."[56]

When religious impulses apparently inspired later works, such as Beethoven's *Missa Solemnis,* which Adorno called his "alienated masterpiece," it did so only in ways that betrayed the impossibility of reversing the transition from the devotional to the aesthetic. "The religiosity of the *Missa,* if one can speak unconditionally of such a thing," Adorno wrote, "is neither that of one secure in belief nor that of a world religion of such an idealist nature that it would require no effort of its adherent to believe in it ... In its aesthetic form the work asks what and how one may sing of the absolute without deceit, and because of this, there occurs the compression which alienates it and causes it to approach incomprehension."[57] Here, aesthetic sublimation meant the opposite of affirmative reconciliation, as the work expressed the current impossibility of an organic totality successfully unifying subject and object, achieved in Beethoven's earlier symphonies. Instead, in the *Missa,* Beethoven "exposed the classical as classicizing. He rejected the affirmative, that which uncritically endorsed Being in the idea of the classically symphonic."[58]

If there is a later equivalent of Christ's Passion, which had once been capable of musical expression with still sacred intent by Bach, it appeared, so Adorno argued, in Alban Berg's human-all-too-human opera *Wozzeck.* The very character of the work, Adorno wrote, "is *Passion.* The music does not suffer within the human being, does not, itself, participate in its actions and emotions. It suffers over him; only for this reason is it able, like the music of the old passion plays, to represent every emotion without ever having to assume the mask of one of the characters of the tragic drama. The music lays the suffering that is dictated by the stars above bodily onto the shoulders of the human being, the individual."[59] Suffering,

56   Ibid., p. 146.

57   Theodor W. Adorno, "Alienated Masterpiece: The *Missa Solemnis*," *Telos,* no. 28 (Summer 1976), p. 120.

58   Ibid., p. 122.

59   Theodor W. Adorno, "The Opera *Wozzeck*," in *Essays on Music,* ed. Richard Leppert, trans. Susan H. Gillespie (Berkeley: University of California Press, 2002), p. 625.

rather than desire, Adorno implied, can be understood as the affect that fuels aesthetic sublimation in a secular world, which transcends the emotional life of the creative subject.

Did a similar attitude inform Adorno's response to the modernist appropriation of so-called primitive culture? To provide a detailed answer would require parsing his complicated analysis of related terms such as "archaic" and "barbaric" in *Dialectic of Enlightenment* and elsewhere, but a few basic points can be ventured now. In *Aesthetic Theory*, while arguing against an ahistorical definition of art, Adorno noted that "much that was not art—cultic works, for instance—has over the course of history metamorphosed into art; and much that once was art is that no longer."[60] If "art" thus defied easy definition, no less dubious was the search for its origins in some primeval need. Nonetheless, Adorno did hazard a speculation about one element in its ur-history that still echoed in the art of today: "It is doubtless that art did not begin with works, whether they were primarily magical or already aesthetic. The cave drawings are stages of a process and in no way an early one. The first images must have been preceded by mimetic comportment—the assimilation of self to its other—that does not fully coincide with the superstition of direct magical influence."[61] The residue of such benign mimesis, which Adorno often contrasted with the subjective domination of nature serving self-preservation, meant that "aesthetic comportment contains what has been belligerently excised from civilization and repressed, as well as the human suffering under the loss, a suffering already expressed in the earliest forms of mimesis."[62] Although such a residue might be called irrational from the point of view of instrumental rationality, it was actually an indication of a more profound and emancipatory ideal of reason preserved in art. Here the relevant sublimation was not of libidinal desire or even the memory of suffering, but rather of the mimetic faculty that had been sacrificed—with the exception of children's play[63]—to the demands of instrumental rationality and the

---

60   Adorno, *Aesthetic Theory*, p. 3.
61   Ibid., p. 329.
62   Ibid., p. 330.
63   For a critique of Adorno's appeal to childhood experience in his treatment of sublimation, see Matt F. Connell, "Childhood Experience and the Image of Utopia: The Broken Promise of Adorno's Proustian Sublimations," *Radical Philosophy*, no. 99 (January/February 2000).

domination of nature. As Peter Uwe Hohendahl notes, "By remaining attached to the primitive, for Adorno the advanced artwork resists the process of Enlightenment ... Adorno recognizes the ambiguity of the modern artwork, its tendency to return to the logic of mimesis."[64]

There was, to be sure, also a regressive potential in the modernist exaltation of the primitive or even the "pre-capitalist," against whose dangerous political implications Adorno warned.[65] In aesthetic terms, Adorno most explicitly discerned it in the music of Igor Stravinsky, which he invidiously compared with Schoenberg's atonal alternative in *Philosophy of New Music*. Likening *The Rite of Spring* to the visual modernists' discovery of African sculpture, Adorno wrote that "it belongs to the years in which 'savages' were first called 'primitives,' to the world of Sir James Frazier, Lucien Lévy-Bruhl, and Freud's *Totem and Taboo* ... When the avant-garde avowed its attachment to African sculpture, the reactionary aim of the movement was still entirely hidden."[66] It was, however, on full display in Stravinsky's embrace of the sacrifice of the individual to the collective, which is enacted without protest in the *Rite of Spring* with its brutal rhythms and convulsive shocks, anticipating the slaughter of the coming First World War.

But unlike many post-colonial and post-modernist critics, Adorno refused to lament the disembedding of what came to be called primitive artifacts from their allegedly "authentic" contexts of origin or advocate the restoration of their cultic functions. In *The Jargon of Authenticity*, he decried attempts to grant priority to the original over the copy, the genuine over the derived, the pure over the impure, the autochthonous over the diasporic. As in his insistence on distinguishing between artworks and the psychology of their creators, he refused to reduce the validity of aesthetic objects to their genetic cultural matrix.[67] Whatever the limits of aesthetic sublimation, it was superior to the repressive de-sublimation that sought to reverse the historical process and regain

64   Peter Uwe Hohendahl, *The Fleeting Promise of Art: Adorno's Aesthetic Theory Revisited* (Ithaca, NY: Cornell University Press, 2013), p. 96.

65   Adorno, *Minima Moralia*, pp. 52–3.

66   Theodor W. Adorno, *Philosophy of New Music*, trans. Robert Hullot-Kentor (Minneapolis: University of Minnesota Press, 2006), pp. 111–12.

67   Theodor W. Adorno, *The Jargon of Authenticity*, trans. Knut Tarnowski and Frederic Will (London: NLB, 1973); see also Martin Jay, "Taking on the Stigma of Authenticity: Adorno's Critique of Genuineness," in *Essays from the Edge: Parega and Paralipomena* (Charlottesville: University of Virginia Press, 2011).

libidinal immediacy, a caution that extended to naïve attempts to return to a pristine version of nature before its domination.[68] Adorno's much derided hostility to jazz can be at least partly understood in these terms, for, so he claimed, "jazz is the false liquidation of art—instead of utopia becoming reality it disappears from the picture."[69] In *Dialectic of Enlightenment*, he and Horkheimer could in contrast define "the secret of aesthetic sublimation" as the ability "to present fulfillment in its brokenness," something denied to the culture industry, which "does not sublimate: it suppresses."[70]

Thus, despite the reservations Adorno expressed against the Freudian reduction of artistic creation to sublimated desire, he could argue that "by re-enacting the spell of reality, by sublimating it as an image, art at the same time liberates itself from it; sublimation and freedom mutually accord."[71] In fact, even Stravinsky's appropriation of primitivism could be understood dialectically as a placeholder for a more emancipatory liquidation. For despite its regressive dangers, it also expresses "the longing to abolish social appearances, the urge for truth behind bourgeois mediations and its masks of violence. The heritage of the bourgeois revolution is active in this disposition of mind."[72] It is for this reason that Stravinsky's music was denounced by fascists, who preferred the restoration of classical kitsch in their art and literal barbarism in their violent actions: "In the Third Reich of countless human sacrifice," Adorno noted, "*The Rite of Spring* would not have been performable."[73]

If we now return in conclusion to the three objections we have noted Adorno made to Freud's theory of aesthetic sublimation when it was used reductively to explain artistic creativity, a somewhat more complicated picture emerges. As in the case of Marcuse, who had defended "non-repressive sublimation" in *Eros and Civilization*, Adorno distinguished between affirmative and critical versions.[74] Rather than adapting to the status quo and channeling the transgressive idiosyncrasies of

---

68   See Deborah Cook, *Adorno on Nature* (Durham, NC: Duke University Press, 2011).

69   Adorno, "Perennial Fashion—Jazz," in *Prisms*, p. 132.

70   Horkheimer and Adorno, *Dialectic of Enlightenment*, p. 111.

71   Adorno, *Aesthetic Theory*, p. 130.

72   Ibid., p. 112.

73   Ibid.

74   Herbert Marcuse, *Eros and Civilization: A Philosophical Inquiry into Freud* (Boston: Beacon, 1955), p. 190.

artists into culturally uplifting consolations for the renunciation of
desire, sublimation can also mean preserving the potential of past
sources of dissatisfaction with the present, such as religious yearning
and the primitivist disdain for contemporary civilization, for future
appropriation. This is why it presents "fulfillment in its brokenness,"
rather than as fully realized. Not only is the memory preserved of past
suffering, but so too are traces of the mimetic impulse that inspired art
in the first place. It is for this reason Adorno can define successful sublimation as guarding in itself "what it sublimates."

This survival also means that, despite Adorno's second complaint
against psychoanalytic reductionism, his fear that the theory of sublimation can spiritualize what was originally a corporeal or material
interest, he never endorsed a simple reversal of that hierarchy. Art,
indeed, culture in general, did involve a certain renunciation of bodily
desires, or rather of their immediate realization, and thus necessarily
involved spiritualization. And as a result, civilization did bring with it
inevitable discontents, as Freud had pessimistically argued, or at least all
previous civilizations had done so. But the alternative was not a simple
restoration of dominated nature or the unmediated de-sublimation of
instinctual desire. Instead, it was necessary to heal the wound by means
of the weapon that had caused it. As Eckart Goebel notes,

> Adorno moves beyond the antithesis of sublimation and the drives.
> Only false sublimation, with adaptation and integration (in Freud:
> narcissistic idealization) as its aim, reproduces the archaic desires of the
> drives as they once were, because they were never changed. Aesthetic
> experience as conceived by Adorno differentiates instinctual desire by
> comprehending sublimation both as differentiation and as a protest
> against the world under "the rule of brutal self-preservation," which
> corresponds to the identical, rigid self.[75]

Finally, because the sublimation of reception rather than production,
the posterior rescue of the endangered effects of prior sublimations,
focuses on created artworks rather than creative artists, it avoids the
dangers of excessive subjectivism. Literally manifest in the rescue of
artworks menaced by destructive, iconoclastic fervor, it honors the

---

75   Goebel, *Beyond Discontent*, p. 224.

primacy of the object, the resistance that the world, both natural and cultural, presents to the domination implied in the narcissistic quest for self-preservation at all costs. What is sublimated need not be reduced to the libidinal needs of the thwarted subject, but rather can be understood as the delicate mixture of spiritual and corporeal, rational and sensual, formal and substantive that humankind has come to call the work of art.

To offer an example of what Adorno may mean, let me turn in conclusion to Leo Bersani's discussion of psychoanalysis and art in *The Freudian Body*. Reading Stéphane Mallarmé's "L'Après-midi d'un faune" as less a transcendence of desire than its active extension, Bersani argues that "the sublimating conscious described by the faun operates on what might be called a principle of accelerating supplementarity . . . Mallarmé encourages us to view sublimation not as a mechanism by which desire is denied, but rather as a self-reflexive activity by which desire multiplies and diversifies its representations."[76] With a certain irony, the faun's desire is neither realized nor repressed, but rather proliferates, while working to undermine his boundaried, integral selfhood. Understood thusly, the "somatic pleasure" which Adorno identified with utopia turns out to be less the restoration of primary narcissistic oneness than an open-ended play of mimetic repetition and displacement. It may begin as "blind," but, because of the experience it has gained through aesthetic sublimation, it learns to see with fresh eyes. Rather than a defense mechanism or a version of symptom formation, sublimation, in this larger sense, draws on the legacy of past cultural creation to enable a future in which the promise of happiness may, against all odds, still be realized.

---

76   Leo Bersani, *The Freudian Body: Psychoanalysis and Art* (New York: Columbia University Press, 1986), pp. 48–9.

3

Blaming the Victim? Arendt, Adorno and Erikson on the Jewish Responsibility for Anti-Semitism

Perhaps the greatest test of dialectical thinking comes when there is no easy way to transcend or even mediate unpalatable alternatives and reach a higher-level reconciliation. Struggling to make sense of the absolute and unfathomable evil that came to be called the Holocaust, intellectuals who were among its fortunate survivors were faced with the choice of turning the Jews into passive scapegoats, randomly chosen for no plausible reason to suffer their fate, or active agents in bringing it about, however unintentionally. Three of the most probing attempts to deal with this dilemma were made by the émigrés Erik Erikson, Theodor Adorno (along with Max Horkheimer) and Hannah Arendt, all of whom speculated on the abiding sources of anti-Semitism and the reasons for its exterminationist turn in their own day. In so doing, they were willing to risk crossing the line that prohibited blaming victims for their victimization, or at least so it might seem at first glance. But rather than mere exercises in Jewish self-hatred, their efforts took seriously the task of explaining why the Jews have held such a prominent place in the cultural imaginary of the West for so long.

If the method of immanent critique were to be applied to their speculations, however, one significant caveat emerges. Anti-Semites often operate with a generic category, attributing this or that trait or behavior to "the Jews" understood as a collectivity (or even more problematically, "the Jew" as a singular type). At times, in their explanations of and ripostes to anti-Semitism, Erikson, Adorno and Arendt also employ comparable rhetorical tropes. In this, they neglect to account for what might be called—to adopt the terminologies of Alain Finkielkraut and Sarah Hammerschlag—the presence of the "imaginary Jew" or the "figural Jew" in their own think-ing.[1] What makes this recognition so difficult, of course, is that such generic thinking not only underpins the accusations of Jew-haters, but also often informs Jewish self-understanding. Indeed, it is arguably one of the preconditions of their survival as "a people" as well as a religion despite all the attempts to destroy or assimilate them over millennia.

And yet, if we take Adorno's insistence on the normative value of non-identity seriously, all identitarian categories should be challenged by what exceeds their conceptual grasp. What might be called the nominalist moment in Critical Theory, its belief that alterity must survive any attempt at reconciliation, suggests that all positive identities—including ethnic or national ones like "the Jews"—are inherently problematic.[2] Or, to be more precise, the cultural construction of categorical identities may exert enormous pressure on the way humans make sense of their world and therefore cannot be easily dispelled, but they should not be reified into eternal or natural kinds.

Ironically, to give the screw one final twist, for Adorno the Jews some-times figured as the exemplar of non-identity itself because of the inability of the dominant cultures in which they survived to digest them. For exam-ple, his oft-quoted claim that "German words of foreign derivation are the Jews of language"[3] shows Adorno's figural use of them in precisely this way. As a result, the Jews serve for him as placeholders for the particularist defense against sublimation he called "idiosyncrasy," which, as we noted in the previous chapter, he insisted was the source of aesthetic creativity.[4]

---

1 Alain Finkielkraut, *The Imaginary Jew*, trans. Kevin O'Neill and David Suchoff (Lincoln: University of Nebraska Press, 1997); Sarah Hammerschlag, *The Figural Jew: Politics and Identity in Postwar French Thought* (Chicago: University of Chicago Press, 2010).

2 For recent explorations of this theme in his work, see Eric Oberle, *Adorno and the Century of Negative Identity* (Stanford, CA: Stanford University Press, 2018); and Oshrat C. Silberbusch, *Adorno's Philosophy of the Nonidentical: Thinking as Resistance* (Cham, Switzerland: Palgrave Macmillan, 2018).

3 Theodor W. Adorno, *Minima Moralia: Reflections on Damaged Life*, trans. E. F. N. Jephcott (London: NLB, 1974), p. 110. For a discussion, see Yasemin Yildiz, "The Foreign in the Mother Tongue: Words of Foreign Derivation and Utopia in Theodor W. Adorno," in *Beyond the Mother Tongue: The Postmonolingual Condition* (New York: Fordham University Press, 2013).

4 For a discussion of the connection, see Jan Plug, "Idiosyncrasies: of Anti-Semitism," in *Language without Soil: Adorno and Late Philosophical Modernity*, ed. Gerhard Richter (New York: Fordham University Press, 2010).

But such a role has its own dangers, as non-conformity to general conventions can easily be stigmatized as pathological. In short, a dialectic that remains negative must find a way to hover over a landscape of theoretical aporias to avoid crash-landing in inhospitable territory.[5]

There are few more comforting responses to the dogged persistence of anti-Semitism than the familiar joke so often repeated in various forms by its victims during the horrible twentieth century: "An anti-Semite claimed that the Jews had caused the war; the reply was: Yes, the Jews and the bicyclists. Why the bicyclists? asks the one. Why the Jews? asks the other." The implication of the joke is straightforward enough: singling out the Jews, it tells us, is entirely arbitrary, and makes as much sense as blaming any other innocent group for something they did not cause. The joke's power comes from the incontrovertible fact that a culprit called "the Jews" has been blamed for so many terrible things for so long by so many detractors that it is impossible to believe that any one group of people could have ever had such powers of conspiratorial malevolence. Against such hyperbolic accusations of evil, it has therefore been tempting to mount a no less unyielding defense of absolute innocence, putting all of the blame on the victimizers' need to find a scapegoat for ills they cannot otherwise explain.

A nagging doubt has, however, haunted the simple inversion of absolute guilt into total innocence—or better put, lack of responsibility—which has seemed, for some, too simplistic a way to explain the stubborn persistence of anti-Semitism. Sigmund Freud, for one, felt the need for a more profound response, and was willing to venture one even if it would inevitably cause more discomfort for the victims than the bicyclist joke. In an often-cited letter to Arnold Zweig in 1934, he posed it in these terms: "Faced with the renewed persecutions, one asks oneself again how the Jew has come to be what he is and why he has attracted this undying hatred."[6] His answer was given in his final work *Moses and Monotheism*, where he speculated that the most profound and abiding cause, along with a welter of others, was the fateful

---

5   This essay, previously unpublished, was presented as a keynote for the conference "Arendt and Antisemitism," organized by Maurice Samuel and Adam Stern at the Yale Center for the Study of Antisemitism in November 2018.

6   Sigmund Freud to Arnold Zweig, September 30, 1934, *Letters*, ed. Ernst L. Freud (London: Hogarth, 1970), p. 421.

invention of monotheism—or rather Moses's appropriation and dissemination of what had been originally an Egyptian idea of the one true God. For belief in that God, who was jealous of his unique status, fueled a stern iconoclastic denial of the visual pleasure characteristic of polytheistic idolatry and a demand for unyielding ethical rigor.[7] Because repressing the desiring, gratification-seeking body was the cost of attaining what Freud called "the lofty heights of spirituality,"[8] the victims of the monotheistic intolerance for pagan sensuality, idolatry and difference were never really reconciled to their loss.

This is not the place to consider yet again the plausibility of Freud's self-acknowledged "historical novel" as an account of the origins of monotheism or the anti-Semitism it helped unleash.[9] I introduce it instead as a prelude to a discussion of three other attempts to enter the dangerous territory of explaining anti-Semitism as more than merely an arbitrary scapegoating of the Jews. These, too, were made by Central European Jews (or in two cases, "half-Jews"), who were forced to migrate by the Nazis and sought to understand the deepest causes of the unprecedented catastrophe that befell their people. Like Freud, these theorists were willing to risk being charged with insensitivity to the plight of the victims of anti-Semitism and giving comfort to the perpetrators. Like Freud, they did not shy away from adopting the rhetoric of what has been called "the conceptual Jew" or "the figural Jew," in which the heterogeneity of actual Jewish experience is subsumed under an essentialized image, inevitably arousing the suspicion that it mimics the fantasmatic imaginary of anti-Semites themselves.[10] Like Freud, they were willing to

7   Sigmund Freud, *Moses and Monotheism*, trans. Katherine Jones (New York: Knopf, 1939).

8   Ibid., p. 112.

9   For the most recent considerations, see Gilad Sharvit and Karen S. Feldman, eds., *Freud and Monotheism: Moses and the Violent Origins of Religion* (New York: Fordham University Press, 2018).

10   Jonathan Judaken, "Blindness and Insight: The Conceptual Jew in Adorno and Arendt's post-Holocaust Reflections on the Antisemitic Question," in *Arendt and Adorno: Political and Philosophical Investigations*, ed. Lars Rensmann and Samir Gandesha (Stanford, CA: Stanford University Press, 2012); and Hammerschlag, *The Figural Jew*. The essentialization of Jewish identity is, of course, a two-way street, as enthusiastic believers in the enduring reality of "the Jewish people" have posited something similar. For a provocative and controversial critique of this assumption, see Shlomo Sand, *The Invention of the Jewish People*, trans. Yael Lotan (London: Verso, 2020). Arendt and Adorno were, to be sure, aware of this danger. Arendt noted that

spin out grand theories that sought answers on a speculative level that went far beyond any possible empirical analysis of discrete historical causes. The theorists in question were among the most influential intellectual legislators of the twentieth century: Erik Erikson, Theodor W. Adorno (along with Max Horkheimer) and Hannah Arendt.

To call attention to the risk they took in speculating on the Jewish role in arousing anti-Semitism is no empty rhetorical gesture, as I know from personal experience. In 2003, I published an essay in *Salmagundi* titled "Ariel Sharon and the Rise of the New Anti-Semitism,"[11] which argued that certain harsh Israeli actions towards the Palestinians had triggered a revival of dormant anti-Semitic bias. Although I carefully distinguished between "cause" and "moral responsibility" and vigorously denied any legitimacy whatsoever to the denigration of "Jews" as a collective category, the outraged response was swift and unyielding. A gaggle of self-proclaimed defenders of the Jews, or, more precisely, of Israel's conduct under all circumstances, denounced the piece as evidence of Jewish self-hatred and blaming the victim.[12] Unexpectedly, I found myself grouped with a host of far more vociferous critics of Israeli policies, including Noam Chomsky, Thomas Friedman, George Steiner, Norman Finkelstein, Judith Butler and Tony Judt, as a cosmopolitan universalist who had cravenly betrayed his inherited ethnic identity. What was meant as a critique of objectionable policies by a

---

during the Enlightenment, "The struggle to emancipate the Jews was not about the Jews, not about an oppressed people; what was *theoretically* demanded was a visible symbol of human liberation, of progress, of the abandonment of prejudice . . . From the start the Jew became *the* Jew, individuals became a principle." "Antisemitism," in *The Jewish Writings*, ed. Jerome Kohn and Ron H. Feldman (New York: Schocken, 2007), p. 67. And Horkheimer and Adorno also recognized the irony of modern Jews who staked their emancipation of the ideal of individual liberty and human rights being once again "debased as a species. They who were never allowed untroubled ownership of the civic right which should have granted them human dignity are again called 'the Jews' without distinction." Max Horkheimer and Theodor W. Adorno, *Dialectic of Enlightenment: Philosophical Fragments*, ed. Gunzelin Schmid Noerr, trans. E. F. N. Jephcott (Stanford, CA: Stanford University Press, 2001), p. 144. For a recent discussion of nominalist alternatives to the conceptual Jew, see Amos Morris-Riech, "The 'Negative Jew' and Individuality," *Jewish Quarterly Review* 97: 1 (Winter, 2007).

11   Martin Jay, "Ariel Sharon and the Rise of the New Anti-Semitism," *Salmagundi*, no. 137/138 (Winter/Spring 2003).

12   Edward Alexander and Paul Bogdanor, eds., *The Jewish Divide over Israel: Accusers and Defenders* (New York: Routledge, 2006); Edward Alexander, *Jews against Themselves* (New Brunswick, NJ: Transaction, 2015).

specific group of right-wing Zionist leaders, which had unintentionally unleashed a no less deplorable anti-Semitic response, was thus turned into a blanket condemnation of "the Jews" as a whole for deserving the hatred directed against them.

If this kind of defensiveness could greet a very modest attempt to explain the triggering of contemporary anti-Semitism—not, *nota bene*, the deeper sources of the abiding prejudice—by specific Israeli actions, you can imagine the risk taken by Freud and our three protagonists when they sought to exhume precisely those sources. They were doing so, after all, at a time when the Jews were most vulnerable, well before a powerful Jewish state could even be accused of stimulating anti-Semitism through its bullying of the non-Jewish people whose land it occupied. By their willingness to speculate on an identifiable Jewish contribution to the prejudice against them, they could be seen as tacitly playing into the hands of those who attributed to Jews allegedly essential characteristics, which had endured over millennia and defied diasporic scattering. They could even be accused of giving comfort to the enemy by identifying and then excoriating some of the same negative traits that were decried by anti-Semites.

But it might also be possible to see another, less malign logic at work in their audacious efforts. Acknowledging some responsibility to the Jews for their fate grants them, after all, the dignity of agency rather than assigning to them a fully passive role in a drama where the only protagonists are their tormentors. One way to honor this dignity is to redirect attention from the dim-witted victimizers, who do not deserve the effort to plumb the alleged depths of their prejudice, to the victims, who were chosen precisely because of the genuinely significant role they have played in the development of civilization.[13] It registers, to give Hannah Arendt's famous phrase a new twist, the banality of evil, or more precisely, the banality of the motives that produced an evil that was

---

13 In *Rigorism of Truth: "Moses the Egyptian" and Other Writings on Freud and Arendt*, ed. Ahlrich Meyer, trans. Joe Paul Kroll (Ithaca, NY: Cornell University Press, 2018), Hans Blumenberg suggests that the common assumption that the enormity of Hitler's genocidal crimes demands no less a profound explanation of the perpetrators' motives might well be a mistake: "It seems to me that analytical profundity can easily tempt [one] to discount a drastic 'superficiality' in the syndrome of hatred of this little people, which spans time and world. Artificial profundities give the matter a dignity that should be accorded those killed, not the murderers" (p. 62).

anything but ordinary. So doing resists the inclination, perhaps most infamously expressed in Jean-Paul Sartre's *Anti-Semite and Jew*, to empty the Jews of any positive content and turn them into little more than a projection of their enemies' malign fantasies.[14] That is, rather than being merely the target of random scapegoating that could have just as easily been directed against bicycle riders, the Jews have at least to some extent earned their unique status as a magnet for hatred because of the remarkable ways they have made a difference in the lives of us all.

But what that exceptional role might have been is, of course, the crucial issue. Significantly, our three protagonists, Erikson, Adorno and Arendt, came to occasionally overlapping, but more often very different, conclusions. By comparing them, we may better understand the overdetermined tenacity of anti-Semitism and the difficulties that prevent its eradication. But in order to preclude in advance the type of simplistic outrage that can greet even far less ambitious efforts such as my *Salmagundi* column, it must be stressed that, in no case, did they consider what they saw as the Jews' inadvertent contribution the sole or even primary source of anti-Semitism, let alone turn their explanations into accusations that might legitimate a prejudice they considered abhorrent. To explain, they made clear, is neither to blame nor to condemn.

Let us begin with Erik Erikson, who first addressed the issue in 1942, even before the full horror of the Holocaust was known.[15] He was one of several émigré psychoanalysts, including Otto Fenichel, Ernst Simmel, Rudolph Loewenstein, Bruno Bettelheim and Erich Fromm, who

---

14   For a comparison of Sartre and Arendt on this issue, see Enzo Traverso, "The Blindness of the Intellectuals: Historicizing Sartre's *Anti-Semite and Jew*," *October* 87 (Winter 1999). For a nuanced analysis of the discrimination Sartre makes between the "inauthentic" Jew, who allows himself to be defined by the anti-Semitic other, and the "authentic" Jew who has the ability to choose his destiny, see Peter E. Gordon, "Out from *Huis Clos*: Sartre, Lévinas and the Debate over Jewish Authenticity," *Journal of Romance Studies* 6: 1–2 (2006). What the authentic Jew does not have, however, are inherent positive characteristics, which would turn his or her existential freedom into essentialist self-constraint.

15   During the war, Erikson published "Hitler's Imagery and Germany Youth," *Psychiatry* 5: 4 (1942), which prefigured the argument in "The Legend of Hitler's Childhood." The following analysis will focus on the latter, much more influential essay. For an account of the relationship between them, see Lawrence J. Friedman, *Identity's Architect: A Biography of Erik H. Erikson* (New York: Scribner, 1999), pp. 166–76.

attempted to analyze fascism as a collective social pathology.[16] His
wartime effort was little noticed, but it achieved considerable attention
when it appeared in revised form as the final section of his influential
essay "The Legend of Hitler's Childhood" in his 1950 collection
Childhood and Society. Erikson began what he called "A Note on Jewry"
by acknowledging the importance of projection on the part of those
who see in the Jews what they are reluctant to recognize in themselves.
Then he added, "While projections are hostile and fearful distortions,
however, they are commonly not without a kernel of profound meaning . . . we must therefore ask in passing what seems to make the Jew a
favorite target of the most vicious projections—and this by no means
only in Germany."[17]

The first possibility Erikson considered derived from the traditional
psychoanalytic speculation that the rite of circumcision, a kind of
masculinity tax demanded by God in his covenant with the Jewish
people, aroused "castration fear" in gentiles who have not undergone the
same loss. Erikson, however, doubted the sufficiency of this argument
and turned to another explanation, which derived from the celebrated
theory of the importance of psychosocial identity that he applied to the
German search for a coherent and strong national identity. That theory
posited a universal conflict in the self between "defensive rigidity and
adaptive flexibility . . . conservativism and progressivism,"[18] which was
played out in the Jewish diaspora as a battle between orthodox dogmatism, insistence on the letter of the Law, and cultural and moral relativism based on an opportunistic adaptation to the demands of specific
contexts. Even non-observant Jews, Erikson argued, often oscillate
between these two extremes. It was, however, their stronger inclination
towards relativism that ultimately accounts for the animus showed
against them. Besides the cynical variant of relativism, which could lead
to nihilistic irresponsibility, there was a responsible version that allowed
Jews to mediate cultural differences and heal conflicts. In the latter,
which Erikson called the result of "Jewish genius," relative values are
"lifted to a plane on which known reality becomes relative to more

---

16   For a discussion of their work (with the exception of Fromm's), see David James
Fischer, "Towards a Psychoanalytic Understanding of Fascism and Anti-Semitism:
Perceptions from the 1940s," *Psychoanalysis and History* 6: 1 (2004), hagalil.com.
17   Erik H. Erikson, *Childhood and Society* (New York: Norton, 1963), pp. 353–4.
18   Ibid., p. 354.

inclusive orders."[19] An example is the way in which Judaism subordi-
nated earthly values to higher religious ones, an argument that echoed
Freud's claim in *Moses and Monotheism* that the Jews had achieved the
"lofty heights of spirituality."

More recently, Erikson continued, three major secular Jewish thinkers,
Marx, Freud and Einstein, had relativized the conscious choices of
humans, subordinating them to forces beyond their control, whether it be
the economy, the unconscious or the physical universe. "We may well
ask," he mused, "whether it is altogether mere historical accident that
Marx, Freud and Einstein, all men of German-Jewish ancestry, have come
to formulate and, moreover, to *personify* radical redefinitions of the very
ground man thought he stood on."[20] Their challenges to conventional
wisdom and established traditions were not, however, threats to the
healthy identities of "strong countries" in untroubled times, "because
their sense of identity is enhanced by progressive redefinition."[21] But the
story was very different "in times of collective anxiety" when "the very
suggestion of relativity is resented, and this especially by those classes
which are about to lose status and self-esteem . . . It is at this point that
paranoid anti-Semitism is aroused by agitators of many descriptions and
purposes, who exploit mass cowardice and mass cruelty."[22]

Erikson's claim that the Jews' relativization of absolute values was the
source of anti-Semitic resentment has sometimes been blamed on his
often remarked ambivalence about his own Jewish identity.[23] Whether

---

19   Ibid., p. 355.
20   Ibid., p. 356.
21   Ibid.
22   Ibid., p. 357. It is ironic to see Freud, who sought to blame the absolutism of the
Hebrew God for arousing resentment, described here as generating anti-Semitism
precisely because of his own relativizing of values.
23   David James Fischer writes: "This stereotyping of the Jews into two simplistic typologies
has the ring of the pejorative; it suggests a heightened ambivalence of the author about his own
Jewish identity. Erikson asserted that Jewish relativism could easily dissolve into 'nihilism,' that
psychological insight could be used to devalue the absolutes of the majority and host countries
that Jews could not defeat by might. My own speculation is that Erikson's ambivalence about his
own Jewishness, his shame, guilt, and possible hatred of himself as a Jew are being expressed
in these passages, just as is his ultimate rejection of Jewishness." "Towards a Psychoanalytic
Understanding of Fascism and Anti-Semitism," hagalil.com. The controversy over Erikson's
ambivalence about his Jewish identity can be traced to a hostile review by Marshall Berman in
the *New York Times* of Erikson's *Life History and the Historical Moment* in 1975. For a discussion
of its impact and Erikson's response, see Friedman, *Identity's Architect*, pp. 429–36.

or not this was the case, his analysis, developed as he admitted only "in passing," does offer one way to explain the intensification of anti-Semitic sentiment in times of social stress and disorientation. It relies on a notion of the Jews having maintained their identity despite experiencing an especially keen conflict between "defensive rigidity" and "opportunistic adaptation," sharpened by "centuries of dispersion." Their turning the latter into a virtue, understood as the provocative relativization of traditional standards and values, resulted in the resentment of those in other groups who were more threatened by a similar loss of certainty in their own culture. In short, "the Jew seemed to remain himself despite dispersion over the world, while the German trembled for his identity in his own country. In fact, these mysterious Jews seemed to be making of intellectual relativity a means of racial self-preservation. To some Germans, this was not understandable without assuming an especially devious chauvinism, a hidden Jewish pact with Fate."[24]

There was much in Erikson's analysis that resonated with the Frankfurt School's attempt to explain the roots of anti-Semitism. His analysis of the family dynamics that spawned Nazism in his 1942 essay was in fact cited approvingly several times in *The Authoritarian Personality*, and in an aphorism titled "On Anti-Semitism," written in 1956, Max Horkheimer repeated without acknowledgment virtually the same argument Erikson had made about the Jews in "The Legend of Hitler's Childhood."[25] But in their most extensive theoretical analysis of the question, the chapter "Elements of Anti-Semitism: Limits of Enlightenment" in *Dialectic of Enlightenment*, published in 1947, Horkheimer and Adorno went well beyond Erikson's psychoanalytic approach, based as it was largely on ego psychological notions of

---

24 Erikson, *Childhood and Society*, p. 353.
25 Theodor W. Adorno, Else Frenkel-Brunswik, Daniel J. Levinson and R. Nevitt Sanford, *The Authoritarian Personality* (New York: Harper, 1964), pp. 231, 370, 376, 762. They cite his 1942 essay, not the one in *Childhood and Society*. In "On Anti-Semitism," in *Dawn and Decline: Notes 1926–1931 and 1950–1969*, trans. Michael Shaw (New York: Continuum, 1978), Horkheimer writes: "The Jews are the enemy because they witness the spiritual God and thus relativize what puffs itself up as the Absolute: idol worship, the nation, the leader . . . every Jew is experienced as a member of the Jewish people, the people that almost two thousand years ago lost their state, and although scattered, were held together by their idea of God. It is thus a people in the highest possible sense of the word, the sense of a substance all others feel their own people cannot equal" (p. 131).

personal identity with little regard for differentiating class factors.[26] Without positing a hierarchy of causation in accord with the generally paratactic mode of presentation Adorno was later explicitly to champion,[27] the chapter included seven discrete sections, which introduced a variety of explanations.[28] In addition to the psychoanalytic, which drew, as had Erikson, on the importance of projection and saw unreflective paranoia as a pathological exacerbation of the inevitable projective element in all knowledge, they introduced several others. Among these were a still Marxist analysis of the importance of economic factors and a recognition of the residual power of Christian hostility towards the recalcitrant remnant that refused to accept the new messiah. Horkheimer and Adorno also posited a complicated relationship between mimesis, mimicry, and the domination of nature, which drew on the larger argument of *Dialectic of Enlightenment* about the costs of instrumental rationality run amuck.

A great deal of exegetical energy has already been spent on explicating and judging their unsynthesized constellation of juxtaposed arguments, and this is not the place to expend still more.[29] What concerns

26   Horkheimer and Adorno, *Dialectic of Enlightenment*. The distance between their understanding of psychoanalysis and Erikson's was indirectly expressed in Horkheimer, Adorno and Marcuse's critique of the neo-Freudianism of their erstwhile colleague Erich Fromm. As Fromm's most distinguished biographer, Lawrence J. Friedman, writes, "Fromm's formulation [of man's basic need of a sense of his own unique identity] was compatible with Erik Erikson's concept of 'psychosocial identity,' although he never acknowledged this." *The Lives of Erich Fromm: Love's Prophet* (New York: Columbia University Press, 2013), p. 187.

27   See, for example, Theodor W. Adorno, "Parataxis: On Hölderlin's Late Poetry," in *Notes to Literature*, vol. 2, ed. Rolf Tiedemann, trans. Shierry Weber Nicholsen (New York: Columbia University Press, 1992).

28   Leo Löwenthal contributed to the first three.

29   See, for example, Dan Diner, "Reason and the 'Other': Horkheimer's Reflections on Anti-Semitism and Mass Annihilation," in *On Max Horkheimer: New Perspectives*, ed. Seyla Benhabib, Wolfgang Bonß and John McCole (Cambridge, MA: MIT Press, 1993); David Seymour, "Adorno and Horkheimer: Enlightenment and Antisemitism," *Journal of Jewish Studies* 60: 2 (Autumn 2000); Anson Rabinbach, "The Cunning of Unreason: Mimesis and the Construction of Anti-Semitism in Horkheimer and Adorno's *Dialectic of Enlightenment*, in *In the Shadow of Catastrophe: German Intellectuals between Apocalypse and Catastrophe* (Berkeley: University of California Press, 1997); "Why Were the Jews Sacrificed? The Place of Anti-Semitism in *Dialectic of Enlightenment*," *New German Critique*, no. 81 (Fall 2000); and "The Frankfurt School and the 'Jewish Question,' 1940–1970," in *Against the Grain: Jewish Intellectuals in Hard Times*, ed. Ezra Mendelsohn, Stefani Hofman and Richard I. Cohen (New York: Berghahn, 2014);

me now is only the role they attributed to the Jews in abetting their own destruction. One critic, Jonathan Judaken, has gone so far as to charge that Horkheimer and Adorno "blame the Jewish victim for having become the target of fascist domination . . . a guiding thread of this entire piece is that the persecution of the Jews is linked to a system of domination that undergirds that persecution, a system for which 'the Jews' have some specific culpability."[30] What precisely were the claims that could solicit such a charge? "The Elements of Anti-Semitism," in fact, offers several distinct possibilities. The first concerns the role the Jews can be said to have played in the rise of capitalism, indeed of modernization broadly understood. "The Jews," Horkheimer and Adorno wrote,

> were the colonizers of progress. Having helped as merchants to disseminate Roman civilization through Gentile Europe, they became, in keeping with their patriarchal religion, representatives of urban, civic, and finally industrial conditions. As bearers of the capitalist modes of existence from country to country they earned the hatred of those who suffered under that system. For the sake of the economic progress which today is their downfall the Jews were from the first a thorn in the side of the craftsmen and farmers whose status capitalism undermined.[31]

In the modern era, the Jews prospered in the sphere of capitalist circulation and finance rather than production, and, when that sphere

---

Jacobs, *The Frankfurt School, Jewish Lives, and Anti-Semitism*, chapter 2; Lars Rensmann, *The Politics of Unreason: The Frankfurt School and the Origins of Modern Antisemitism* (Albany: SUNY Press, 2017); Judaken, "Blindness and Insight," and Julia Schulze Wessel and Lars Rensmann, "The Paralysis of Judgment: Arendt and Adorno on the Antisemitic Question," in Rensmann and Gendesha, *Arendt and Adorno*. For my own earlier attempt to deal with this issue, see Martin Jay, "The Jews and the Frankfurt School: Critical Theory's Analysis of Anti-Semitism," in *Permanent Exiles: Essays on the Intellectual Migration from Germany to America* (New York: Columbia University Press, 1985).

30   Judaken, "Blindness and Insight," pp. 192–3. Rabinbach also notes that "the 'Elements of Antisemitism,' it might be argued, ultimately holds the Jews accountable for their own fate." "Why Were the Jews Sacrificed?," p. 62. In contrast, Wessel and Rensmann write, "Adorno hardly ever links antisemitism to the actual behavior of Jews, though he discusses their different reactions to and relationship with dominant society." "The Paralysis of Judgment," p. 203.

31   Horkheimer and Adorno, *Dialectic of Enlightenment*, p. 143.

declined, so too did their useful function as intermediaries for the real powers of society, thus leaving them vulnerable to attack as displaced targets of anger at those occluded powers.[32] To the extent that their analysis was still informed by a Marxist critique of capitalism, Horkheimer and Adorno implicitly empathized with the anger of those who were its victims.[33] Thus, although they could appreciate August Bebel's celebrated characterization of anti-Semitism as "the socialism of fools," a phrase he borrowed from the Austrian liberal Ferdinand Kronawetter, they tacitly acknowledged that it also had an affinity, however distorted, with the forces that might bring about the genuine socialism they hoped would ultimately triumph.[34]

In addition to this economic explanation, Horkheimer and Adorno also echoed Freud's argument in *Moses and Monotheism* about the costs of Judaism's elevation of transcendental spirit over base materiality and sensual pleasure, which they connected to their general characterization of Enlightenment as the domination of nature.[35] "God as spirit," they argued,

> is the principle opposed to nature; it not only stands for nature's blind cycle as do all the mythical gods, but offers liberation from it. But in its remote abstractness, the incommensurable has at the same time

32   Horkheimer and Adorno's claim about the decline of the sphere of circulation was premised on the rise of state capitalism advanced by Friedrich Pollock, their colleague at the Institute of Social Research. More recently, this decline has been reversed; indeed, the globalization of capital markets and the dangerous expansion of speculation in dubious credit instruments has spurred renewed anti-Semitic animus (for example, against targets like George Soros).

33   Here, Horkheimer and Adorno talk only of precapitalist victims, but, in an aphorism composed in the 1920s when his Marxism was most militant, Horkheimer could argue that "as the material base of ghetto life was left behind, the willingness to sacrifice life and property to one's religious beliefs also became a thing of the past. Among bourgeois Jews, the hierarchy of goods is neither Jewish nor Christian but bourgeois. The Jewish capitalist brings sacrifices to power, just like his Aryan class colleague. He first sacrifices his own superstition, then the lives of others, and finally his capital. The Jewish revolutionary in Germany is not different from his 'Aryan' comrade. He commits his life to the liberation of man." *Dawn and Decline*, p. 43.

34   August Bebel acknowledged the provenance of the phrase in Herman Bahr, *Der Anti-Semitismus: Ein Internationales Interview* (Berlin: S. Fischer, 1894), p. 21.

35   Rabinbach discusses their debt to Freud and the importance of their common stress on the prohibition of images (*Bilderverbot*) in "Why Were the Jews Sacrificed?," p. 57.

become more terrible, and the pitiless statement "I am who am," which tolerates nothing beside itself, surpasses in its inescapable power the blinder and therefore more ambiguous judgment of anonymous fate. The God of Judaism demands what he is owed and settles accounts with the defaulter.[36]

Because of their sublimation of pagan sacrifice into symbolic ritual behavior, the Jews created the template for later sacrificial behavior, including the sacrifice of workers' surplus labor in capitalist production. Since the Jews were implicated in the long, civilizing mission of Enlightenment, understood as beginning well before the modern era, they were vulnerable when nature ultimately revenged itself for its domination. "The Jews themselves, over the millennia, have played their part in this, with enlightenment no less than with cynicism. As the oldest surviving patriarchy, the incarnation of monotheism, they converted taboos into maxims of civilization while the others were still enmeshed in magic."[37] Calling the Jews the primary culprits for the rise of modern capitalism and the domination of nature was surely problematic, but there was a modicum of justification, so Horkheimer and Adorno implied, in their being assigned some responsibility, a risky conclusion that was in fact candidly considered in their correspondence during this period.[38]

But *Dialectic of Enlightenment* also ventured another explanation for anti-Semitism rooted in a much more admirable aspect of the complex role the Jews played in human history, one which has in fact aroused gentile envy rather than anger. "Reconciliation," Horkheimer and Adorno wrote, "is Judaism's highest concept, and expectation its whole meaning."[39] Surviving despite all that has been done to them for millennia, nomads with no settled place in the world, they somehow embody, at least in the minds of their enemies, the utopian traits that genuine reconciliation betokens: "happiness without power, reward without work, a homeland without frontiers, religion without myth. These features are outlawed by the ruling powers because they are secretly

---

36   Horkheimer and Adorno, *Dialectic of Enlightenment*, p. 145.
37   Ibid., p. 153.
38   For a discussion, see Rabinbach, "Why Were the Jews Sacrificed?," pp. 62–3.
39   Horkheimer and Adorno, *Dialectic of Enlightenment*, p. 165.

coveted by the ruled."[40] The Jewish intellectual is especially stigmatized because he is allowed the luxury of remunerated thought without the burden of physical labor. The cosmopolitan rootlessness and eternal wandering of the Jews, and their apparent ability to thrive without engaging in productive labor, have earned them the reproach of parasitism, which, Horkheimer and Adorno insisted, would more accurately be directed at capitalists of all ethnic backgrounds. Instead of being parasites, the Jews actually foreshadow a state of bliss in a "land of milk and honey" where the burden of toil is lifted. Paradoxically, for Horkheimer and Adorno, the Jews are, on the one hand, complicit in the domination of nature and capitalist modernization, and, on the other, the stubborn remnants of a condition prior to that process in which happiness can be sought without the exercise of power or domination.

In another way as well, the Jews arouse envy for something Erikson had also noted: their defiant ability to retain a meaningful communal identity against all efforts to eradicate or assimilate them. Stubbornly resisting two millennia of demands to accept a false messiah, they embody idiosyncratic resistance to homogenization. Incurring hatred on the part of those threatened by heterogeneity and otherness, they nonetheless prefigure a world in which difference is not denigrated and the false equivalences of the exchange principle no longer prevail. In short, their being singled out as more than a random target of hatred can only be understood by acknowledging both their regrettable contribution to the modern world with all of its flaws *and* their laudable resistance to the world they have helped create.

For all of these reasons, *Dialectic of Enlightenment* challenged the view that anti-Semitism is more than the random scapegoating of a fungible target. Or, rather, it seemed to do so until the last of the seven sections of "Elements of Anti-Semitism," which was added after the end of the Second World War, apparently by Horkheimer. It begins with this bald, counterintuitive assertion: "But there are no longer any anti-Semites,"[41]

---

40   Ibid.

41   Ibid., p. 165. It might be speculated, however, that Horkheimer and Adorno were not expressing their own position here, but ironically reporting what seems to have been the prevailing opinion in postwar America. This point is made by Fabian Freyenhagen, "Adorno and Horkheimer on Anti-Semitism," in *A Companion to Adorno*, ed. Peter E. Gordon, Espen Hammer and Max Pensky (Hoboken, NJ: Wiley, 2019), pp. 103–22.

and goes on to explain that "anti-Semitic views always reflected stereo-typed thinking. Today only that thinking is left. People still vote, but only between totalities. The anti-Semitic psychology has largely been replaced by mere acceptance of the whole fascist ticket, which is an inventory of the slogans of belligerent big business."[42] The Jewish masses themselves, Horkheimer and Adorno suggested, "are no more immune to ticket thinking than the most hostile youth organization."[43] There is, however, a positive implication that can be drawn from this new state of affairs. Because anti-Semitism is now merely "one item in an interchangeable ticket," there is, they argue, "irrefutable reason to hope for its end."[44] But if ticket mentality as a whole persists as a pathological expression of "the rage against difference" marking the dialectic of enlightenment from its beginnings, that end is surely not in sight.[45] Ending on this note of unrec-onciled ambiguity, "Elements of Anti-Semitism" leaves the reader with a range of possible explanations without an overarching synthesis bringing them together.

To turn, finally, to Arendt, it is clear that she was no less vehemently hostile to the contingent explanation of anti-Semitism than her two fellow exiles. In fact, as early as an unpublished prewar text on that very subject, she specifically invoked the bicycle rider joke in order to debunk it for promoting a simplistic "ventilation theory" in which "a scapegoat has to be found for national discontent."[46] Repeating her dismissal of the joke at the beginning of *The Origins of Totalitarianism*, she wrote: "The theory that Jews are always the scapegoat implies that the scapegoat might have been anyone else as well. It upholds the perfect innocence of the victim, an innocence which insinuates not only that no evil was done but that nothing at all was done which might possibly

---

42   Ibid., p. 166.
43   Ibid., p. 171.
44   Ibid.
45   The persistence for the Frankfurt School of anti-Semitism as a threat even in America is shown by their participation in the *Studies in Prejudice* project with the American Jewish Committee after the war, as well as their unsuccessful attempt to sponsor a movie that might help alleviate it. See the discussions in David Jenemann, *Adorno in America* (Minneapolis: University of Minnesota Press, 2007), chapter 3; and Thomas Wheatland, *The Frankfurt School in Exile* (Minneapolis: University of Minnesota Press, 2009), chapter 6.
46   Hannah Arendt, "Antisemitism" (circa 1938–9), in *The Jewish Writings*, p. 47.

have a connection with the issue at stake."[47] But if the dubious scapegoat theory were actually "one of the principle attempts to escape the seriousness of antisemitism,"[48] no less problematic was the ahistorical fantasy of the eternal nature of the prejudice, which sometimes was invoked by Jews and their sympathizers to help cement Jewish identity at a time when it was increasingly fragile. Although she expressed understanding, even sympathy, for the Jewish desire never "under any circumstances to discuss their share of the responsibility,"[49] Arendt refused to flinch from the possibility that some responsibility there was. To be sure, when she spoke of "their share of the responsibility," Arendt was not referring to the genocidal, exterminationist version of anti-Semitism that had led to the Holocaust. For "neither the fate of European Jewry not the establishment of death factories," she insisted, "can be fully explained and grasped in terms of anti-Semitism."[50] But they had at least been prepared by the long-standing prejudice against the Jews, whose partial origins in Jewish behavior she was determined to acknowledge.

Unlike Freud, Erikson or Adorno, Arendt did not, however, turn to psychoanalytic explanations of projection or resentment against Judaism's alleged overly spiritualized repression of sensual pleasure to explain those origins. Stressing the historical roles played by assimilation, secularization, the rise and fall of the modern nation-state and the transformation of older forms of Christian hatred of the Jews into their modern variants, she also took seriously what she saw as the Jews' own contribution to their predicament. As Richard Bernstein has noted in his insightful account of Arendt's complicated response to "the Jewish question," the issue was "not one of blame, guilt or even *moral* responsibility. It is, rather, a question of political responsibility: of how the Jews have (and have not) responded to the concrete political situations in which they have found themselves."[51] Consonant with her belief in the importance of

---

47 Hannah Arendt, *The Origins of Totalitarianism* (Cleveland: World, 1964), p. 5.

48 Ibid., p. 7.

49 Ibid.

50 Hannah Arendt, "Social Science Techniques and the Study of Concentration Camps," in *Essays in Understanding, 1930–1954*, ed. Jerome Kohn (New York: Harcourt, 1994), p. 235. Elsewhere, she went so far as to say that "the foundations of antisemitism are found in developments that have very little to do with Jews." "Antisemitism," p. 75. But "very little" did not mean "nothing at all."

51 Richard J. Bernstein, *Hannah Arendt and the Jewish Question* (Cambridge, MA: MIT Press, 1996), p. 56.

political action as the locus of positive freedom, and her dismay at its relegation to marginal status by social and economic forces in modern mass society, Arendt lamented the long-standing effects of the traumatic loss of Jewish political sovereignty during the Roman period:

> Jewish history offers the extraordinary spectacle of a people, unique in this respect, which began its history with a well-defined concept of history and an almost conscious resolution to achieve a well-circumscribed plan on earth and then, without giving up this concept, avoided all political action for two thousand years. The result was that the political history of the Jewish people became even more dependent upon unforeseen, accidental factors than the history of other nations, so that the Jew stumbled from one role to the other and accepted responsibility for none.[52]

This avoidance of political activity was exacerbated, she argued, by the second great catastrophe suffered by the Jewish people, the failure of the messianic Sabbatian movement in the seventeenth century, which led to an even further retreat from the world—what she was to call in *The Human Condition* "world-alienation"—into apolitical mysticism.[53] "The catastrophe of this victory of mystical thought," she wrote in a 1948 review of Gershom Scholem's *Major Trends in Jewish Mysticism*,

> was greater for the Jewish people than all other persecutions had been, if we are to measure it by the only available yardstick, its far-reaching influence upon the future of the people. From now on, the Jewish body politic was dead and the people retired from the public scene of history.[54]

Or to put it another way, the traumatized Jews had rejected worldliness for the hope of redemption in another life.

---

52 Arendt, *The Origins of Totalitarianism*, p. 8.
53 Hannah Arendt, *The Human Condition* (Chicago: University of Chicago Press, 1958), pp. 230–1.
54 Hannah Arendt, *The Jew as Pariah: Jewish Identity and Politics in the Modern Age*, ed. Ron H. Feldman (New York: Grove, 1978), pp. 104–5. Richard Bernstein argues that she erred in following Scholem's claim that Sabbatianism was a political as much as a religious movement. See *Hannah Arendt and the Jewish Question*, p. 60.

In this life, however, the results were nothing less than disastrous. For the Jewish loss of a positive political community ultimately produced a foolish reliance on two mirages when the isolation of the ghetto was exchanged for social and economic assimilation: belief in universal human rights, which allegedly existed beyond the sovereign power of citizenship in a specific polity, and faith in the assurances of liberal states that they would honor minority rights for those without that power. It is because both hopes proved vain with the decline of liberalism and the transformation of the juridical subject into a superfluous, mere "human being" that Arendt was able to begin *The Origins* by stressing the importance of anti-Semitism as the precursor of the possible fate of anyone rendered stateless in the totalitarian age. Although arousing less outrage than her later excoriation in *Eichmann in Jerusalem* of the Jewish councils for collaborating with the Nazi machinery of annihilation, Arendt's accusation against her people was in fact far more sweeping. For centuries, she charged, they had succumbed to a passive, apolitical alienation from the world that doomed them to dependence on the goodwill of others. As she put it when she was awarded the Lessing Prize of the city of Hamburg in 1959, it is the lot of "pariah peoples" to suffer

> so radical a loss of the world, so fearful an atrophy of all the organs with which we respond to it—starting with the common sense with which we orient ourselves in a world common to ourselves and others and going on to the sense of beauty, or taste, with which we love the world—that in extreme cases, in which pariahdom has persisted for centuries, we can speak of real worldlessness. And worldlessness, alas, is always a form of barbarism.[55]

To call pariah peoples in general, and the Jews in particular, "barbarians" may well seem a shocking, even heartless assertion, and the feeling is not lessened when Arendt goes on to explain that worldlessness means a loss of the necessary distance between humans, the pluralism of difference, that is a necessary premise of political action. For, although the positive result of that loss may be a compassionate closeness that can "breed a kindliness and sheer goodness of which human beings are otherwise scarcely capable," it comes at a very high cost: "The charm and

---

55 Hannah Arendt, *Men in Dark Times* (New York: Mariner, 1968), p. 13.

intensity of the atmosphere that develops is also due to the fact that the pariahs of this world enjoy the great privilege of being unburdened by care for the world."[56]

Pariah peoples as barbarians "unburdened by care for the world"—if Arendt can be seen as channeling some of her teacher/lover Martin Heidegger's most controversial sentiments, it is perhaps in this passage that it is most evident. Although Richard Bernstein has sought to defend her ardent endorsement of "*amor mundi*," love for the world, as expressing "one of the most glorious strands in the tradition of Judaism"[57] rather than being Heideggerian in origin, there seems little direct evidence to buttress this claim. Erikson, it will be recalled, had pointed to the remarkable ability of Jews to maintain their collective identity in diasporic dispersion as a source of anti-Semitic resentment on the part of other peoples whose identity was more precarious. Arendt argued, instead, that the closeness and solidarity that gave Jews cohesiveness as a pariah people was built on the problematic grounds of mutual compassion and tribal, in-group solidarity rather than worldly activism in the political realm. This mistaken choice, she argued bitterly, was manifest in the secularized version of the religious notion of the chosen people, which persisted even among assimilated Jews:

> Out of the belief in chosenness by God grew that fantastic delusion, shared by unbelieving Jews and non-Jews alike, that Jews are by nature more intelligent, better, healthier, more fit for survival—the motor of history and the salt of the earth . . . [secularization] engendered a very real Jewish chauvinism, if by chauvinism we understand the perverted nationalism in which (in the words of Chesterton) "the individual is himself the thing to be worshipped; the individual is his own ideal and even his own idol." From now on, the old religious concept of chosenness was no longer the essence of Judaism; it became instead the sense of Jewishness.[58]

What Scholem famously found lacking in Arendt—"love for the Jewish people"—and Walter Laqueur called her long-standing "animosity

---

56   Ibid., pp. 13–14.
57   Bernstein, *Hannah Arendt and the Jewish Question*, p. 188.
58   Arendt, *The Origins of Totalitarianism*, p. 74.

towards the Jews as a group"[59] grew out of her uncompromising disdain for ethnic rather than political solidarity.[60]

In *The Human Condition*, Arendt had, in fact, argued that "love, by its very nature, is unworldly, and it is for this reason rather than its rarity that it is not only apolitical but antipolitical, perhaps the most powerful of all antipolitical forces."[61] The reason is that "it destroys the in-between which relates to and separates us from others."[62] One can therefore see why she would resist calls to "love the Jewish people," although how this argument comports with her defense of *amor mundi*, which honors precisely that in-between, is not fully clear.

Much more can be said—and has in many places over the years— about Arendt's refusal to accept the terms of Scholem's rebuke, but let me return in conclusion to the comparison that has been at the center of this exercise: the alternative attributions of responsibility for anti-Semitism given to the Jews by Erikson, Adorno and Horkheimer, and Arendt. As we have seen, all of them, along with Sigmund Freud, posited some responsibility of the Jews for their troubles denied by the bicycle rider joke. They agreed that honoring the victims over the victimizers necessitated crediting them with something extraordinary, either for good or for ill, which had set them apart from other possible targets of the free-floating resentment of anti-Semites. But they differed over what that was. For Erikson, it was the ability to maintain a coherent identity, even under conditions of physical dispersion and the relativization of values, which aroused the envy of those still struggling to define who they were. For Adorno and Horkheimer, several other historical roles were crucial. Among them were the Jews as the "colonizers of progress" and pioneers of finance capitalism, the Jews as the advocates of

---

59   The accusation was made and discussed in the letters Scholem and Arendt exchanged in 1963 after the publication of *Eichmann in Jerusalem*, reprinted in Arendt, *The Jew as Pariah*, pp. 240–1. Walter Laqueur, "The Arendt Cult: Hannah Arendt as Political Commentator," in *Hannah Arendt in Jerusalem*, ed. Steven E. Aschheim (Berkeley: University of California Press, 2001), p. 58.

60   It should be noted that once Israel was established, Arendt, like Horkheimer and Adorno, was fully committed to its survival, and had no qualms about supporting it in its wars with the Arabs. In fact, Young-Bruehl records that Arendt even contributed to Meir Kahane's Jewish Defense League in both 1967 and 1973! *Hannah Arendt: For Love of the World* (New Haven, CT: Yale University Press, 1982, p. 456.

61   Arendt, *The Human Condition*, p. 218.

62   Ibid., p. 217.

dominating spirit over dominated matter and sensuality (a claim echoing Freud), and the Jews as the contrary embodiment of utopian alternatives to the toil of everyday life, of "happiness without power, reward
without work, a homeland without frontiers, religion without myth."
For Arendt, it was the worldlessness of a people that had lost its will to
engage in politics, believing instead that it could somehow rely in the
modern era on abstract human rights and the goodwill of liberal governments, or reacting to liberalism's failure with a version of integral, tribal
Zionism that undercut the pluralist promise of genuine political action.

What can be made of these very different assignments of Jewish
responsibility for their plight, which, let it be stressed again, were never
the entirety of the explanations given by our protagonists for anti-Semitism nor meant as an accusation of guilt? What has to be first registered
is the sheer fact that all of them found it necessary to seek such a cause
at all, which united them in refusing the exculpatory logic of the bicycle
rider analogy. Their shared willingness to speculate on Jewish responsibility might, of course, be simply dismissed as expressing their ambivalence about their own Jewish identities, which we have already
mentioned in the cases of Erikson and Arendt. Adorno, the son of a
Catholic mother who baptized him into that faith and an assimilated
Jewish father who had contempt for the *Ostjuden*,[63] was no less ambivalent, at least until the Holocaust compelled him to identify unequivocally with its victims. But, however much they may have struggled with
their personal identities, attributing their speculations merely to an
expression of Jewish self-hatred only serves to trivialize in advance
whatever insights, however uncomfortable, they might have provided.

Rather than impugning their motives, therefore, it would be more
fruitful to evaluate the merits of their arguments. They cannot easily be
synthesized into a coherent position. Erikson and Adorno drew on
psychoanalysis, if with different nuances, whereas Arendt had no use for

---

63 According to Stefan Müller-Doohm, Oskar Wiesengrund had a "somewhat
ostentatious aversion to everything that was consciously Jewish. This hostility was
directed in the first instance at the so-called Eastern Jews . . . his son Teddie, too, was on
his own testimony not immune to the arrogance assimilated Jews felt towards the East
European Jews." *Adorno: A Biography*, trans. Rodney Livingstone (Malden, MA: Polity,
2005), p. 19. For a nuanced account of Adorno's complicated identity and its changes
over time, see Evelyn Wilcock, "Negative Identity: Mixed German Jewish Descent as a
Factor in the Reception of Theodor Adorno," *New German Critique*, no. 81 (Fall 2000).

Freud.[64] Unlike the others, Adorno maintained at least an element of the Marxist economic analysis that had motivated earlier Frankfurt School accounts, such as Horkheimer's controversial prewar essay "The Jews and Europe."[65] Arendt was alone in focusing on the retreat from politics and the world-alienation of a pariah people content to put survival—mere life—over positive freedom. At times, to be sure, their positions did overlap. Arendt's lament about the vain reliance on abstract human rights protected by liberal states was anticipated in *Dialectic of Enlightenment*, where Horkheimer and Adorno argued that "liberalism had granted the Jews property, but without the authority to command. The purpose of human rights was to promise happiness even where power was lacking."[66] Similarly, Erikson's admiration for the sustaining of a common identity based on openness to the relativity of values comports with Arendt's hope for an agonistic politics without absolutes as an alternative to world alienation, which she saw undermined by Zionist tribalism.[67] But by and large, they left us with a welter of different suggestions about the role Jews might have played in stimulating enmity, which are *a fortiori* like the "Elements of Anti-Semitism" chapter in *Dialectic of Enlightenment* in defying synthetic coherence.

---

64   Adorno and Arendt were fierce intellectual rivals in other ways as well, with radically different assessments of Marx and Heidegger, and despised each other on a personal level. Arendt had been furious at Adorno since the 1920s for the role she thought he had played in undermining her first husband Günther Stern's *Habilitationsschrift*, remarking that "that one's not coming into our house!" Young-Bruehl, *Hannah Arendt*, p. 8. Adorno's disdain for her is shown in his adamant refusal to allow her any participation in the editing of Walter Benjamin's work. On February 17, 1960, he wrote to Scholem: "In the case of Hannah Arendt I am intransigent, not only on account of my low estimation of this lady, who I consider an old washerwoman, but above all because I know what Benjamin thought of her and her earlier husband." Theodor W. Adorno and Gershom Scholem, *Briefwechsel, 1939–1969*, ed. Asaf Angermann (Frankfurt: Suhrkamp, 2015), p. 192. Ironically, Stern, after he had changed his name to Günther Anders, was awarded the Adorno Prize by the city of Frankfurt in 1983.

65   Max Horkheimer, "The Jews and Europe" (1939), in *The Frankfurt School and Religion: Key Writings by the Major Thinkers*, ed. Eduardo Mendieta (New York: Routledge, 2005).

66   Horkheimer and Adorno, *Dialectic of Enlightenment*, p. 141.

67   Erikson's own attitude towards Zionism was more positive. Shortly after the creation of the state of Israel he visited family in Haifa. According to Friedman, "He confessed that he was so impressed with the Jewish state that if he had not been an American citizen, he would almost certainly have become an Israeli." *Identity's Architect*, p. 173.

In evaluating them as individual explanations, we also have to be very cautious, because it is hard to know what kinds of evidence we might bring to bear to confirm or refute them. Although purporting to be historical rather than essentialist, their explanations tend to invoke either the persistence of long-standing traits or the enduring effects of primordial acts that have reverberated through the ages.[68] The inventors of monotheism and spiritual repression of the body, the original dominators of nature, the colonizers of capitalist progress, the stubborn adherents of communal identity despite diasporic dispersion—all of these are so vast in scope and sweeping in their inclusion of disparate cases that it would take a team of experts to judge their plausibility. Perhaps the only real exception is Arendt's claim about the political indifference and worldlessness of the Jews in exile, which she claims is purely historical and thus undermines the assumption of eternal anti-Semitism. Of all of the explanations we have listed, hers is the one that can best be evaluated on the basis of actual historical developments, or more precisely, against the apparent end of that exile with the creation of the State of Israel.

Recent students of Jewish political thought—and here I am thinking in particular of Michael Walzer and his colleagues who in 2003 launched a multivolume series, *The Jewish Political Tradition*—have provided a more complete and complex understanding of Jewish ruminations on political authority and organization than was available to Arendt.[69]

---

68   Dana Villa even charges that Horkheimer and Adorno's explanation "winds up being little more than a variation on the old theme of an eternal anti-Semitism." "Genealogies of Total Domination: Arendt, Adorno and Auschwitz," *New German Critique* 34: 1 (Winter 2007), p. 27.

69   Michael Walzer, Menachem Lorberbaum, Noam J. Zohar and Madeleine Kochen, eds., *The Jewish Political Tradition*, vol. 1, *Authority* (New Haven, CT: Yale University Press, 2003); vol. 2, *Membership* (2006); vol. 3, *The Community* (2018); vol. 4, *Politics in History* (forthcoming). See also Michael Walzer, *In God's Shadow: Politics in the Hebrew Bible* (New Haven, CT: Yale University Press, 2012). They have, however, conceded Arendt's point that the Jews were not very concerned with popular sovereignty or pluralism strictly speaking. Indeed, as even evidenced by the Hebrew Bible, which antedates the diasporic loss of sovereign power, the ancient Jews, unlike the Greeks, had no explicitly political theory because they trusted in God's laws rather than worrying about how men's could be legitimately made. However, during the centuries that followed, they have argued, the institution of the *kahal,* the executive board running autonomous Jewish communities, was more than the mere "housekeeping" façade derided by Arendt. Full political sovereignty, after all, need not be the essence of the political, as Arendt herself may have tacitly conceded in her preference for a Jewish homeland over a Jewish state.

Historians have also challenged Arendt's categorical assertion that "Jewish history . . . for two millennia has been made not by Jews but by those people who surround them."[70] But the most pressing question concerns Arendt's disillusionment with actual existing Zionism. For if her main lament about Jewish history concerned the willingness of a pariah people to withdraw from politics, why, one might wonder, did she turn against the Zionism she had once fervently embraced just when it was on the verge of establishing the first Jewish state in almost two millennia?[71]

Arendt made clear her reasoning in several essays composed in the mid-1940s expressing her bitter disappointment at the victory of the Revisionist Zionism of Vladimir Jabotinsky over the accommodation with Arabs she had supported as a member of Judah Magnes's Brit Shalom.[72] Juxtaposing the goal of a "Jewish *homeland*" in a binational state, which she endorsed, with a "Jewish *state*," which she found problematic, Arendt attacked the assumption of "eternal anti-Semitism" as an excuse for the embrace of an integral, tribal nationalism that was ultimately antipolitical: "It is nothing less than the uncritical acceptance of German-inspired nationalism. This holds a nation to be an eternal organic body, the product of inevitable natural growth of inherent qualities; and it explains peoples, not in terms of political organizations, but in terms of biological superhuman personalities."[73] The antipolitical

---

For a recent ingenious attempt to derive a very different version of politics in the Talmud, one based on deterritorialization and agonistic argumentation, see Sergey Dogopolski, *Other Others: The Political after the Talmud* (New York: Fordham University Press, 2018).

70   Arendt, "Antisemitism," in *The Jewish Writings*, p. 48.

71   For accounts of Arendt's disillusionment with Zionism, see Young-Bruehl, *Hannah Arendt*, chapter 5; Amnon Raz-Krakotzkin, "Binationalism and Jewish Identity: Hannah Arendt and the Question of Palestine," Moshe Zimmerman, "Hannah Arendt, the Early 'Post-Zionist,' " and Richard J. Bernstein, "Hannah Arendt's Zionism," in Aschheim, ed., *Hannah Arendt in Jerusalem*; Tuija Parvikko, *Arendt, Eichmann and the Politics of the Past* (Helsinki: University of Helsinki Press, 2008), chapter 1; and Steven E. Aschheim, *At the Edges of Liberalism: Junctions of European, German, and Jewish History* (New York: Palgrave Macmillan, 2012), chapter 5.

72   Five of these essays, written from 1942 to 1950, are collected in Arendt, *The Jew as Pariah*. They are reprinted, along with other minor essays from the period, in *The Jewish Writings*.

73   As she put it in "To Save the Jewish Homeland; There Is Still Time" (May 1948), "The real goal of the Jews in Palestine is the building up of a Jewish homeland. This goal must never be sacrificed to the pseudo-sovereignty of a Jewish state." *The Jew as Pariah*, p. 192.

inclinations of the Revisionists were shown, among other things, by their resorting to terrorism, which replaced argumentation with violence. Although a staunch advocate of a Jewish Army to fight the Nazis, Arendt understood that, although war may have been, as Clausewitz famously put it, the continuation of politics by other means, the opposite was not true. Abstract norms, not cynical Realpolitik, had to be followed: "The only political ideas an oppressed people can have are freedom and justice. Democracy can be their only form of organization."[74]

Significantly, in the unfinished essay on anti-Semitism she had written before the war and the growing power of Zionist Revisionism, Arendt had already rejected the nationalist historiography that "strips the relationship between Jews and their host nation of its historicity and reduces it to a play of forces (like those of attraction and repulsion) between two natural substances that will be repeated everywhere that Jews live."[75] Although Jabotinsky and his followers were explicit in their embrace of this model, Arendt contended that it was initially Herzl's vision of a Jewish state that had anticipated their position. It, too, was based on a rigid assumption of the ahistorical nature of anti-Semitic hatred and the need for a polity based on ethnic identity rather than pluralist politics. Instead of a *demos* of equal citizens, it turned "the Jewish people" into an exclusive *ethnos* understood in tribal terms. Instead of a people, it has understood them as a nation. Zionism, she feared, had embraced "the dangerous illusion of the possibility of *autonomous Jewish politics*."[76]

As a result, celebrating the establishment of the Jewish state as an antidote to the anti-Semitism engendered by the Jews' retreat from politics, she concluded, was misguided. Instead of alleviating hatred for the Jews, it would only exacerbate it. "Even more unrealistic but just as influential [as the claim that other nations would welcome a new nation-state]," she argued, "was Herzl's belief that the establishment of a Jewish state would automatically wipe out anti-Semitism."[77] So anxious, in fact, was Arendt about the negative effects of its creation as an ethno-nationalist rather

---

74 Arendt, "Jewish Politics" (1942), in *The Jewish Writings*, p. 241.
75 Arendt, "Antisemitism," pp. 50–1.
76 Ibid., p. 57, italics in original.
77 Arendt, "The Jewish State Fifty Years After" (May 1946), in *The Jew as Pariah*, p. 172.

than pluralist polity that she could ponder the worst possible scenario in 1946:

> The utopian and ideological elements with which [Herzl] injected the new Jewish will to political action are only too likely to lead the Jews out of reality once more—and out of the sphere of political action. I do not know—nor do I even want to know—what would happen to Jews all over the world and to Jewish history in the future should we meet with a catastrophe in Palestine. But the parallels with the Sabbatai Zevi have become terribly close.[78]

Arendt's dire prediction has, of course, not been realized, at least not yet, but many of the qualms she felt when Israel was created have also not been stilled by subsequent history. Although her contrast between an ethno-nationalist state and pluralist democracy may have been exaggerated—at least for a while, Israel tried to be both—the tide seems to be turning in the direction she feared.

But what about Arendt's even more sweeping charge, that of worldlessness or world alienation, which was at the root of her analysis not only of hatred of the Jews, but also of the totalitarian temptation that menaced the modern world at large. To do full justice to her argument, we would have to dive into the deep waters of *The Human Condition*, a book she had once in fact wanted to entitle *Amor Mundi*,[79] and address the vexed question of her debts to and departures from Heidegger, for whom the numinous term "world" was enormously important.[80] All that we can say now is that, for Arendt, world alienation meant an unhealthy withdrawal from public interaction, the atrophy of the

---

78   Ibid., p. 177.

79   Young-Bruehl, *Hannah Arendt*, p. 324.

80   For two very different evaluations, see Dana Villa, *Arendt and Heidegger: The Fate of the Political* (Princeton, NJ: Princeton University Press, 1996); and Richard Wolin, *Heidegger's Children: Hannah Arendt, Karl Löwith, Hans Jonas and Herbert Marcuse* (Princeton, NJ: Princeton University Press, 2001). For an analysis of Heidegger's use of the term, see the entry on it in Michael Inwood, *A Heidegger Dictionary* (Oxford: Blackwell, 1999). It was already an important concept for Husserl, who used it to mean the transcendental horizon of disclosure of phenomena. See the discussion in Peter Eli Gordon, "Realism, Science, and the Deworlding of the World," in Hubert L. Dreyfus and Mark A. Wrathall, eds., *A Companion to Phenomenology and Existentialism* (Malden, MA: Wiley-Blackwell, 2006).

interstitial space of intersubjective appearances, the loss of a shared *"sensus communis,"* and the withering of the durable institutions that raise humans above the state of nature. It was thus very different from the "self-alienation" lamented by existentialists like Sartre. Carried to an extreme, it abetted the homelessness—often literal as well as metaphorical—that was becoming the fate of modern men and women in general. In this sense as well, to give the formula of Horkheimer and Adorno a bitterly ironic twist, the Jews could rightly be understood as the "pioneers of progress." For by fostering an exaggerated love of the self and elevating the value of mere life or survival at all costs, they had anticipated the loss of *amor mundi* that led to the nightmare politics of the twentieth century.

How persuasive was Arendt's claim that world alienation was the fate of, let alone pioneered by, the Jews as the canaries in the mine of modernity? As in the case of her rejection of Herzlian Zionism as merely tribal ethno-nationalism and thus inherently antithetical to agonistic pluralism, it is not, I would argue, fully convincing. Ironically, Arendt herself had originally attributed an exaggerated love of the self largely to Christian sources, in particular the writings of Saint Augustine, to whose legacy she devoted her dissertation.[81] Denigrating the value of the public sphere and the corruption of mundane existence, he had extolled love of God and the quest for personal salvation. And, insofar as the *vita contemplativa*, which Arendt often invidiously compared to the *vita activa*, was a legacy of Greek philosophy, in particular Plato, it is hard to single out the Jews as the vanguard of alienation from the world, at least in terms of other-worldly theory trumping this-worldly practice. As for the love of life at all costs, it may have come to characterize the Jews in the diaspora, insofar as they were determined to maintain their collective identity as well as their individual existence. The Israeli cult of Masada to the contrary notwithstanding, Jews, unlike Christians, were generally hesitant to celebrate sacrificial martyrdom.[82] Indeed, after the

---

81   Hannah Arendt, *Die Liebesbegriff bei Augustin: Versuch einer philophischen interpretation* (Berlin: Springer, 1929). For an account of its importance, see Ronald Beiner, "Love and Worldliness: Hannah Arendt's Reading of Saint Augustine," in *Hannah Arendt: Twenty Years Later*, ed. Larry May and Jerome Kohn (Cambridge, MA: MIT Press, 1997).

82   For a discussion of the exceptions, see Shmuel Shepkaru, *Jewish Martyrs in the Pagan and Christian Worlds* (Cambridge: Cambridge University Press, 2005).

fall of the Second Temple, even animal sacrifice was abandoned. But to say the least, it is hard to begrudge them their concern for survival against the backdrop of two thousand years of Christian and Islamic attempts to supersede their religion, and the cost of assimilation being understood as the abandonment of their communal identity, not to mention the history of literal threats to their individual survival as human beings, culminating in the Holocaust. If the epithet "barbarian" means anything, it surely cannot be applied to a pariah people for whom "mere life"—both as a community of fate and as individual members of that community—was so often in such jeopardy.

In short, Arendt seems to have held the Jews responsible for opposing mistakes, both of which incited anti-Semitic hostility. First, they too long accepted their role as passive victims of history, putting mere life over the life of freedom that can come only from political activism. As such they exemplified the world alienation that was a mark of barbarism rather than civilization. And second, when they seemed to be returning to healthy historical activism by realizing the Zionist project of a Jewish homeland, they made the wrong choice in defining it as an exclusivist tribal nation-state rather than a pluralist democratic polity. Thus, although her attempt to locate the Jewish contribution to anti-Semitic hostility may have sought to be more historical than those of Adorno, Horkheimer and Erikson, at least in positing a possible way of breaking old patterns, its ultimate implication is no less discouraging. For, if the bicycle rider joke remains a false consolation, as I think it does, we are left with the sobering thought that whether or not all the speculative causes provided by the protagonists of this exercise are equally plausible, their cumulative effects seem all too potent. Perhaps the frequency of proximate triggers can be lessened and unnecessary provocations avoided, as I tried to argue in *Salmagundi* a decade and a half ago, but the dynamite they can ignite seems, alas, destined to be explosive for a very long time to come.

4

The Authoritarian Personality and the Problematic Pathologization of Politics

The Frankfurt School's continuing relevance has perhaps been nowhere as apparent as in the widespread revival of interest in its explorations of the deeper sources and contemporary manifestations of authoritarian populism. In these increasingly troubled times, the ghosts of the 1930s and 1940s seem to haunt our political landscape. Latter-day "prophets of deceit" employ many of the same demagogic techniques trenchantly exposed by Leo Löwenthal (along with Norbert Guterman) in their 1949 contribution to the Studies in Prejudice *series produced under Institute auspices.[1] Here, qualitative content analysis is informed by psychological and sociological insights into the structural underpinnings of the authoritarian worldview.*

1 Leo Löwenthal and Norbert Guterman, *Prophets of Deceit: A Study of the Techniques of the American Agitator* (New York: Harper, 1949). It was reissued in a new edition in 2021 and retranslated into German by Susanne Hoppmann-Löwenthal the same year, generating extensive commentary. For my own thoughts on its current relevance, see Katrin Stoll, "Leo Lowenthal's Legacy: The Relevance and Response of Critical Theory to Authoritarianism, Austerity and Anti-Semitism Today: An Interview with Martin Jay," *Studia Literaria Historica* 10 (2021). Adorno studied the propaganda techniques of one agitator in particular in *The Psychological Technique of Martin Luther Thomas's Radio Addresses* (Stanford, CA: Stanford University Press, 2000). Another study commissioned by the Institute was conducted by Siegfried Kracauer, but remained unpublished in English until the present day because of Adorno's doubts about its methods. See Kracauer, *Selected Writings on Media, Propaganda and Political Communication,* ed. Jaeho Kang, Grahame Gilloch and John Abromeit (New York: Columbia University Press, 2022).

The most influential volume in the series then and now was The Authoritarian Personality *(1950), based on studies conducted by the Institute in cooperation with the Berkeley Public Opinion Study Group.*[2] *Hailed when it first appeared as a methodological breakthrough in using survey techniques along with qualitative analyses of typical cases, it was also criticized for its apparent prioritizing of psychological over social explanations and its implicit political biases. As a result of the latter, it was marginalized in mainstream social science for two generations. But, baffled by the recent upsurge of authoritarian populism, often attracting working-class whites, many current commentators have returned to an analysis that assigns to its supporters flawed personalities that are predisposed to being seduced by irrational appeals, even against their own interests.*

Rather than revisit the earlier debates that swirled around The Authoritarian Personality, *this essay addresses two larger issues: the cross-cultural applicability of a characterological model generated by European theoretical assumptions to empirical data from postwar America, and the inadvertent costs of pathologizing political opponents. Not only is there a danger of foreclosing in advance the dialogic practices of deliberative democracy, however naïvely idealized they may seem, but there is also the potential exculpation of wrongdoers who can claim they were not responsible for their morally dubious acts. These were warnings that, ironically, were already voiced by Frankfurt School theorists themselves in considering the limitations of characterological types in explaining the abiding appeal of authoritarianism.*

In September 2019, an international conference at Beijing Normal University titled "Aesthetics, Society and the Travels of Critical Theory" brought together more than fifty scholars to discuss the legacy of the Frankfurt School and other twentieth-century European theorists. The papers ranged widely, with frequent attempts made to compare aspects of Critical Theory with Chinese intellectual traditions, but one potential theme was conspicuous by its absence. As far as I could tell from the papers I heard in Western languages and the abstracts I read

---

2   Theodor W. Adorno, Else Frenkel-Brunswick, Daniel J. Levinson and R. Nevitt Sanford, *The Authoritarian Personality*, 2 vols. (New York: Harper, 1949); reissued by Verso with a new preface by Peter E. Gordon in 2019.

of others in English, no one attempted to enter the dangerous territory where Frankfurt School ideas might be applied with critical intent to contemporary China.[3] Not surprisingly, in the highly charged atmosphere prior to the celebration of the seventieth anniversary of the Communist revolution, when unsettling events in Hong Kong threatened to undermine the official story of national pride in the accomplishments of the regime, it would have been risky, to say the least, to ruminate on the actual relevance of the ideas that were being so lavishly praised in the abstract.

The result was that no one sought to apply Friedrich Pollock's analysis of "state capitalism" to an economy that was rapidly transitioning away from anything remotely resembling the socialism for which Marx had so fervently yearned. No one asked if Herbert Marcuse's critique of "one-dimensional man" or Adorno's of "the administered world" might help make sense of contemporary Chinese society, or if the "culture industry" model developed in *Dialectic of Enlightenment* might plausibly characterize its mass culture. Nor did anyone wonder if the type of rationality fueling China's rapid modernization was more instrumental than communicative in the sense Habermas has sought to develop. And, finally, to come to the point of this chapter, no one dared to ask if the empirical methods developed by the Frankfurt School and its colleagues in *The Authoritarian Personality* might profitably be employed to investigate the psychological profiles of the average citizen of a country clearly governed in an authoritarian fashion.

As a result of these unaddressed questions, it was hard not to conclude that Critical Theory had been coopted as window dressing for essentially uncritical purposes, falling in line with the blatant disconnect between the radical Marxism still publicly endorsed by official dogma and the aggressively capitalist practice that has characterized China since the reforms of Deng Xiaoping. Although perhaps it might provide

3   This impression confirms the conclusion reached by Guohua Zhu and Xiangchun Meng in "From the 'Other' to the 'Master Narrative': The Chinese Journey of the Frankfurt School," *Comparative Literature and Culture* 20: 3 (2018): "Notwithstanding the critical appropriation of Adorno's aesthetics and theory of the Culture Industry, the Chinese reception of Critical Theory has been by and large a process of de-politicization. Critical Theory has apparently lost its battlefield in China. It fails to fully mobilize the Chinese intellectuals in their critical reflections on Chinese conditions of modernity, even though many Chinese scholars have been attracted to and inspired by the insights of Critical Theory" (p. 4), docs.lib.purdue.edu.

some leverage for those marginalized members of a Chinese New Left who seek intellectual sustenance in the heterodoxies of Western Marxism, there was little evidence of any danger that it might inspire a serious critique of today's China, one that might question the orthodox narrative promoted by the Communist Party. Or, at least, so I thought when the conference ended.

As is often the case, however, hasty impressions from a quick trip to a foreign country whose language is not your own can prove untrustworthy. For at least one conclusion that I had drawn had to be modified when I returned home and gained the access to the internet that had been blocked while I was in Beijing. There I discovered that a robust literature does, in fact, exist that has at least considered the applicability of *The Authoritarian Personality* to the post-revolutionary Chinese case. Although, to be sure, it does not seem to have emanated from mainland China itself, it at least shows that the question of the relevance of the study to the Chinese case has indeed been posed. In fact, as early as the 1960s, it was adduced to characterize the alleged national character of the Chinese people, albeit in a neutral rather than critical way.[4] But, as demonstrated by Anita Chan's 1985 *Children of Mao: Personality and Political Activism in the Red Guard Generation*,[5] it could also be introduced to explain the psychology—or more precisely, the "social character"—of the anti-Confucian militants of the Cultural Revolution, which she saw as a troubling, albeit passing, episode in modern Chinese history.[6] Although not all of the literature depended on extensive survey

---

4   See, for example, A. F. Wright, "Values, Roles and Personalities," in *Confucian Personalities*, ed. A. F. Wright and D. Twitchett (Stanford, CA: Stanford University Press, 1962), pp. 3–23; and P. N. Singh, S. C. Huang and G. Thompson, "A Comparative Study of Selected Attitudes, Values and Personality Characteristics of American, Chinese and Indian Students," *Journal of Social Psychology* 57 (1962), pp. 123–32. The latter study concluded that Indian students were even more authoritarian than the Chinese.

5   Anita Chan, "Political Socialization and the Authoritarian Personality in China," in *Children of Mao: Personality and Political Activism in the Red Guard Generation* (London: Palgrave Macmillan, 1985). She argues that seven of the ten traits of the authoritarian personality described by Adorno and his colleagues—the exceptions are superstitious beliefs, general destructive and aggressive inclinations, and an exaggerated concern with sex—were shared by the Red Guard militants. Rather than evidence of a general Chinese national character, they demonstrate a historically specific "social character" unleashed by Mao's decision to launch the Cultural Revolution.

6   "The particular climate that encouraged the development of the authoritarian 'social character' no longer prevails," Chan concluded. "The 1980's are not the 1960's;

research in the field using the study's famous "F-scale" to measure psychological predilections for authoritarianism, the appropriateness of the category in this context has indeed been vigorously discussed.

The current state of the debate was helpfully summarized in 2016 by the Taiwanese scholar Chin-Lung Chien in an essay called "Beyond Authoritarian Personality: The Culture-Inclusive Theory of Chinese Authoritarian Orientation."[7] Chien claims that the most recent scholarship shows increasing skepticism towards the cross-cultural validity of a theory and method originally generated in a very different cultural context. Endorsing what anthropologists call an "emic" rather than "etic" point of view, one that draws on indigenous psychological characteristics rather than allegedly universal ones, he argues that Chinese culture has traditionally respected high status and willingly bestows authority on figures—in particular, the ruler (traditionally, the emperor), parents and teachers—who are assumed to earn it. Sensitivity to authority is keen and social interactions often involve judging who would be the relevant authority in a particular situation. Filial piety within the family is generalized to other areas of society, so that hierarchical relationality rather than egalitarian individualization has long been considered both normal and normative in China.

Acknowledging the power of vertical authority-dependence does not mean, however, that there are no limits to the obedience of those who willingly subordinate themselves. Confucian relationality goes in both directions, and authority earns its legitimation by the benevolence with which it treats those under its care. Accordingly, disobedience is permitted when the obligations of the authority are not honored, as evidenced by the popular saying "If you're not benevolent, I'm not righteous." Although the recent restoration of respect for Confucianism in China might be seen as a cynical weaponization of the tradition in the service of maintaining the power of the ruling Communist Party and its nationalist ideology, public opinion survey research seems to indicate that there is actually a high level of governmental responsiveness to citizen complaints, which has led to a surprising trust among the populace of

---

and the children of Deng are not the children of Mao." *Children of Mao*, p. 225. Chan noted that the term "social character" had been introduced by Erich Fromm to designate a collective rather than individual syndrome.

7   Chin-Lung Chien, "Beyond Authoritarian Personality: The Culture-Inclusive Theory of Chinese Authoritarian Orientation," *Frontiers in Psychology* 7: 924 (2016).

their leaders.[8] A second exception to the rule of accepting authority without reservations concerns the distinction made between public acceptance and private resistance, which may seem like inconsistency or even hypocrisy, but is considered a sign of maturity in Chinese culture. Compartmentalization allows for a distinction between social values and personal interests, which loosens the grip of authority even in traditional Chinese society.

I am not, of course, in a position to judge the validity of the literature on the applicability of the "authoritarian personality" template in China. But noting that the category has been invoked to cover both traditional Confucian respect for authority and the Cultural Revolutionary disdain for parents and teachers in the service of obeying only Mao and the Party does, I think, spur us to question the universal applicability of the contrasting syndromes presented in *The Authoritarian Personality*. These, it will be remembered, are exemplified by the two ideal typical figures called "Mack" and "Larry," one a "high-scorer" on the F-scale, the other a "low-scorer." Commentators, to be sure, have often noted a certain wobble in the characterization of both personality types. High scores have sometimes been taken to signify personalities that would be better called "fascist" or "totalitarian" than "authoritarian." The syndrome of low-scorers has been no less difficult to label in straightforward terms. In the Institute's pioneering, although unpublished, study directed by Erich Fromm of workers' attitudes in the later Weimar period, the opposition had been between "authoritarian" and "radical" personalities, with subcategories like "conservative-authoritarian" and "rebellious authoritarian" complicating the picture.[9] In *The Authoritarian Personality*, "radical" was replaced either by "democratic" (at least as

---

8 Wengang Tang, "The 'Surprise' of Authoritarian Resilience in China," *American Affairs* 2: 1 (Spring 2018), pp. 101–17. According to one survey, conducted in 2008, 78 percent of respondents in China agreed with the statement "my government would respond to people's needs," compared with 36 percent in Taiwan, 33 percent in Japan and 21 percent in Korea.

9 Erich Fromm, *The Working Class in Weimar Germany: A Psychological and Sociological Study*, ed. Wolfgang Bonss, trans. Barbara Weinberger (Leamington Spa, UK: Berg, 1984). Fromm would continue to underline the importance of the "rebellious" authoritarian character, as distinguished from a genuinely revolutionary one, in *The Fear of Freedom* (London: Routledge & Kegan Paul, 1963), p. 146. Although the title in the British edition was changed from the American *Escape from Freedom*, the text is the same.

implied by the frequent use of "anti-democratic" as a synonym for "authoritarian") or, more frequently, "genuine liberal," which was the most positive of the typological characterizations offered by Adorno in his discrimination between low-scorers.[10] The implied harmonious combination of the two into a coherent "liberal democratic" personality, when in fact the two political philosophies have often been at odds, never seems to have been squarely defended. Nor was the important distinction between liberal and socialist addressed, which is made embarrassingly manifest in the index where the reference for "Socialism" says *"see* Liberalism."[11]

But, however the high- and low-scorers might be labeled in describing the American subjects who had been tested, they would not easily map on to the relevant dichotomy in the Chinese case, which, if Chin-Lung Chien is right, cries out for an indigenous psychological approach. Although exceptions can surely be found, the primary alternative there would seem to be between something like "traditional authoritarian" and "revolutionary authoritarian" personalities, depending on which authorities are obeyed and which defied. Significantly, in his preface to the study, Horkheimer had argued that "the central theme of the work is a relatively new concept—the rise of an 'anthropological' species we call the authoritarian type of man."[12] What this terminology suggests is that it should be understood as a modern phenomenon, which is not specific to any one culture. But if the Chinese case is taken seriously, it may be questionable to conclude that "authoritarian personalities" have emerged only in the modern era and that their existence always follows one model.[13]

---

10   Adorno et al., *The Authoritarian Personality*, p. 781. The instability of the categorization of the anti-authoritarian personality is exemplified by the evolution in Fromm's usage, from the "radical" and "revolutionary" to the "mature person: a person who does not need to cling to others because he actively embraces and grasps the world, the people, and the things around him." Fromm, "The Authoritarian Personality," *Deutsche Universitätszeitung* 12: 9 (1957), p. 3.

11   Adorno et al., *The Authoritarian Personality*, p. 988.

12   Max Horkheimer, preface to *The Authoritarian Personality*, p. lxxi.

13   This is not to say, however, that it lacks purchase outside the United States and might not be productively applied today. For attempts to extend it to present-day authoritarian populist movements in America and Europe, see Jeremiah Morelock, ed., *Critical Theory and Authoritarian Populism* (London: Westminster, 2018); and Paul K. Jones, *Critical Theory and Demagogic Populism* (Manchester: Manchester University Press, 2020).

Similarly, there would also likely be far fewer examples in Chinese history of that "genuine liberal" type with "a strong sense of personal autonomy and independence" who is "antitotalitarian . . . without the element of hesitation and indecision" so clearly valorized by the authors of *The Authoritarian Personality*.[14] Although one might advocate the nurturance of such personalities and refuse to exclude their development in contemporary China on the dubious grounds that they are inherently and forever only "Western," it is clear that they cannot be understood as representing anything like a "normal" model against which the "pathology" of authoritarianism can be measured in all cultures. Nor, of course, may it be unproblematic in defining the normative type of a "healthy" character in the West either.[15]

Imposing the high-/low-scorer dichotomy onto the Chinese case, however one labels the personalities they typically represent, may ironically seem to express the very ethnocentrism that the authors of *The Authoritarian Personality* themselves considered a symptom of high-scoring on the F-scale. Even if "ethnocentrism" may be too charged a label to use, what is clear is that the local context in which *The Authoritarian Personality* was composed influenced the ways in which its categories were composed. As Adorno's "Remarks" on the book written in 1948 clearly indicate, the Holocaust and the continuing menace of hostility towards the Jews, even when it seemed to be in abeyance in postwar America, was a prime motivating factor for the study.[16] Daniel Levinson explicitly noted in the opening of the third chapter of the book, "The Study of Anti-Semitic Ideology," that "one of the most clearly antidemocratic forms of social ideology is prejudice, and within this context anti-Semitism provides a fruitful starting point for a social psychological study . . . the irrational quality in anti-Semitism stands out in even casual everyday conversations."[17] The broader discussions

---

14   Max Horkheimer, preface to *The Authoritarian Personality*, p. lxxi.

15   For a critique of this assumption, see Benjamin J. Fong, "The Psychic Makeup of the New Anthropological Type," *South Atlantic Quarterly* 117: 4 (October 2018), pp. 757–71.

16   Theodor W. Adorno, "Remarks on *The Authoritarian Personality*," in Adorno et al., *The Authoritarian Personality*. Horkheimer and Adorno (with the help of Leo Löwenthal) had composed the chapter "Elements of Anti-Semitism" in *Dialectic of Enlightenment* shortly before.

17   Daniel Levinson, "The Study of Anti-Semitic Ideology," in Adorno et al., *The Authoritarian Personality*, p. 57.

of ethnocentrism, fascism and authoritarianism in general that follow draw heavily on the initial characterization of anti-Semitic prejudice and its psychological underpinnings. Although Adorno was at pains to argue that it was generated largely from above by governmental manipulation rather than spontaneously from below, and that it was more an objective social pathology than an individual one, the major premise of the study was that it could only be understood—and possibly combatted—if its unconscious motivations were confronted.

It is not surprising that anti-Semitism played such a central role in the *Studies in Prejudice* in general and *The Authoritarian Personality* in particular, an understandable outcome of the circumstances of its genesis and the personal experiences of many of its authors. Noting this fact is not, let me hasten to add, to endorse in any way the charge later made by unapologetic anti-Semites like the psychologist Kevin MacDonald that the entire project was somehow an attempt by Jews "to undercut gentile family structure" and "subvert the entire social categorization scheme underlying gentile society."[18] This is pernicious nonsense. But it does seem clear that highlighting anti-Semitic prejudice as a prominent component of the F-scale does not easily translate into a methodological tool that will illuminate the pre-political psychology of Chinese authoritarianism, whether understood as an enduring legacy of Confucianism or as an ephemeral explosion during the Cultural Revolution. For not only is bias against Jews absent on an explicit level, but it would also be very difficult to find any functional equivalent of it in Chinese culture, even if there are inevitable examples of prejudice in its long history (for example, bias against certain people from different regions, such the Cantonese hostility towards the Hakka, which fueled the so-called Punti–Hakka Clan Wars in the nineteenth century).

The uncertain applicability of the method developed in *The Authoritarian Personality* to cases outside the culture out of which it emerged is not, however, the main issue I want to address in this paper. For, even when it is confined to the American and European contexts that originally generated it, a more general question must be posed,

18 Kevin MacDonald, *Culture of Critique: An Evolutionary Analysis of Jewish Involvement in Twentieth-Century Intellectual and Political Movements* (Westport, CT: AuthorHouse, 2002), p. 178. For a thorough demolition of MacDonald's racist arguments, see Nathan Cofnas, "Judaism as a Group Evolutionary Strategy: A Critical Analysis of Kevin MacDonald's Theory," *Human Nature* 29: 2 (June 2018), pp. 134–56.

which concerns the problematic application of psychological categories to political convictions and behavior. In particular, I want to open the question of what it means to introduce the charge of "pathology" to explain and stigmatize political discourse and behavior. I do so with the frank acknowledgment that raising it has already been weaponized by the targets of the analysis themselves. Thus, the aforementioned Kevin MacDonald, whose anti-Semitic agenda is unapologetically explicit, calls the chapter of his book *Culture of Critique* that treats *The Authoritarian Personality* "The Frankfurt School of Social Research and the Pathologization of Gentile Group Allegiances."[19] As ludicrous as it is to impute the distinction between high- and low-scorers on the F-scale to a covert agenda of identity politics, the implications of pathologizing political positions are nonetheless worth considering.

The vocabulary of pathology is, of course, originally derived from medicine, where it refers to diseases that disturb the normal equilibrium of a healthy organism. As Foucault pointed out in *The Birth of the Clinic*, the modern human sciences were deeply indebted to medical discourse as the first place where the individual could be divided into a unique living subject and an inert object of scientific typification.[20] Because of its explicit roots in a discourse about nature, the distinction between normal and pathological has sometimes overlapped with the charged opposition between natural and unnatural (although, of course, disease and death are no less "natural" than health and life). In the spectrum of antonyms to "normal," pathological clusters at one end with "abnormal" rather than at the other with "extraordinary." It was apparently first applied to mental illnesses by the psychiatrist and philosopher Karl Jaspers in his 1913 *General Psychopathology*.[21] Precisely what to include in the category has, of course, been a source of ongoing controversy, as is the importance of the purely physical component in its etiology.

Emerging in part in the context of the extrapolation of biological categories, often evolutionary in nature and racist in application, to social and cultural phenomena, it brought with it a cargo of questionable assumptions. It was not by chance that Jaspers's pioneering book

---

19   MacDonald, *Culture of Critique*, chapter 5.

20   Michel Foucault, *The Birth of the Clinic*, trans. A. M. Sheridan (London: Tavistock, 1973), p. 197.

21   Karl Jaspers, *General Psychopathology*, 2 vols., trans. J. Hoenig and Marian Hamilton (Baltimore: Johns Hopkins University Press, 1997).

has been flagged for positing "the close relationship of race and mental illness, citing in great detail the claims that the Jews as a race were disposed to mental illness."[22] As Foucault has made us all aware, the nosological attempts of psychologists and psychiatrists well before Jaspers to categorize and treat mental illness were tacitly grounded in moral and religious assumptions that compromised their claims to scientific neutrality. Without denying the pain of those who can genuinely be said to suffer from mental disturbances, there was often a slippery slope that led to the inclusion of nonconformists, dissenters, and "deviants" in the category of pathological exceptions to cultural norms. However one judges the validity of Foucault's arguments about the malign practices of "governmentality" and "biopower," it is difficult to restore full faith in the innocence of categories of pathology transferred from physical conditions to mental states. For, as Georges Canguilhem made clear as early as his 1943 study *The Normal and the Pathological*, the opposition was already culturally inflected when it was applied to medical and biological phenomena in the nineteenth century.[23] When it was extended with dubious results to cultural and aesthetic phenomena, most notably modernism, by critics like Max Nordau in his 1892 screed *Degeneration*, its potential for abuse became clear.[24]

Even greater caution has to be exercised, I would argue, when the language of pathology is extrapolated from the discourses of medicine and psychology to social and political attitudes and behaviors. Based on the analogy of the society or polity to a natural organism with conditions of health and disease, and experiencing generative and degenerative trajectories of growth and decline, it can be traced as far back as

---

22 Sander L. Gilman and James M. Thomas, *Are Racists Crazy? How Prejudice, Racism, and Antisemitism Became Markers of Insanity* (New York: New York University Press, 2016), p. 23.

23 Georges Canguilhem, *The Normal and the Pathological*, trans. Carolyn R. Fawcett (Cambridge, MA: MIT Press, 1991). This translation was of an expanded edition of the book in 1966 and included an introduction by Foucault. For a discussion, see Mike Gane, "Canguilhem and the Problem of Pathology," *Economy and Society* 27: 2/3 (1998), pp. 298–312.

24 Max Nordau, *Degeneration* (Lincoln: University of Nebraska Press, 1993); for an account of the larger discourse of degeneration in literary terms, see Barbara Spackman, *Decadent Genealogies: The Rhetoric of Sickness from Baudelaire to D'Annunzio* (Ithaca, NY: Cornell University Press, 1989).

Plato's *Republic*,[25] but gained added currency in the nineteenth century in the work of social theorists as disparate as Herbert Spencer, Cesare Lombroso and Émile Durkheim.[26] The analogy raised a number of troubling questions that still bedevil any attempt to apply it in a naïve, unreflective fashion. Does "health" correspond to an assumed standard of normality (or normalcy) and "illness" to deviance from that norm?[27] Is normality a descriptive category based on statistical evidence revealing the "average" or "mean" of a current behavioral sample, or a presumed past equilibrium that has somehow been disturbed in the present? Or is it rather a normative category, employed with critical intent and indicating a condition that has yet to be achieved? If a normative category, is it identified with continuing evolutionary change based on the survival of the fittest, as Social Darwinists claimed, or with ever-expanding economic development, as modernization theorists have argued? Or are there other values, such as social justice, equality and stability, which can serve as the criteria of a healthy society or polity? Conversely, does the counter-notion of pathology merely refer to what is marginal or eccentric in the current society or does it have the added normative weight of a potential that might, alas, be actualized in the future (as was often said of the latent fascist lurking inside the current authoritarian personality)?

Furthermore, are the pathogens that disturb the putative normal equilibrium external to a functioning system, which they disrupt, or are they built into the system from within, like the aging of cells, and inevitably compel it to decay? If the former, can they be understood in terms of an imbalance caused by the mere intrusion of a foreign body or instead by its scale, a bit like Plato's *pharmakon*, which can be a cure or a poison depending on the dosage level?[28] If the latter, is the argument that decay is organically inevitable a vain gesture to lament the completed

---

25 See Sara Brill, "Political Pathology in Plato's *Republic*," *Apeiron* 49: 2 (2016), pp. 127–61.

26 See Walter M. Simon, "Herbert Spencer and the 'Social Organism,' " *Journal of the History of Ideas* 21: 2 (April/June 1960), pp. 294–9.

27 The term "normalcy" gained currency in the 1920 American presidential election, when Warren Harding promised a return to it. For a consideration of its literary uses, see Heinz Ickstadt, "The Creation of Normalcy," *Revue Française d'Études Américaine*, no. 85 (June 2000), pp. 6–22.

28 The latter usage is adopted by Carl J. Friedrich in "Political Pathology," *Political Quarterly* 37: 1 (January 1966).

life-cycles of cultural or social collectivities, which like Oswald Spengler's "civilizations" inevitably decline, or should efforts be made to prolong their lifespan?

Is there, whether we place the cause of decline externally or internally, a necessary congruence between individual health and the health of the social body, or are there tensions between them, as Thomas Malthus and other analysts of the dangers of overpopulation by well-fed breeders have averred?[29] Is mere system-maintenance, no matter the cost for certain unfortunate elements of the whole, a sufficient criterion of "health" or "functionality"? Or are there other values that might justify disrupting the smooth functioning of a system, perhaps even undermining its survival? Is there an echo of the distinctions between pure and polluted, clean and unclean, ordered matter and the matter out of place that is called dirt, in the contrast between healthy and ill social and political behavior and beliefs? If the metaphors of "health" and "disease" prove problematic, is the situation improved by translating them into the more capacious and less explicitly medical vocabulary of "functional" and "dysfunctional"? For the question always has to be answered: functional for whom or what purpose?

In addition to these fundamental questions, there is also the issue of what is considered a social or political pathology in more specific terms. When the vocabulary of social pathology became popular in the nineteenth century, it was often applied by sociologists to such phenomena as crime, alcoholism and suicide. But of course, other forms of alleged "degeneration," ranging from outlaw sexual behavior, a bohemian lifestyle and modern art to anarchistic politics and nihilistic anomie, could be described as pathological. More ominously still, entire groups, often understood in racial terms, could be categorized as inherently pathological, with the implied conclusion that they had to be eliminated through whatever means were necessary. But at a certain point in the twentieth century, as Sander Gilman and James Thomas show in their 2016 study *Are Racists Crazy?*, two major shifts occurred in which the diagnosis of pathology used to stigmatize different races as inherently degenerate began to be applied in new ways. First, it was mobilized to

---

29 See Catherine Gallagher, *The Body Economic: Life, Death, and Sensation in Political Economy and the Victorian Novel* (Princeton, NJ: Princeton University Press, 2005).

explain the damage done to the victims of that stigmatization by historical processes, for example, the costs borne by Jews who sought to assimilate to gentile society or by African Americans who bore the scars of
slavery and Jim Crow and were the pioneers of integration. Often a
version of what psychoanalysts had called the neurotic defense mechanism of "identification with the aggressor" was used to explain an internalized self-hatred that might allow it to be understood sympathetically
rather than censoriously. Although the unintended consequence could
be the continuing labeling of outsider groups as psychologically
damaged—as shown by the uproar unleashed by Daniel Patrick
Moynihan's controversial account of the disintegration of the Black
family[30]—at least the explanation was now historical rather than ontological, and the fault was attributed to external pressures rather than
hard-wired, internal flaws.

Second, and for the purposes of this paper, more importantly, the
diagnosis of pathology could ultimately be applied not only to the
victims of racism, whether understood as their ontological or historical
fate, but instead to the perpetrators, whose irrational prejudice was a
sign of a deeper malady.[31] The story Gilman and Thomas tell of this
transformation, which emerged full blown only as a reaction to the
Holocaust, includes such works Wilhelm Reich's 1934 *The Mass
Psychology of Fascism*, Erich Fromm's 1941 *Escape from Freedom*,
Richard Brickner's 1943 *Is Germany Incurable?* and Ernst Simmel's 1946
edited collection *Anti-Semitism*, whose subtitle tellingly called the prejudice "a social disease."[32] They also place *The Authoritarian Personality*
at a crucial point in that narrative. Gilman and Thomas see that work
and the *Studies in Prejudice* in general as major contributions to what

---

30   Daniel P. Moynihan, *The Negro Family: The Case for National Action* (Washington,
DC: Office of Policy Planning and Research, US Department of Labor, 1965).

31   Gilman and Thomas, *Are Racists Crazy?*, chapters 4 and 5. The transition is
emblematized by Horkheimer's claim, made in 1946: "One is tempted to say that though
the Jews, who have changed much in the course of history, are certainly no race, the anti-
Semites in a way *are* a race, because they always use the same slogans, display the same
attitudes, indeed almost look alike." Cited on p. 184.

32   Ernst Simmel, *Anti-Semitism: A Social Disease* (New York: International
Universities Press, 1946). Simmel's own contribution to the collection, which emerged
from a conference including Horkheimer, Adorno and two other authors of *The
Authoritarian Personality*, was bluntly titled "Anti-Semitism and Mass Psychopathology,"
by which he explicitly meant a collective "psychosis."

they call "the 'rising tide' of post-war scholarship on both the pathological conditions of prejudice and racism, and their psychopathological consequences on the targets of prejudice and racism."[33]

Although that tide receded for a number of years, it is clearly on the rise again, and for obvious reasons. As a result, the current relevance of *The Authoritarian Personality* is now very much in evidence, as shown by its recent republication by Verso with an excellent introduction by Peter E. Gordon, as well as special journal issues, anthologies and conferences.[34] For all of its often acknowledged methodological flaws, there is much to be learned by reopening the issues raised by the study and from considering the conclusions it reached. But a few words of caution should be heeded before a wholesale application to contemporary events can be advocated. They concern the universal applicability of the theory, which we have raised in connection with the Chinese case, and with the problematic implications of pathologization itself.

Both compel us to confront the costs of conceptual subsumption and homogenizing typicality. Among the most consistent bugaboos of Critical Theory, targeted with special vehemence in Horkheimer and Adorno's *Dialectic of Enlightenment*, was the reduction of particular instances to exemplars of general types, the nonfungible to abstract equivalences, the nonidentical to the identical. Although functional in the service of species self-preservation, conceptualization had as its cost the reduction of the other to the same, the homogenization of difference, and the reification of fluid life into inert categories. It thus abetted the domination of nature and the subject's priority to the object. A stalwart of aesthetic modernism, Adorno never followed Georg Lukács in echoing Engels's praise for literary realists like Balzac who provided a "truthful reproduction of typical characters in typical circumstances."[35] Instead, he valued the idiosyncratic as a marker of resistance to conformism.[36] What might be called the nominalist impulse in Critical Theory

---

33   Gilman and Thomas, *Are Racists Crazy?*, p. 196.

34   See, for example, the special issue of *South Atlantic Quarterly*.

35   Friedrich Engels to Margaret Harkness, April 1888: marxists.org.

36   Axel Honneth, "Idiosyncrasy as a Tool of Knowledge: Social Criticism in the Age of the Normalized Intellectual," in *Pathologies of Reason: On the Legacy of Critical Theory*, trans. James Ingram (New York: Columbia University Press, 2009). For a discussion of its contradictory implications, see Jan Plug, "Idiosyncrasies: of Anti-Semitism," in *Language without Soil: Adorno and Late Philosophical Modernity*, ed. Gerhard Richter (New York: Fordham University Press, 2010).

resisted the naturalization of categorical generalizations and rigid oppositions, which should be understood instead as historically created and
thus potentially open to de-reification.[37]

From this perspective, the resort to abstract personality types in the
Institute's work would seem to be a contradiction.[38] Accordingly, even a
sympathetic observer like Espen Hammer has lamented that "Adorno,
in *The Authoritarian Personality*, gets himself into a conflict with his
own requirement that experience should be interpreted and not classi-
fied. The very rigidity of the criteria being used—their reified character—may easily prevent them from revealing historically complex and
dynamic truths."[39] The discourse of pathologization, after all, inevitably
reads apparently idiosyncratic surface appearances—medical, psychological or social—as symptoms of deeper patterns which can fruitfully
be characterized in more typological and systemic terms.

But, as was always the case with the resolutely dialectical tenor of
Critical Theory, there was inevitably a counterargument against the
implications of a radical nominalism that dismissed all typification as
inherently coercive. It was made by Adorno in chapter 19 of *The
Authoritarian Personality*. Here he confronted head-on the criticism
that "typologies tend towards pigeonholing and transform highly flexi-
ble traits into static, quasi-biological characteristics, while neglecting,
above all, the impact of historical and social factors."[40] Acknowledging
that the psychiatric typologies of mental diseases introduced by nine-
teenth/early twentieth-century figures like Emil Kraepelin and Cesare
Lombroso have been discredited, he also conceded that "the critique of
psychological types expresses a truly humane impulse, directed against
that kind of subsumption of individuals under pre-established classes

---

37   For an account of the nominalist impulse in Adorno, and its limits, see Martin
Jay, "Adorno and Musical Nominalism," *New German Critique*, no. 129 (September
2016), pp. 5–26.

38   Even from other perspectives, the tension between nominalist and realist
impulses in their creation of types has been criticized. See John Levi Martin, "*The
Authoritarian Personality*, 50 Years Later: What Lessons Are There for Political
Psychology?," *Political Psychology* 22: 1 (2001), pp. 4–5. He argues that high scorers on
the F-scale are identified nominalistically and then assumed to belong to an ontologically
real personality type.

39   Espen Hammer, *Adorno and the Political* (London: Routledge, 2006), p. 63.

40   Adorno, "Types and Syndromes," in *The Authoritarian Personality*, p. 744.

which has been consummated in Nazi Germany."[41] In fact, Adorno even went on to say that "the rigidity of constructing types is itself indicative of that 'stereopathic' mentality which belongs to the basic constituents of the potentially fascist character."[42]

And yet despite all its pitfalls, Adorno argued that the typological approach is justified under present circumstances, in which "the marks of social repression are left within the individual soul . . . people form psychological 'classes,' inasmuch as they are stamped by variated social processes . . . large numbers of people are no longer, or rather never were, 'individuals' in the sense of traditional nineteenth-century philosophy."[43] In other words, society has created the stereotypes which typological theories merely register. Here Adorno defended ontological realism, albeit one based on the existence of historical rather than natural kinds. As a result, an undialectical nominalism "would be tantamount to renouncing the conceptual medium or any theoretical penetration of the given material, and would result in an irrationality as complete as the arbitrary subsumptiveness of the 'pigeonholing' schools."[44] Because such typifications are reflections of social pressures rather than natural kinds, the method of *The Authoritarian Personality* can be justifiably called a "*critical* typology."[45] High-scorers on the F-scale are more easily identified as fitting a uniform syndrome than low-scorers precisely because rigidity of psychological structure is evidence of an authoritarian personality, which emerges from social pressures to conform.[46] Such a personality, however, is best understood by drawing on the clinical categories of classical psychoanalysis, in particular the "sado-masochistic character" limned by Erich Fromm in the work he did for the Institute before his neo-orthodox revisionist turn.[47] There was a fit between the social and psychological level, because, as Horkheimer had argued in the Institute's unfinished project in the 1930s on authority and the family,

41 Ibid., p. 745–6.
42 Ibid., p. 746.
43 Ibid., p. 747.
44 Ibid., p. 748.
45 Ibid., p. 749.
46 This distinction helps explain the confusingly imprecise characterizations of the less rigid types posited as the opposite of the authoritarian: revolutionary, radical, democratic, liberal.
47 Adorno, "Types and Syndromes," p. 759.

"external social repression is concomitant with the internal repression of impulses."[48]

Was such a smooth transition between the two levels of explanation really persuasive? And if so, what was the criterion of normality against which the pathology of authoritarianism might be measured? Although *The Authoritarian Personality* seemed to assume that such a transition was indeed possible, largely because social pressures had so penetrated into the interiority of the self that the individual psyche was merely a shell of what it once had been, Adorno was less certain in other writings from this period. In fact, in several places he insisted that the two levels, the social and psychological, had to be kept distinct enough to allow for some sort of resistance to an over-socialized concept of human nature, which could draw its strength from biological desires that could not be fully blunted or satisfied in the present world.[49] Against the reductively harmonistic concept of "social character," adopted by Fromm when he abandoned Freud's libido theory, it was necessary to keep the tension between the two levels of analysis in play because, in reality, a complete absorption of one into another, despite everything, had not taken place.

Whatever Adorno's ambivalence about the collapse of the sociological and psychological in *The Authoritarian Personality*, the question of where precisely to locate the pathological source of high scores on the F-scale remained unclear. If psychopathology and social pathology were in lockstep, each reinforcing the other, was one ultimately primary and the other secondary? Perhaps the best way to address this question would be to turn to the suggestions offered by the authors of *The Authoritarian Personality* to treat the pathology of authoritarianism. Adorno, as we know from his dismissive statements in *Minima Moralia*, written in the same years that he helped create the empirical surveys for the *Studies in Prejudice*, had no use for Freudian therapy as a way to alleviate personal suffering.[50] All it did, he scornfully charged, was to

---

48   Ibid.

49   Theodor W. Adorno, "Sociology and Psychology, Part I," *New Left Review* 1: 46 (November/December 1967), pp. 67–80; "Part II," 1: 47 (January/February 1969), pp. 79–97.

50   See, for example, Theodor W. Adorno, *Minima Moralia: Reflections from Damaged Life*, trans. E. F. N. Jephcott (London: NLB, 1974), p. 61: "The therapeutically much-lauded transference, the breaking of which is not for nothing the crux of analytic treatment, the artificially contrived situation where the subject performs, voluntarily and calamitously, the annulment of the self which was once brought about

reconcile emotionally troubled souls to the miserable society in which they were embedded. In *The Authoritarian Personality*, he extended this skepticism to the claim that psychological weapons could be mobilized to cure collective prejudices: "Psychological 'treatment' of prejudiced persons is problematic because of their large number as well as because they are by no means 'ill,' in the usual sense, and, as we have seen, at least on the surface level are often even better 'adjusted' than the non-prejudiced ones."[51] In other words, even if it did not manifest itself in aberrant psychological behavior, the true pathology was on the deeper level of the social. For high-scorers on the F-scale could appear well adjusted according to the norms of the present order and thus not manifest any overt signs of illness.

To take the logic of this argument to its endpoint, we can say that for Adorno prejudicial attitudes and beliefs, such as anti-Semitism or ethnocentrism, were merely manifest symptoms of latent deformations. More ominously still, even when such noxious beliefs were consciously denied, it was possible to detect by indirect means the same characterological defects in an alarming number of respondents.[52] But, on a more fundamental level, such psychopathological symptoms were themselves expressions of deep-seated social pathologies that affected virtually everyone in the society. If the very existence of genuine "individuals" in the nineteenth-century classical liberal sense was threatened, treating their symptoms on a personal level was thus doomed to fail. And a mass "cure" in which large populations of suffering patients were willing to undergo collective therapy through a lengthy process of transferential working through—with whom?—was even less plausible. The prospects for fundamental change were thus bleak, at least without a wholesale change in the prevailing social order, which had pretty much remained in place even after the defeat of fascism. It was as if the symptoms of the irrational mass behavior that had so distressed the theorists of the

---

involuntarily and beneficially by erotic self-abandonment, is already the pattern of the reflex-dominated, follow-my-leader behavior which liquidates, together with all intellect, the analysts who have betrayed it."

51   Adorno, *The Authoritarian Personality*, p. 748.

52   The importance of the indirect revelation of subconscious beliefs for Horkheimer and Adorno, who scorned the straightforward sampling of overt opinions favored by American empiricists, is discussed in David Jenemann, *Adorno in America* (Minneapolis: University of Minnesota Press, 2007), pp. 42–4.

"crowd" in the late nineteenth century, such as Gustave Le Bon, and fueled the rise of fascism were lurking just beneath the surface in many people who were not roaming the streets in search of someone to lynch.

Underlying this pessimism was a much more rigorous norm of a non-pathological social order than indicated by the models of a democratic or "genuine liberal" personality assigned to low-scorers on the F-scale. Hidden behind the Aesopian language they adopted in America was the still Marxist assumption, to borrow Fabian Freyenhagen's paraphrase, that "put in medical language, *capitalism is modern society's pathogen.*"[53] The implied alternative was, of course, socialism, which was itself based on a very high normative standard. As Axel Honneth pointed out, the early Frankfurt School's "basic distinction between 'pathological' and 'intact, non-pathological' relations" defined social health as a rational society. The ultimate source of this standard, Honneth argued, was the political philosophy of Hegel, who "was convinced that social pathologies were to be understood as the result of the inability of society to properly express the rational potential already inherent in its institutions, practices, and everyday routines."[54]

By acknowledging this normative standard and its implications for politics, we can come to the crux of the problem raised by extending the category of the pathological from a medical to a psychological to a social malady and then still further to include political beliefs. By characterizing political opponents as suffering from deep-seated pathological personality traits and calling their beliefs irrational, while denying them even the possibility of a personal therapeutic cure, there is little possibility of taking any of their grievances seriously, reasoning with them about the means to address them, and persuading them to change.[55] The tacit

---

53   Fabian Freyenhagen, "Critical Theory and Social Pathology," in *The Routledge Companion to the Frankfurt School*, ed. Peter E. Gordon, Espen Hammer and Axel Honneth (New York: Routledge, 2019), p. 414. Italics in original. He argues that beginning with Habermas, this assumption was jettisoned in favor of the idea that pathology was defined by an imbalance among the differentiated spheres of modernity.

54   Honneth, *Pathologies of Reason*, pp. 22–3.

55   For an attempt to address this problem from within the Frankfurt School tradition of radical psychoanalysis, see Jessica Benjamin, "'The Wolf's Dictionary': Confronting the Triumph of a Predatory World View," *Contemporary Psychoanalysis* 53: 4 (2017), pp. 470–88. She urges the adoption of a "third space" that goes beyond the split between "us" and "them," in which "we recognize the general idea that not just some, but all, individuals are entitled to dignity, to have their rights and their suffering respected" (p. 476).

dehumanization of the targets of such critiques will be familiar to anyone who remembers the attempts by conservative critics of the New Left, such as Lewis Feuer, to denounce their protests as little more than the irrational working out of adolescent Oedipal fantasies of patricide.[56]

In *Are Racists Crazy?*, Gilman and Thomas discern what they call "an ominous tone" in Horkheimer's contribution to Ernst Simmel's collection *Anti-Semitism: A Social Disease*: "He talks about the need for 'mental sanitation', a 'planned program of *international* mental hygiene', education in 'psychological slums', and also . . . the types of films people 'need' to see. Such projects seem to echo the pathologies associated with authoritarianism and repression, rather than attempt to eliminate them."[57] We are, in other words, uncomfortably close to the abuse of psychiatric hospitals in the Soviet Union or re-education camps for the Uighur in Xinjiang Province in China.[58]

As it turns out, these precise words are misattributed by Gilman and Thomas, coming as they do from the subsequent essay in the collection written by the psychoanalyst Simmel and not from Horkheimer's.[59] Thus, it might seem prudent to hesitate before seeing them as the explicit outcome of the migration of pathology from medical and psychological discourses to their social and political equivalents in *The Authoritarian Personality*. But, wrongly attributed or not, they do point to a major difficulty in the project's underlying assumptions. For if you hold to rationality as the standard of non-pathological social health, you have to make be willing to defend the universal validity of your understanding of the term. If you embrace an emphatic Hegelian notion, which posits the historical realization of reason understood in the manner of nineteenth-century German Idealism at its most metaphysically speculative, you have to be prepared to explain to Chinese believers in a Confucian notion of legitimate traditional authority why they are provincial and culture-bound, while you are not.

---

56 Lewis S. Feuer, *The Conflict of Generations: The Character and Significance of Student Movements* (New York: Basic Books, 1968).

57 Gilman and Thomas, *Are Racists Crazy?*, p. 185.

58 For a short history of the problematic use of psychiatry for political purposes, see Robert van Voren, "Political Abuse of Psychiatry: An Historical Overview," *Schizophrenia Bulletin* 36: 1 (2010), pp. 33–5.

59 Ernst Simmel, "Anti-Semitism and Mass Psychopathology," in Simmel, *Anti-Semitism*, p. 75.

If, on the other hand, you understand rationality in the way more recent Frankfurt School members such as Jürgen Habermas have—that is, as an intersubjective process of communicative interaction in which both giving justifications and listening to those of others works to build a consensus based on persuasion rather than coercion or manipulation[60]—you face another dilemma. Treating your political opponents with condescension as inherently incapable of reasoning because of their underlying personality flaws, consigning them in some cases to the tellingly labeled "lunatic fringe," short-circuits the possibility of ever achieving the normative goal against which you measure their alleged pathology. In other words, once you stigmatize political others as typical cases of latent psychological disorders—or, in the infamous words of Hillary Clinton, as "deplorables"—and relentlessly dismiss the justifications they give of their opinions,[61] you make it very hard for them to participate in a deliberative democracy that relies on communicative rationality. It may be a pipe dream, of course, to believe such a utopia can ever exist, but if so, you cannot then in good faith continue to call social and political orders that fail to achieve an unattainable norm "pathological."

Even if you eschew pathologizing an opponent's political opinions as symptoms of individual psychological disturbances—thus allowing them to maintain some remnant of personal dignity—you run into another dilemma when you see a society as a whole as inherently pathological. In an essay published in 1961 titled "Opinion Delusion Society," Adorno insisted that "so-called pathological opinion, the deformations due to prejudice, superstition, rumor, and collective delusion that permeate history, particularly the history of mass movements, cannot at

---

60   For an attempt to trace the development of Critical Theory's ideas about reason, see Martin Jay, *Reason after Its Eclipse: On Late Critical Theory* (Madison: University of Wisconsin Press, 2016).

61   Skepticism towards surface opinions was also more consistently directed at high-scorers than low-scorers. According to one critic, "Despite several portions of Larry's interview that must have served as red flags to such Freudian theorists, his comments were never subjected to the critical and dismissive scrutiny that Mack's were. It seems that Lows were in effect handed a "Get Out of Neurosis Free" card, as can be seen in [the authors'] interpretation of Larry's view of gender relations, which were plainly stereotyped, superficial, morally rigid, unashamedly egotistical, and put adherence to conventional morality above inner feeling: all High traits." Martin, "*The Authoritarian Personality*, Fifty Years Later," p. 8.

all be separated from the concept of opinion per se."[62] That is, a politics trusting in the validity of public opinion, even "normal" rather than what is deemed "pathological" opinion, reflects a debased and contingent version of truth, which fails to do justice to the object of knowledge. "Truth," Adorno insisted, "has no place other than the will to resist the lie of opinion."[63]

But who will have the capacity to exercise that will and come to know or recognize what is true, and how might it manifest itself in the world of politics, which is anything but a disinterested search for a singular truth beyond mere opinion?[64] Adorno himself admitted that "if there really is no correct life in the false life, then actually there can be no correct consciousness in it either."[65] Without an explanation for how you and your like-minded friends have somehow escaped the damage of that false life and been able to get access to a truth denied to everyone else, then it will be hard to escape the reproach that you have been elevating your own relative opinions into more absolute truths. Discriminating between different childhood family experiences will not suffice, especially if you have declared the general obsolescence of the liberal individual with ego strength, nurtured in a family that once provided a haven in a heartless world, but no longer does so. Insisting on the orthodox Freudian distinction between libidinal desires and social character, the biological and the cultural, will also not be a sufficient response, as it does not accord well with the counterargument that social pathology directly imprints itself on the psyches of modern men and women. Nor does it comport with the description in *The Authoritarian Personality* of the "genuine liberal," "who cannot stand any outside interference with his personal convictions and beliefs, and . . . does not want to interfere with those of others either,"[66] which

---

62 Theodor W. Adorno, "Opinion Delusion Society," in *Critical Models: Interventions and Catchwords*, trans. Henry W. Pickford (New York: Columbia University Press, 1998), p. 106. Elsewhere in the essay, he more explicitly defines pathological opinion as "hardened opinion, reified consciousness, the damaged capacity for full experience" (p. 119).

63 Ibid., p. 121.

64 See Martin Jay, *The Virtues of Mendacity: On Lying in Politics* (Charlottesville: University of Virginia Press, 2010) for a critique of the idea of politics as a search for single, unequivocal truths.

65 Adorno, "Opinion Delusion Society," p. 120.

66 Adorno et al., *The Authoritarian Personality*, p. 781.

indicates a pluralist who tolerates different opinions rather than searching for a univocal concept of truth.

There is one final issue that needs to be addressed, which takes us in
the opposite direction from the points just made. Although there may
well be an underlying ethical component in the Frankfurt School's idea
of social pathology, as Fabian Freyenhagen has contended,[67] when
applied in practice, it may have an unintended consequence. For, in
addition to condescendingly demeaning those who are labeled authoritarian personalities, precluding in advance their ability to engage in
rational political discourse, the pathologization diagnosis can also have
an inadvertently exculpatory function when judging their deeds after
the fact. That is, it can be invoked to mitigate the moral responsibility of
the people—both individuals and communities—who are stigmatized
as psychopathological for the choices they have made. Often linked to
the discussion of evil, whether radical or banal, associated with commentators on the Holocaust like Hannah Arendt, Susan Neiman and Richard
Bernstein,[68] this objection was raised even earlier by an unexpected
critic. In a 1943 review of Richard Brickner's Is Germany Incurable?,
Erich Fromm worried that seeking to apply psychiatric categories to
something as nebulous as the "German character" might "become a
substitute for valid ethical concepts . . . they tend to weaken the sense
for moral values, by calling something by a psychiatric term when it
should be called plainly evil."[69]

Fromm's uneasiness with the potential ethical implications of pathologization was ironically borne out after the war, when the Institute of
Social Research, having returned to Germany, organized focus group

67 Freyenhagen, "Critical Theory and Social Pathology," p. 412. He contrasts
ethical with moral in the following way: "whereby ethics has to do with the good and
flourishing (and the bad and lack of flourishing), and morality has to do with justice and
the right (and injustice and the wrong)." He further argues that the early Frankfurt
School was more normatively invested in the former than the second and third
generation, which based critique more on the latter.

68 Hannah Arendt, Eichmann in Jerusalem: A Report on the Banality of Evil (New
York: Viking, 1963); Susan Neiman, Evil in Modern Thought: An Alternative History of
Philosophy (Princeton, NJ: Princeton University Press, 2002); Richard J. Bernstein,
Radical Evil: A Philosophical Interrogation (Malden, MA: Wiley, 2002) and The Abuse of
Evil: The Corruption of Politics and Religion since 9/11 (Cambridge: Polity, 2005).

69 Erich Fromm, "What Shall We Do with Germany?," review of Richard M.
Brickner, Is Germany Incurable?, Saturday Review, May 29, 1943, p. 10; cited in Gilman
and Thomas, Are Racists Crazy?, p. 122.

discussions rather than using survey research to reveal Germans' attitudes towards their responsibility for Nazism. *Group Experiment*, as it was known, was directed by Friedrich Pollock, but Adorno contributed a qualitative assessment of the findings in a chapter called *Guilt and Defense*, which has been translated as a separate book.[70] In it, he noted the way in which a too hasty acceptance by participants in the discussions of their pathologized diagnosis as authoritarian personalities could serve as an excuse for reprehensible behavior: "These too can degenerate into the stereotype that fends off consciousness of actual responsibility, insofar as the subject reifies itself as an object of pathology without seriously applying the implicit criticism of the subject to himself."[71]

By expressing such qualms, both Fromm and Adorno signaled their awareness of the dangers of unreflective social and political pathologization, dangers which have not entirely been ignored by current commentators as well. Thus, Amy Allen has recently written: "Drawing on psychoanalysis can lend itself to a tendency to pathologize those we disagree with, to identify phenomena such as Trumpism or Brexit with regressive psychological phenomenon or authoritarian personality structures, thereby implicitly positioning those of us who are critical of these phenomena as more psychologically mature than our political opponents. Although this can be satisfying, we should be wary of the comforts and seductions of those satisfactions."[72]

Is it possible, let me ask in conclusion, to harness the insights of *The Authoritarian Personality*, whose relevance today seems so obvious, without succumbing to the counterproductive condescension and self-satisfaction that accompanies the slippage from medical to psychological to social to political uses of the discourse of pathologization? Is it possible to acknowledge that we too live what Adorno would have called

70 Friedrich Pollock, Theodor W. Adorno and Colleagues, *Group Experiment and Other Writings: The Frankfurt School on Public Opinion in Postwar Germany*, ed. and trans. Andrew J. Perrin and Jeffrey K. Olick (Cambridge, MA: Harvard University Press, 2011); Theodor W. Adorno, *Guilt and Defense: On the Legacies of National Socialism in Postwar Germany*, ed. and trans. Jeffrey K. Olick and Andrew J. Perrin (Cambridge, MA: Harvard University Press, 2010).

71 Adorno, *Guilt and Defense*, p. 87. My thanks to Robert Hullot-Kentor for drawing this passage to my attention.

72 Amy Allen, "Psychoanalysis, Critique and Praxis," *Critique and Praxis*, 13/13, April 4, 2019, blogs.law.columbia.edu.

"damaged lives" and should think twice before dividing the world into the normatively healthy and the deplorably sick? Is it possible to invoke a normative notion of a future rational society against which we measure the alleged irrationality of our own without disrespecting the opinions and values of others? Is it, in short, possible to find ways to take seriously the suffering of those who resort to stereopathic solutions without ourselves imitating precisely that flawed approach by stigmatizing and marginalizing those whose politics we find repugnant? There are no easy answers to these questions, but it is imperative in our increasingly fragile democracy to try to find them.

5

The Age of Rackets? Trump, Scorsese and the Frankfurt School

The Frankfurt School's controversial critique of "the culture industry" claimed it was under the sway of commercial interests and that it blunted social discontent rather than genuinely reflecting the tastes and fulfilling the needs of its consumers. Read symptomatically, however, its products might reveal occluded truths of the society out of which they emerged. The eminent director Martin Scorsese's 2019 hit movie The Irishman *is a case in point.[1] Interpreted through the lens of the half-forgotten analysis of "racket society" begun, but never completed by Horkheimer and his colleagues during the Nazi era, it reveals how much the universalizing abstractions of moral principle, the rule of law and impersonal market relations have been replaced by ad hoc transactional interactions of loyalty based on protection and obedience. In other words, it is the emblematic movie of the era of Donald Trump, which remains even more relevant the more we learn about his presidency after he was voted out of office.*

Like virtually all attempts to characterize social or cultural totalities in simplified terms, the original "racket society" analysis overshot its target and underestimated the resilience of the impersonal abstractions that had seemingly been supplanted. It remains uncertain, however, if its new

---

1 Another choice example would be the award-winning HBO television series *Succession*, whose first season was in 2018. Its portrayal of a ruthless, power-hungry, unscrupulous family fighting over the inheritance of its founder's media empire reveals how the poison of the racket society permeates that sphere, as *The Irishman* did with trade unions, politics and the judiciary.

relevance will prove as temporary as it did when it was initially elaborated by the Frankfurt School to make sense of Nazi gangsterism. For merely restoring the sway of impersonal abstractions may not address the grievances that contribute to the rise of racket society in the first place. Formal equivalences, after all, underpin not only the impersonal rule of law and democratic citizenship, but also the exchange of commodities under capitalism. How the claims of the idiosyncratic and the non-identical can be recognized without undermining the defenses against arbitrary abuse erected by abstract formalism is still to be determined.[2]

Much has been made of late of the prescience of the Frankfurt School in anticipating the rise of populist nationalism in general and Donald Trump in particular.[3] By and large, the focus has been on their critiques of the culture industry, the authoritarian personality, the techniques of right-wing agitators and anti-Semitism. Another aspect of their legacy has, however, been largely ignored, which supplements their insights into the psychological and cultural sources of the problem and deepens their analysis of the demagogic techniques of the agitator. Its relevance can be fully appreciated if we take a detour through Martin Scorsese's widely acclaimed film *The Irishman*, which chronicles the career of mob hitman Frank Sheeran, among whose most notable victims—or so the real Sheeran claimed to his biographer Charles Brandt—was Teamsters Union president Jimmy Hoffa.

Whether or not the movie convincingly solves the mystery of Hoffa's disappearance and presumed death in 1975, it brilliantly succeeds in painting a vivid picture of a violent, amoral world in which power relations are transactional and the threat of betrayal haunts even the

---

2   A shortened version of this essay appeared in the *Los Angeles Review of Books*, April 5, 2020.

3   See, for example, Alex Ross, "The Frankfurt School Knew Trump Was Coming," *New Yorker*, December 5, 2016; Sean Iling and Stuart Jeffries, "If You Want to Understand the Age of Trump, Read the Frankfurt School," *Vox*, December 27, 2016, vox.com; Christian Fuchs, "How the Frankfurt School Helps Us to Understand Donald Trump's Twitter Populism," *HuffPost*, January 18, 2017, huffingtonpost.co.uk; and more substantially, Christian Morelock, ed., *Critical Theory and Authoritarian Populism* (London: Westminster, 2018); Paul K. Jones, *Critical Theory and Demagogic Populism* (Manchester: Manchester University Press, 2020); and Jeremiah Morelock, ed., *How to Critique Authoritarian Populism: Methodologies of the Frankfurt School* (Leiden: Brill, 2021).

most seemingly loyal friendships. It is a world only fitfully beholden to legal constraints and unmoved by appeals to mercy, a quality whose absence is underlined by the thoroughly marginalized roles it assigns to women. Despite the introduction of a priest who takes Sheeran's confession at the end of his life and suggests he can somehow will into existence the regret he is unable to feel, the film provides no real avenue of redemption for him to escape the earthly hell in which he has been living.

In certain respects, *The Irishman* may seem an elegiac reflection on the rich genre of Mafia epics that gave us three *Godfather*s, six seasons of *The Sopranos*, and several classics by Scorsese himself. But, as emblematized by the lame device of attributing Sheeran's fluency in Italian to his military service in the Second World War—as if GIs had the time to read Dante on the beaches of Salerno—the movie does not really immerse us in the culture and protocols of the Mafia. Because of his non-Italian background, Sheeran cannot become a "made man," and Hoffa's German and Irish background means he is also immune to inclusion in any Mafia "family." Although Robert De Niro and Al Pacino, the actors who so vividly portray them, inevitably invite us back into the universe created by Mario Puzo and Francis Ford Coppola, the territory of the story they inhabit is bigger. It can be called, to anticipate the larger point I want to make, a "racket society," which extends well beyond any ethnically circumscribed crime syndicate.

What makes *The Irishman* such a powerful depiction of that society is its insistence that the practices and mores of the Mob have permeated many other institutions. It appears most obviously in the trade union movement, where the powerful International Brotherhood of Teamsters, whose overflowing pension fund serves as a piggy bank for loans to gangsters, becomes even more corrupt when Hoffa—incarcerated for jury tampering, attempted bribery and fraud—is replaced by Frank Fitzsimmons. It also appears in the judicial system, where judges can be bought, juries gotten to and lawyers allowed to use all the tricks in their playbook to defeat justice. And, most appallingly, it permeates the world of politics, where John Kennedy is elected because of illegal vote-tampering in Illinois, the Bay of Pigs is invaded to bring casino owners back to Havana, Hoffa is paroled by Nixon because of a campaign contribution and possibly, just possibly, the Mob hires Lee Harvey Oswald as its hitman. Such is the immersion of politics in the racket society that the gangsters are utterly incredulous when Bobby Kennedy has the audacity to break ranks and go after Hoffa.

However conjectural these claims may be, *The Irishman* is actually a movie that may be telling us as much, if not more about our own world than that of Frank Sheeran and Jimmy Hoffa. To flesh out this conjecture, it will be helpful to consider that often neglected legacy of the Frankfurt School to which I have already alluded: its tentatively developed exploration of what it called "racket society." The concept was first developed during another, even more fraught period in history, when Max Horkheimer and his colleagues at the Institute of Social Research were in their American exile searching for a way to make sense of the Nazi regime that had driven them from Germany. Unhappy with the rigid categories of class analysis bequeathed to them by traditional Marxist theory, which had failed to anticipate the rise of fascism, and exasperated by the inability of the working class to play the revolutionary role assigned by that theory, they sought other explanations for what had happened. In the America to which they had fled in 1934, awareness of the increasing prominence of the "rackets" and "racketeering"—the *Encyclopedia of Social Sciences,* published in that very year, already had an entry on it—was mounting.[4] So too was popular fascination, as evidenced by the first cinematic treatment of the theme, Lewis Milestone's 1928 silent film *The Racket.* Significantly, the term had often been promoted by champions of big business who wanted to discredit labor unions, the most salient example being Gordon L. Hostetter and Thomas Quinn Beesley's *It's a Racket!* of 1929. They defined it as "any scheme by which human parasites graft themselves upon and live by the industry of others, maintaining their hold by intimidation, force, and terrorism."[5] What made the parasites especially menacing was their informal institutionalization into what became known as "organized" or "syndicated" crime. Surviving the end of Prohibition, when it had first emerged to prominence, it thrived in such illegal enterprises as

---

4 Murry I. Gurfein, "Racketeering," *Encyclopedia of Social Sciences* (New York: Macmillan, 1934). The etymology of the term is in dispute, with some claiming it referred to the exorbitant "rackrents" charged by greedy landlords (satirized in Maria Edgeworth's 1800 novel *Castle Rackrent*) and others attributing it to the noises used by pickpockets to distract their victims.

5 Gordon L. Hostetter and Thomas Quinn Beesley, *It's a Racket!* (Chicago: Les Quin, 1929), p. 4.

prostitution, drug-dealing, numbers-running, fencing stolen goods and gambling, and could easily spill over into other forms of corruption, including political.

It was tempting for German emigres to see parallels in the recent events they had escaped in Europe. Bertolt Brecht's "parable play" of 1941, *The Resistible Rise of Arturo Ui*, satirized Hitler's ascent to power through the fiction of a 1930s Chicago mobster who sought to control the cauliflower racket through violence, intimidation and protection. Unproduced in his lifetime, it was, however, one of Brecht's least successful efforts.[6] Theodor W. Adorno was later to criticize the play for conjuring away the true horror of fascism by turning it into "an accident, like misfortunes and crimes" rather than "the product of the concentration of social power."[7] But ironically, despite their often tense relationship with Brecht during their exile in Southern California, he and his colleagues had themselves begun to ponder the larger implications of rackets in the late 1930s and sought to work out their ideas during the war. The results were mixed, to be sure, with plans for a full-scale study resulting in only unpublished essays, leaving what Rolf Wiggershaus has called "an unfinished torso."[8]

Traces of the argument did survive in their later work, often in cryptic form, but, after it ceased to play a prominent role in their deliberations, it was ignored by most early interpreters of their legacy (the present author included). Recently, however, interest in their fragmentary analysis of rackets has quickened, especially in Germany. Beginning

---

6 As Frederic Ewen notes in his biography of Brecht, "To an audience dominated by memories of a horror unprecedented in civilized or uncivilized history, perpetrated by a nation once allegedly dedicated to humanism, Arturo Ui could only appear as a distorted parodistic puppet, and the analogy with American gangsterism as trivial . . . Neither 'epic' theater, nor the '*Verfremdung*' device could be just to so weighty a historical subject. Gangsterism is scarcely a phenomenon that could adequately describe Nazism and its atrocities." *Bertolt Brecht: His Life, His Art, and His Times* (New York: Citadel, 1967), pp. 374–5.

7 Theodor W. Adorno, "Commitment," in *Notes to Literature*, 2 vols., trans. Shierry Weber Nicholsen (New York: Columbia University Press, 1992), vol. 2, p. 83. In his "Extorted Reconciliation: On Georg Lukács' *Realism in Our Time*," he further accused Brecht of making fascism "socially extraterritorial and thereby easily 'stoppable,' 'resistible' at will," and thus ultimately making the Ui/Hitler character lose "its plausibility even within the play itself." *Notes to Literature*, vol. 1, p. 222.

8 Rolf Wiggershaus, *The Frankfurt School: Its Theories, History and Political Significance*, trans. Michael Robertson (Cambridge, MA: MIT Press, 1994), p. 319.

with an essay by Michael Greven in 1994 and culminating in 2019 with a book of over 600 pages by Thorsten Fuchshuber, "racket theory" has been treated as at least a partial refutation of the charge that Critical Theory suffered from a "political deficit."[9] Although slower to arrive in America, it is becoming a subject of debate here as well, with recent symposia on its implications and even an undergraduate research seminar at Williams College devoted to its exploration.[10]

The dogged persistence of capitalism and unexpected rise of fascism required both an economic and a political explanation. Some Institute figures, most notably the political scientist Franz Neumann, retained the more traditional Marxist notion of monopoly capitalism, which suggested that the system's contradictions remained unresolved and intensified class struggle was still a strong possibility. But others followed Friedrich Pollock in positing a new stage of capitalism, in which the state had managed to dull those contradictions, manage cyclical economic crises and undermine the working class's revolutionary consciousness.[11] Ultimately siding with Pollock, if with some hesitations, were Horkheimer and Adorno, even if the latter initially balked at

---

9   Michael Th. Greven, "Zur Kontinuität der 'Racket-Theorie': Max Horkheimers politisches Denken nach 1945," in *Kritische Theorie und historische Politik: Theoriegeschichtliche Beiträge zur gegenwärtigen Gesellschaft* (Opladen: Springer, 1994); and Thorsten Fuchshuber, *Rackets: Kritische Theorie der Bandenherrschaft* (Freiburg: Ça Ira, 2019). For a precis of his argument, see Fuchshuber, "Saving Mediation: The Topicality of Max Horkheimer's Post-liberal Concept of the Political," on the *Telos* website (March 24, 2016): telospress.com. Other German scholars, including Wolfgang Pohrt, Gunzelin Schmid Noerr, Volker Heins, Manfred Gangl, Lars Rensmann, Philipp Lenhard and Gerhard Scheit, have debated its implications. Scheit's "Rackets" is translated into English in Beverly Best, Werner Bonefeld and Chris O'Kane, eds., *The SAGE Handbook of Frankfurt School Critical Theory* (London: SAGE, 2018).

10   See the symposium in Nonsite.org, 18 (January 2019), which included comments by James Schmidt, John Lysaker, Chris Cutrone, Nicholas Brown and David Jenemann. The senior seminar in Political Science was directed in the fall of 2019 by Nimu Njoya: catalog.williams.edu. An even earlier consideration of the racket theory can be found in Peter M. R. Stirk, *Twentieth-Century German Political Thought* (Edinburgh: Edinburgh University Press, 2006), chapter 4.

11   For an account of the conflicting responses to Pollock's argument, see Wiggershaus, *The Frankfurt School*, pp. 280–91. He ultimately concludes that "Neumann's analysis of the relations between the party, the state, the armed forces and the economy made it clear that his differences of opinion with Pollock were basically quibbles about words. The development which Neumann described clearly pointed in the same direction as that for which Pollock had chosen the unhappy term 'state capitalism'" (p. 289).

the implication that "state capitalism" might actually reduce the suffering of those who were its victims.[12] Domination still prevailed, and, indeed, under fascism it was more nakedly and ruthlessly exercised. The inequality of class society under capitalism had by no means ended, but it now operated in a more directly political way.

Although Critical Theory was often taxed in later years for its relative indifference to politics because it was unable to find a way to link radical theory and revolutionary praxis, ironically it now upheld a darker version of the "primacy of the political" that sought to explain domination in essentially non-economic terms. As Horkheimer put it baldly in an unpublished memorandum called "Rackets and Spirit," written in 1942, "The basic form of domination is the racket . . . The most general functional category exercised by the group is protection."[13] His correspondence from the same year shows that he had high hopes for a coordinated application of the rackets model to many different sectors of modern life, which would resurrect the initial interdisciplinary program of the Institute.[14] At the basis of his enthusiasm was the belief that that the centrality of the mode of production and the economically defined classes it spawned had in fact been characteristic only of the period of classical liberal capitalism, which was now over. Instead, earlier forms of more direct rule had returned in a new guise. Before the rise of a more or less consolidated ruling class confronting an increasingly united working class, whose interaction was mediated by wage relations in the marketplace and the rule of formal law, there had been a welter of competing associations or cliques, run by elites who provided protection to their underlings, backed up by the threat of force, in return for obedience. In his essay "The End of Reason," published in 1941, Horkheimer claimed that "procurers, condottieri, manorial lords and

---

12 The claim that Horkheimer unequivocally supported Pollock's position, made, for example, by Gunzelin Schmid Noerr in his "Editor's Afterword" to *Dialectic of Enlightenment*, ed. Gunzelin Schmid Noerr, trans. Edmund Jephcott (Stanford, CA: Stanford University Press, 2002), is challenged in Greven, "Zur Kontinuität der 'Racket-Theorie.' "

13 Max Horkheimer, "Die Rackets und der Geist," in *Gesammelte Schriften*, vol. 12, *Nachgelassene Schriften 1931–1949*, ed. Gunzelin Schmid Noerr (Frankfurt: Fischer, 1985), pp. 287–8.

14 See, in particular, his letter of October 1, 1942, to Leo Löwenthal, in Max Horkheimer, *Gesammelte Schriften*, vol. 17, *Briefwechsel 1941–1948*, ed. Gunzelin Schmid Noerr (Frankfurt: Fischer, 1996), pp. 342–3.

guilds have always protected and at the same time exploited their clients. Protection is the archetype of domination."[15] Now in the post-liberal age, whether it be called monopoly or state capitalism, organizational tendencies were leading to the restoration of such direct, unmediated power arrangements. A congeries of competing cliques retained the loyalty of their clientele by trading protection for obedience, abandoning any pretense to represent general interests or universal principles.

In perhaps his most extensive elaboration of the racket theory, an unpublished essay called "On the Sociology of Class Relations," circulated to his Institute colleagues in 1943, Horkheimer spelled out his explicit departure from classical Marxism:

> The racket model, as was typical for the relationship between rulers and ruled, is now representative for all human relationships, even for those inside the working class. The difference between rackets in Capital and in Labor lies in the fact that by capitalistic rackets, the entire class profits, while the racket in Labor functions as a monopoly only for the leader and the labor aristocracy.[16]

Now, rather than focusing on the ambivalent psychological makeup of the working class or their ideological prejudices, as the Institute had in several studies that began in Weimar and continued in exile, he offered a structural analysis in which the proletariat, rather than opposing the capitalist ruling class, has mimetically internalized its pattern of domination.[17] At whatever level of the current society, the model of protection rackets has become increasingly prevalent.

---

15 Max Horkheimer, "The End of Reason," in *The Essential Frankfurt School Reader*, ed. Andrew Arato and Eike Gebhardt (New York: Continuum, 1978), p. 35.

16 Max Horkheimer, "Zur Soziologie der Klassenverhältnisse," *Gesammelte Schriften*, vol. 12, pp. 101–2. "Labor aristocracy" is, of course, a term dating to Kautsky and popularized by Lenin to denounce elites within the labor movement who fail to identify with the lot of their less fortunate comrades. The English original of this essay has recently appeared online with comments by James Schmidt, John Lysaker, Chris Cutrone, Nicholas Brown and David Jenneman: nonsite.org.

17 Erich Fromm, *The Working Class in Weimar Germany: A Psychological and Sociological Study*, ed. Wolfgang Bonss, trans. Barbara Weinberger (Leamington Spa, UK: Berg, 1984); in the early 1940s, they prepared a lengthy analysis of anti-Semitism in American labor, which was never published. See Catherine Collomp, "'Anti-Semitism among American Labor': A Study by the Refugee Scholars of the Frankfurt School of Sociology at the End of World War II," *Labor History* 52: 4 (November 2011), pp. 417–39.

The return of the racket model of social organization had meant a concomitant weakening of the universalizing mediations that had obscured its functioning during the heyday of liberal capitalism. One such mediation was the apparently impersonal marketplace based on an ideological faith in the possibility of justly rewarding personal merit and industry. As the Institute's political theorist Otto Kirchheimer put it, "*Racket* connotes a society in which individuals have lost the belief that compensation for their individual efforts will result from the mere functioning of impersonal market agencies."[18]

In exposing the lies of bourgeois equality of opportunity and the fairness of market mechanisms, the return of racket society might be construed as potentially emancipatory, or at least as brutally honest in stripping the ideological veil from actual domination. But what it also undermined was the dialectical promise that such ideologies always contain. Thus, in his fragment "Rackets and Spirit," Horkheimer would argue that "each racket conspires against the spirit and all are for themselves. The reconciliation of the general and the special is immanent in the spirit; the racket is its irreconcilable contrast and its obfuscation in the ideas of unity and community."[19] Equally problematic was the explicit repudiation of the rule of law and the ideal of popular sovereignty, both of which were mocked by the unapologetically particularist self-interest of protective solidarity. Thus, to cite Kirchheimer again, "It is the experience of an associational practice which implies that neither the individual's choice of an association nor the aims that the latter pursues are the result of conscious acts belonging to the realm of human freedom."[20] Along with the weakening of mediating universal ideologies went the erosion of an autonomous self who is capable of surviving outside the protective cocoon of the racket.

Although traces of the racket society model can be discerned in Horkheimer's postwar *Eclipse of Reason*,[21] and his joint work with

18   Otto Kirchheimer, "In Quest of Sovereignty" (1944), in *Politics, Law and Social Change: Selected Essays of Otto Kirchheimer*, ed. Frederic S. Burin and Kurt L. Schell (New York: Columbia University Press, 1969), p. 180.

19   Horkheimer, "Die Rackets und der Geist," p. 290.

20   Kirchheimer, "In Quest of Sovereignty," p. 180.

21   See, for example, the characterization of the labor movement: "The fact that labor unions are monopolistically organized does not mean that their members—aside from labor aristocracy—are monopolists. It does mean that the leaders control labor supply, as the heads of great corporations control raw materials, machines, or other

Adorno, *Dialectic of Enlightenment*,[22] the unfinished essays developing it were only posthumously published and the interdisciplinary project involving other Institute members remained unrealized. A number of speculative suggestions have been advanced to account for its virtual disappearance from the Frankfurt School's ongoing attempt to make sense of the grim world in which its members found themselves.[23] With the defeat of fascism in 1945 and the survival, however fragile, of liberal democratic institutions, the sweeping claims of the theory, which posited the end of one epoch in human history and the beginning of another, now seemed exaggerated. The affinity of the racket society model for a monopoly analysis of late capitalism, defended most strongly by Franz Neumann, also made it an awkward handmaiden of the Institute's alternative idea of "state capitalism" elaborated by Friedrich Pollock.[24] Whereas the former implied a more anarchic, or at least poly-cratic, struggle of competing protection racketeering factions, and one

---

elements of production. Labor leaders manage labor, manipulate it, advertise it, and try to fix its price as high as possible. At the same time, their own social and economic power, their positions and incomes, all vastly superior to the power, position, and income of the individual worker, depend upon the industrialist system. The fact that organizing labor is recognized as a business, like that of any other corporate enterprise, completes the process of the reification of man." Max Horkheimer, *Eclipse of Reason* (New York: Oxford University Press, 1947), p. 148.

22   In early drafts of the text, the phrase "system of big rackets" appeared, but was replaced in the final version by "the completely organized system of domination," Max Horkheimer and Theodor W. Adorno, *Dialectic of Enlightenment*, ed. Gunzelin Schmid Noerr, trans. Edmund Jephcott (Stanford, CA: Stanford University Press, 2002), p. 207. Euphemisms for other sensitive terms, such as "monopoly," were also frequently introduced in the published text.

23   In *Rackets*, Fuchshuber argues that part of the explanation may be Horkheimer's inability to convince other Institute members of the validity of the theory, although he attributes it primarily to substantive weaknesses as well as the changed political circumstances after the defeat of Nazism and the onset of the Cold War, which led to the substitute idea of "the administered world" (p. 566–7).

24   For an overview of the conceptual history of "state capitalism," which situates Pollock's argument, see Nathan Sperber, "The Many Lives of State Capitalism: From Classical Marxism to Free-Market Advocacy," *History of the Human* Sciences 32: 3 (July 2019), pp. 100–25. Pollock was, to be sure, himself a supporter of the racket society model, at least in the early 1940s. See the discussion in Philipp Lenhard, *Friedrich Pollock: Die graue Eminenz der Frankfurter Schule* (Frankfurt: Suhrkamp, 2019), pp. 256–7. For another consideration of the issue, which also concludes that state capitalism and racket society were essentially compatible, see Manfred Gangl, "The Controversy over Friedrich Pollock's State Capitalism," *History of the Human Sciences* 29: 2 (2016), pp. 23–41.

which might descend into unstable chaos, the latter tended towards an emphasis on the organization of a "command economy" from above, employing instrumental rationality to steer the system and mollify its contradictions. Although there is some uncertainty about the timing and the unqualified extent of Horkheimer and Adorno's adoption of Pollock's argument, it seems clear that it underlies their later notion of an "administered world" and was also operative in Herbert Marcuse's idea of a "one-dimensional society."

Another possible source of their hesitation was the growing realization that the mediating ideologies seemingly stripped away by the resurgence of rackets might still have some weak power to resist the full implementation of the system. In "Rackets and Spirit," Horkheimer had conceded that "in the true idea of democracy, which leads a repressed, underground existence in the masses, the hint of a society free from rackets has never been entirely extinguished."[25] Reflecting as an émigré from Nazism in 1944 on the still vital role of liberal democratic values despite their dubious ideological function, Adorno conceded that "we owe our life to the difference between the economic framework of late capitalism, and its political façade. To theoretical criticism the discrepancy is slight: everywhere the sham character of supposed public opinion, the primacy of the economy, in real decisions, can be demonstrated. For countless individuals, however, the thin, ephemeral veil is the basis of their entire existence."[26] In addition, the power of ideologies of a less benign kind—in particular, the exterminationist anti-Semitism that fueled Nazism—to trump the purely transactional patron–client relationships of the racket model needed to be acknowledged. For, as the German historian Philipp Lenhard later noted, it is one thing to be a gangster, another to be an ideologically motivated mass-murderer.[27]

Finally, there may have been some second thoughts about the wholesale characterization of organized labor as entirely corrupted by rackets,

---

25 Horkheimer, "Die Rackets und der Geist," p. 291.

26 Theodor W. Adorno, *Minima Moralia: Reflections from Damaged Life*, trans. E. F. N. Jephcott (London: NLB, 1974), pp. 112–13.

27 Philipp Lenhard, "Racket und Antisemitismus," *Prodomo*, no. 21 (April 2019), p. 11. The complicated relationship between the Institute's understanding of anti-Semitism and the racket society model is discussed in Fuchshuber, *Rackets*, pp. 476–507. He ties it to the erosion of mediating principles that might have challenged the program of annihilation.

mimetically duplicating the monopoly structure of capital. In 1942, when the Institute could still see fascism in apocalyptic terms as a world-wide menace, Horkheimer had written, "The historical course of the proletariat leads to a turning point: it can become a class or a racket. Racket means privileges within national borders, class means world revolution. The leaders have taken the choice away from the proletariat: they have chosen the racket."[28] Within the Institute, however, the stark-ness of the opposition had begun to raise doubts. In a letter responding to the circulated draft of Horkheimer's "On the Sociology of Class Relations," Marcuse cautioned in 1943: "You must be especially careful to avoid the impression that you take the 'transformation of the class struggle into adaptation' as a fait accompli and as the whole story . . . the coordination of the working class as a whole with the apparatus of the monopolistic society has not been successful, not in this country, certainly not in Germany and France, probably not in Britain."[29] When the dust settled after the war, the radical alternative posited by Horkheimer, like the famous opposition posited by Rosa Luxemburg during the previous world war "between socialism and barbarism," seemed melodramatically excessive. Although as the subsequent exam-ple of Hoffa's Teamsters shows, there was certainly a potential for unions to be corrupted, it would have been clearly unfair to consider all of them inherently rackets, a dangerous exaggeration that could play too easily into the hands of union-busting propagandists on the right.

Mentioning Hoffa brings us back to the initial question of this essay: to what extent is the morass of lethal venality detailed in *The Irishman* and anticipated by the Frankfurt School's "racket society" theory part of our own world today? For those who seek parallels, perhaps the most explicit contemporary exemplars of a racket society can be found in so-called failed states in which "warlords" struggle for spoils and power with scarcely any respect for the rule of law or general interests.[30]

---

28 Max Horkheimer, "Geschichte der amerikanischen Arbeiterschaft" (1942), in *Gesammelte Schriften*, vol. 12, p. 260.

29 Marcuse to Horkheimer, September 1943, in Herbert Marcuse, *Technology, War and Fascism*, vol. 1, *Collected Papers of Herbert Marcuse*, ed. Douglas Kellner (New York: Routledge, 1998), p. 246.

30 The concept of a "failed state" is not without its critics, who argue it covers too many disparate cases and relies on a Western notion of what a "successful state" looks like. See Charles T. Call, "The Fallacy of the Failed State," *Third World Quarterly* 29: 8 (2008), pp. 1491–507.

Somalia, Libya, Afghanistan, Sudan are just the most obvious examples, but others approaching or recovering from failure can easily be adduced. The crony capitalism of Brazil, for example, has recently been analyzed with specific reference to the Frankfurt School's racket theory.[31] Some commentators, such as Fuchshuber, have even applied it to cases like the Islamic State although it might be argued that because ISIS adheres to a fundamentalist Wahhabist interpretation of Islam it is actually motivated by a powerful mediating ideology rather than the maximization of pure power and the plundering of material assets.[32] But in other cases, a toxic mix of paramilitary organizations, drug- and arms-trafficking, hostage-taking and kidnapping, child military recruitment, sexual assault and indifference to civilian hardships combined with the often exorbitant personal enrichment of those in power, provides unmistakable affinities with the racket model limned by Horkheimer and his colleagues. The mollifying effects of mediating or universalizing ideologies or institutions are diminished, and self-preservation becomes a function of obedience to the most plausible protector. State sovereignty, popular or not, is weakened to the point of virtual extinction, as legitimate authority is replaced by raw power and the monopoly of force famously assigned by Max Weber to the modern state is shattered.

Even when the strong sovereign state is not shattered—for example in Putin's Russia—it may be possible to discern aspects of a racket society in the ways in which oligarchs and remnants of the old Soviet *nomenklatura* have turned a fragile democracy into a kleptocracy.[33] Outside of politics, of course, there are many manifestations of racketeering, which despite everything still haunts the labor movement, and can be found in other institutions from Big Pharma and international sporting federations, such as FIFA, to college admissions offices. And it has even

31 Stefan Klein and Ricardo Pagliuso Regatieri, "Unfettered Capitalism: On Rackets, Cronies and *Mafioso*," *Tempo Social* 30: 3 (2018), pp. 67–84.

32 Fuchshuber, in "Saving Mediation," argues that they are compatible. In *Rackets*, he also tries to make a case for the Islamic Republic of Iran (pp. 606–7). For an application of the Frankfurt School's racket theory to an earlier phase of modern Iranian history, see Olmo Gölz, "The Dangerous Classes and the 1953 Coup in Iran: On the Decline of Lutigari Masculinities," in *Crime, Poverty and Survival in the Middle East and North Africa: The "Dangerous Classes" since 1800*, ed. Stefanie Cronin (London: I. B. Taurus, 2019).

33 See Karin Dasisha, *Putin's Kleptocracy: Who Owns Russia?* (New York: Simon & Schuster, 2015).

infected the Catholic Church, whose ongoing pedophile scandal compounded by its appallingly record of covering it up has, along with the recent shenanigans at the Vatican Bank, given new meaning to "the protection of God."

How does the racket society model help us understand our own current political situation? The United States remains, of course, a long way from being a failed state or a kleptocracy of oligarchs. And yet there are sufficient warning signs to be concerned by tendencies moving in an ominous direction. Despite all the obvious caveats, the racket society model may have something to teach us, even if only as a cautionary example. In 2016, after all, we elected a president who is almost too perfectly cast as a protagonist in a racketeering narrative, allowing commentators easily to label him, as did David Frum recently, "a gangster in the White House."[34] Not only was he notorious for running numerous business scams and engaging in dubious real estate deals before his election—the Wikipedia article on his "legal affairs" takes ten minutes to read and includes a section devoted entirely to allegations of his "business links to organized crime"—but he continued to operate in the same way with relative impunity once he was inaugurated (in fact, his inauguration committee was soon itself investigated for influence peddling). The list of Trump's former underlings who served, are serving, or will soon serve jail time—Paul Manafort, Michael Cohen, Michael Flynn, Rick Gates, George Papadopolous and Roger Stone—is almost matched by one listing his former enablers who have denounced him as a dangerous fraud—Omarosa Manigault Newman, Anthony Scaramucci, Tom Barrack and the hapless Michael Cohen. He even managed, along the way, to acquire a favored son-in-law whose father was a convicted felon for illegal campaign contributions, tax evasion and witness tampering. Cohen's successor as Trump's personal lawyer, Rudy Giuliani, once celebrated for his prosecutorial role in the Mafia Commission Trial in 1985–6, in which the heads of New York's "Five Families" were charged under RICO (the Racketeer Influenced and Corrupt Organizations Act of 1970) for extortion, labor racketeering and murder for hire, earned a very different kind of notoriety through

---

34   David Frum, "A Gangster in the White House," *Atlantic*, December 28, 2019, theatlantic.com.

his involvement with the accused campaign finance law violators Lev Parnas and Igor Fruman.

Trump's habitual choice of shady friends and his own gangsterish conduct in his personal affairs, perhaps best emblematized by his hush payments to porn star Stormy Daniels, are echoed in the way he often operates on the public stage. Intimidating witnesses, threatening retaliation against whistleblowers who "rat" on him, demanding personal loyalty from subordinates over adherence to the law, mocking the emoluments clause of the Constitution—these are just the most egregious examples. In foreign relations, the doctrine of America First means Trump treats long-standing allies in a transactional way, turning NATO and our alliance with South Korea into protection rackets in which payments have to be increased to assure security, and tariff policy is used to coerce obedience. His unapologetic affinity for strongmen who dominate countries with the same indifference to the rule of law and enrich themselves in the process makes unmistakably clear his values and priorities. And the supine acquiescence he has extorted from the Republican Party, exemplified by the loyalty he commands among politicians in Congress terrified of being challenged in primary fights, shows how successful protection can be in ensuring obedience. Kim Jong Un may be mockable as "little rocket man," but Trump has no less richly earned the nickname "big racket man."

In *Minima Moralia*, Adorno drew on the racket society model to explain the ways in which a demagogic leader and his followers mirror each other. It is difficult not to hear a chillingly accurate anticipation of the relationship between Trump and his base:

If society, as a contemporary theory teaches, is really one of rackets, then its most faithful model is the precise opposite of the collective, namely the individual as monad. By tracing the absolutely particular interests of each individual, the nature of the collective in a false society can be most accurately studied, and it is by no means far-fetched to consider the organization of divergent drives under the primacy of the ego answering the reality principle as, from the first, an internalized robber band with leader, followers, ceremonies, oaths of allegiance, betrayals, conflicts of interests, intrigues and all its other appurtenances. One need only observe outbursts in which the individual asserts himself energetically against his environment, for instance rage. The enraged man always appears as the gang leader of his own self, giving his unconscious the order to pull no punches, his eyes shining with the satisfaction of speaking for the many that he himself is. The more someone has espoused the cause of his own aggression, the more perfectly he represents the repressive principle of society. In this sense more than in any other, the proposition is true that the most individual is the most general.[35]

It is telling that virtually all of Trump's machinations are performed in the glare of publicity, which may seem to contradict the conspiratorial secrecy normally attributed to racketeering behavior. Even when Trump's covert plots are exposed, as when he extorted Ukraine to produce dirt on a political opponent, he defiantly and shamelessly owned his bad behavior and tried to turn the resulting impeachment to his own political advantage. Indeed, it is hard not to suspect that much of his appeal to those who stubbornly support him no matter what new outrage he commits or past scandal is revealed may well be due to the subversive glamour in popular culture that has accrued over the years to gangsters and mobsters. From Edward G. Robinson's Little Caesar and James Cagney in *The Public Enemy* to Marlon Brando's Don Vito Corleone and James Gandolfini's Tony Soprano, we have fallen in love with powerful rogues who play by their own rules. Fittingly, there is a "Mob Museum" in—where else?—Las Vegas, which boasts that "no trip is complete without a souvenir photo as a suspect in a police lineup."

Trump may, to be sure, seem more of a common grifter and con artist than a violent hit man, although his order to assassinate Qasem Soleimani provides chilling evidence that he may also aspire to the latter model. But in any case, like the Frank Sheeran depicted in *The Irishman*, he knows how to make his audience, or at least his unshakable "base," root for him, whatever their qualms, because of his apparent toughness, survival skills and disdain for moral and cultural pieties. Like Jimmy Hoffa, who apparently gained new admirers after his depiction in *The Irishman*, he has been lauded for getting something done, however ugly the means.[36] In addition, for at least some of his male admirers, Trump's

---

35   Adorno, *Minima Moralia*, p. 45.
36   For a recent pushback against the positive reassessment of Hoffa, see Barry Eidlin, "We Shouldn't Be Nostalgic for Hoffa," *Jacobin*, January 2, 2020, jacobinmag.com.

blatant sexism and contempt for strong women seems to arouse the same emotions that accompanied Cagney's infamous grapefruit in the face of Mae Clarke in *The Public Enemy*. Nothing was lost, after all, when videos surfaced of Trump's sleazy palling around with the likes of Jeffrey Epstein; it would have been disappointingly out of character had they never been buddies.

The Frankfurt School's "racket society" analysis faltered, to be sure, when it was initially introduced to help explain the rise of fascism. Not only did it fail to do justice to the complexities of the phenomenon, which drew on ideological as well as power-political motivations, but it was also too ambitious in suggesting that an epochal page had been turned in the history of global capitalism. Its melodramatic characterization of the labor movement in having to choose between world revolution or rackets was insultingly dismissive of the honorable alternatives that still existed then and continue to allow many workers to be on the side of progressive politics. Jimmy Hoffa, it must be admitted, was in the future of the labor movement, but the future of the movement was not Jimmy Hoffa.[37]

It would be no less simplistic, let it be admitted, to claim that the racket society model does full justice to our current situation either. Too many other long-term trends, as well as the happenstance of unexpected events, have led us to this fateful conjuncture. But by drawing attention to certain disturbing patterns in contemporary political culture, indeed to the ways in which an unmediated dialectic of domination and protection operates in many different social and cultural contexts, it allows us to understand why *The Irishman* seems so much the quintessential movie for our times. And when we grasp the mirroring effect of actual rackets and their often-romanticized representation in the entertainment industry, it helps us appreciate even more how a figure like Trump, who inhabits both worlds, has benefited from that fateful interaction. For it is not despite his audacious self-presentation as a devious, unscrupulous, morally tone-deaf bully who values personal loyalty over

---

37 Ironically, from 1999–2022, the general president of the International Brotherhood of Teamsters was James P. Hoffa, Jimmy Hoffa's only son, but he is an admired, progressive figure with no taint of racketeering. This is not to say that other American labor leaders have avoided scandals, for example, in the United Auto Workers, but the movement as a whole is neither as strong as it once was or as corrupt as it sometimes seemed on the verge of becoming.

principle, boasts that only stupid people pay taxes or get drafted, and has more henchmen than real friends that he can run his rackets so successfully. It is because of it.

Only by comparing *The Irishman* with the other great labor racketeering film in American cinematic history can we realize how far we have come. *On the Waterfront*, which appeared in 1954, powerfully depicts the tortured journey of a whistleblower who overcomes his complicity with the Mob and family loyalties to defy the violent boss who runs Hoboken's longshoremen's union. Without any of the ethnic overtones that allows Scorsese's film to be seen by some as a sunset Mafia fable, it provides a more unfiltered take on labor racketeering and its consequences. It has, to be sure, long been haunted by the allegation that it allegorically heroizes a stool pigeon to excuse the naming of names by its director Elia Kazan and writer Budd Schulberg during the anticommunist hysteria of the McCarthy era. The mixed reaction Kazan still received when he was given a lifetime achievement award at the Oscars in 2008—presented, ironically, by Martin Scorsese and Robert De Niro—shows that forgiveness was a long time coming and by no means universal.[38]

However one judges the apologetic subtext of the film, on its own terms *On the Waterfront* vividly illustrates the racket society explored by Horkheimer and his colleagues. The conflict it depicts is not between capital and labor, but rather within the labor movement where domination is reproduced on a more confined scale within a class. The film does, however, present a somewhat more hopeful vision of how a racket society can be successfully resisted than *The Irishman*. Not only is there an explicit religious spokesman for moral conscience in Karl Malden's powerfully portrayed waterfront priest Father Barry, but the film grants a woman, the hero's girlfriend Edie Doyle, played by Eva Marie Saint, an active role in resisting the power of the Mob. And through what can only be called the selfless "passion" of the once hapless boxer Terry Malloy, rendered with consummate conviction by Marlon Brando, does a possibility of apparent redemption shine through. As the film ends, the spell of Lee J. Cobb's brutal mobster Johnny Friendly is broken, and

---

38 For a recent attempt at a balanced assessment on the part of a leftist critic of Kazan's actions, see Kathy M. Newman, "Revisiting *On the Waterfront*," *Jacobin*, July 15, 2014, jacobinmag.com.

the longshoremen defy the protection racket that has kept them so long in his thrall. That their mere returning to work is the measure of redemption, rather than challenging the larger capitalist context in which they remained enmeshed, may for some mark the limit of the film's critical reach. But in comparison with *The Irishman*, where Frank Sheeran survives to old age, albeit alone with his memories and scorned by his daughter, it is something worth celebrating.

If *The Irishman* depicts a world more akin to our own than *On the Waterfront*, it is because no successful Terry Malloys have yet arisen to bring down from within the protection racket of our Oval Office Johnny Friendly. The spell is a long way from being broken for his obdurate base, who seem to have as much respect for courageous whistleblowers as the unforgiving critics of Elia Kazan did under very different circumstances a while ago. We may not live in a full-blown racket society, or at least not yet, but we are perhaps even closer to it than we were when a group of exiles from Nazi Germany were trying to make sense of the dark times in which they were immersed. For a long while, they seem to have been on the wrong track, as even they themselves concluded. Today, when a second term for an impeached but exonerated racketeer-in-chief seems a distinct possibility, we cannot, alas, be so sure.

6

Go Figure: Fredric Jameson on Walter Benjamin

No figure in the larger orbit of the Frankfurt School has exemplified the futility of seeking to homogenize its legacy into a coherent and systematic corpus of ideas more than Walter Benjamin. His tragic inability to escape European fascism and join his colleagues at the Institute of Social Research in their American exile was sadly emblematic of his unbridgeable distance from their common project. At times more stringently Marxist and at others more unapologetically theological than other Institute members, he was, as Adorno once put it, à l'écart de tous les courants.[1]

The undeniable fecundity of Benjamin's oeuvre, much of it unfinished, gnomically expressed and posthumously published, has generated an interpretive tsunami that shows no signs of losing its momentum.[2] One of the earliest appreciations in the anglophone world came from the American literary critic Fredric Jameson, who for some six decades has found creative ways to demonstrate the abiding value of Marxism to explicate a wide variety of cultural phenomena. In 2020, he reopened what he called his "Benjamin files" and published a new book that occasioned this extended

---

1   Theodor W. Adorno, "A l'écart de tous les courants," in *Über Walter Benjamin*, ed. Rolf Tiedemann (Frankfurt: Suhrkamp, 1970). The essay concludes wistfully by wondering if Benjamin might not have found a balance between his intellectual autonomy and the support of a group had he survived and come to America.

2   This kind of generalization is, of course, hard to substantiate, although the n-grams showing how often his work is cited in English and French are still trending upward (in German there was a dip after 1995).

reflection on both Benjamin's legacy and Jameson's reading of it.[3] Pushing back against the prevalent view, to which he himself had once subscribed, that Benjamin's melancholic nostalgia was in tension with his radical aspirations, Jameson sought instead to square his "theological code" with historical materialism.

Doing so, however, strains even Jameson's interpretative resources. Finding a way to incorporate Benjamin's idiosyncratic utopian agenda, which includes restoring cosmic harmonies, recovering an Adamic ur-language and the redemption of all souls, known as "apocatastasis," into a plausible progressive program is, after all, not easy. For all of Jameson's herculean efforts, including an attempt to reconcile Erich Auerbach's ruminations on repetitive figurae with a Lukácsian faith in the metanarrative of "world history,"[4] this task eludes him. Benjamin remains an ambiguous figure in the tradition of Critical Theory, both a source of many remarkable insights and an eccentric outlier whose most rhapsodic investments defy any attempt to mobilize them for meaningful action in our flawed—but not "fallen"—world.

In 1969, the journal *Salmagundi* published an essay by Fredric Jameson, then a young professor of literature at the University of California, San Diego, that was arguably the first English-language attempt to engage seriously with the then still obscure German cultural critic Walter Benjamin.[5] Two years later, "Walter Benjamin; or, Nostalgia" was included in Jameson's *Marxism and Form*, a work that announced the arrival of a major voice in the emerging discourse of literary theory,

---

3   Fredric Jameson, *The Benjamin Files* (London: Verso, 2020). This review essay appeared in *History and Theory* 61: 1 (2022).

4   Jameson remains willing to wager on something called "world history" as a potentially redemptive narrative, showing his continuing debt to Lukács's *History and Class Consciousness*. For my reservations about its plausibility, see Martin Jay, "Fidelity to the Event? Lukács' *History and Class Consciousness* and the Russian Revolution," in *Genesis and Validity: The Theory and Practice of Intellectual History* (Philadelphia: University of Pennsylvania Press, 2022).

5   Fredric Jameson, "Walter Benjamin, or Nostalgia," *Salmagundi*, no. 10/11 (Fall 1969/Winter 1970), pp. 52–73. This was also the year that the first English-language collection of Benjamin's work was made available as *Illuminations: Essays and Reflections*, ed. Hannah Arendt, trans. Harry Zohn (New York: Schocken, 1969). Jameson drew on the two volumes of Benjamin's *Schriften*, edited by Theodor W. Adorno and Gretel Adorno, with the help of Friedrich Podszus, which had been published by Suhrkamp Verlag in 1955.

which so energized—if often in the form of polemical donnybrooks—the humanities as a whole for the generation that followed.[6] It also made clear that a reinvigorated version of Marxism—experimental, in dialogue with other theories, sensitive to formal questions, and engaged with aesthetic modernism rather than dismissive of it—would play a leading role in what became known as "the theory wars" of the last decades of the twentieth century.

As indicated by the title of his essay, Jameson focused on the laments for a lost past prior to the depredations of capitalism he saw scattered throughout Benjamin's oeuvre. Like the melancholics who dominated the Baroque *Trauerspiels* he had written about in his failed *Habilitationsschrift*, Benjamin, he wrote, "is himself foremost among these depressed and hyperconscious visionaries who people his pages."[7] And yet, although nostalgia is often understood as fueling fascist anti-modernism, "there is no reason why a nostalgia conscious of itself, a lucid and remorseless dissatisfaction with the present on the grounds of some remembered plenitude, cannot furnish as adequate a revolutionary stimulus as any other: the example of Benjamin is there to prove it."[8]

Now, after more than a half-century has passed, Jameson has returned to Benjamin, albeit with an enriched and somewhat altered appreciation of his work. Referring to the frequent assignment of Benjamin to the ranks of "left melancholics," Jameson apologetically confesses that "I count myself, in one of the earlier American studies of Benjamin, as responsible as anyone else for this misconception" (p. 69) and adds that he wants "to shake off the now-conventional image of a nostalgic Benjamin" (p. 219).[9] In its place, *The Benjamin Files* offers a series of

---

6   Fredric Jameson, *Marxism and Form: Twentieth-Century Dialectical Theories of Literature* (Princeton, NJ: Princeton University Press, 1971), pp. 60–83.

7   Ibid., p. 71.

8   Ibid., p. 82.

9   Benjamin himself coined the term "left melancholics" in his 1931 essay on Erich Kästner's poetry. See his "Left-Wing Melancholy," in *Walter Benjamin: Selected Writings*, vol. 2, *1927–1934*, ed. Michael W. Jennings, Howard Eiland and Gary Smith, trans. Rodney Livingstone and others (Cambridge, MA: Harvard University Press, 1999), pp. 423–7. For a recent consideration of the tradition of left melancholy, see Enzo Traverso, *Left-Wing Melancholia: Marxism, History, and Memory* (New York: Columbia University Press, 2016). He accepts the phrase and applies it to Benjamin but argues that it can sustain possible future resistance.

intense, imaginative and idiosyncratic readings of nine of Benjamin's canonical works (as well as some more obscure texts), which leave him redefined as a "time traveler from some messianic future" (p. 42).

A great deal has changed in the five decades since Jameson's pioneering essay. From an intriguing rumor, Benjamin has become one of the most potent figures in the pantheon of our major cultural influencers. The two volumes of Benjamin's *Schriften*, on which Jameson based his essay, have now become seven in the *Gesammelte Schriften*, and an even longer definitive edition is in the works. His voluminous correspondence is also now widely available, translations into English abound, and the thousands of commentaries on him in many languages defy anyone's efforts to master them all. For his part, Jameson has published more than a score of books on an astonishingly wide variety of subjects, from the most arcane recesses of Hegelian dialectics to the latest fads in popular culture, and he himself has been the subject of a dozen or so book-length commentaries. Still unapologetically Marxist, even defiantly utopian, he has managed to earn the abiding respect of many across the political spectrum, as evidenced by the prestigious Holberg Prize he was awarded in 2008. Although now in his late eighties, he shows no signs of slowing down. In short, *The Benjamin Files* is an event not only in the reception of Walter Benjamin but also in the still-unfolding career of an extraordinary intellectual in his own right.[10]

To attempt an adequate review of this book would therefore require a stereoscopic vision that brings into focus two distinct moving images, a metaphor that Benjamin himself employed.[11] Or perhaps to borrow another image imaginatively developed by Benjamin and approvingly adopted by Jameson, it would require placing them into a constellation of juxtaposed points of light in order to illuminate the cultural/political landscape of the past century. And it would do so while respecting both the differences and the similarities between the two historical moments

---

10   For a recent example of the ongoing reception of Jameson's ideas in disciplines other than literary criticism and philosophy, see Keith B. Wagner, Jeremi Szaniawski and Michael Cramer, eds., *Fredric Jameson and Film Theory: Marxism, Allegory and Geopolitics in World Cinema* (New Brunswick: Rutgers University Press, 2022).

11   See Walter Benjamin, "N [Re the Theory of Knowledge, Theory of Progress]," in *Benjamin: Philosophy, Aesthetics, History*, ed. Gary Smith (Chicago: University of Chicago Press, 1989), p. 44, where he cites approvingly a remark of Rudolf Borchardt. "N" is the letter assigned by Benjamin to one of the Convolutes (or bundle of papers) left in his unfinished *Arcades Project*.

in which each author produced his work. This would be a tall order indeed, and it would require far more time and a great deal more ingenuity than this commentator possesses.

Instead, let me fall back on another tactic effectively introduced by Benjamin in his remarkable ruminations on Charles Baudelaire and focus only on "some motifs" in *The Benjamin Files* that may repay close attention.[12] They will be four in number: what Terry Eagleton many years ago called "the politics of style,"[13] especially its destructive inclinations; the uncomfortable place of theology in a social theory claiming to be historical materialist; the plausibility of resurrecting cosmological similitudes; and, finally, the power of *figurae* to disrupt the smooth flow of historical time. Doing justice to each would warrant a formidable tome of its own, but we will have to be satisfied with only a few critical reflections and the hope that they will open up new horizons in our ongoing encounters with both Benjamin and Jameson.

Jameson shares with Benjamin a keen awareness that critical thought with a political intent demands not only powerful substantive arguments but also bold formal experimentation. However much language may be a "prison-house," to borrow the phrase from Friedrich Nietzsche that Jameson adopted for the title of one of his earlier books,[14] it is always possible to rattle the bars of its cages and invite its inmates to view the world outside with fresh eyes. Benjamin's challenges to conventional prose and established scholarly and critical genres have been widely remarked: his suppression of the expressive subjectivity of the writer, his ambition to write a book entirely of citations, his hostility to linear argumentation in favor of synchronic "thought-images" (*Denkbilder*), his adoption of the visual technique of montage for anti-discursive purposes, and so on. So too has his insistence that destruction is a necessary step in the practice of genuine cultural criticism, a preliminary stage to any constructive re-constellation of the ruins that

---

12   Walter Benjamin, "On Some Motifs in Baudelaire," in *Walter Benjamin: Selected Writings*, vol. 4, *1938–1940*, ed. Howard Eiland and Michael W. Jennings, trans. E. F. N. Jephcott and others (Cambridge, MA: Harvard University Press, 2006), pp. 313–55.

13   Terry Eagleton, "Fredric Jameson: The Politics of Style," *Diacritics* 12: 3 (1982), pp. 14–22.

14   Fredric Jameson, *The Prison-House of Language: A Critical Account of Structuralism and Russian Formalism* (Princeton, NJ: Princeton University Press, 1975).

follow. Benjamin not only celebrated the virtues of "the destructive character" but also identified with children who are "irresistibly drawn to the detritus created by building, gardening, housework, tailoring, or carpentry. In waste products they recognize the face that the material world turns to them and them alone. In putting such products to use they do not so much replicate the works of grown-ups as take materials of very different kinds, and, through what they make with them in play, place them in new and very surprising relations to one another."[15]

Despite important differences, in certain respects, Jameson, whose own notoriously digressive, convoluted, "difficult" style has been the subject of sustained scrutiny,[16] emulates Benjamin. Most notably, he eschews the hypotactic constraints of building an argument, considering and rejecting alternatives, and producing plausible conclusions. Instead, the rhetoric of his presentation often seems more associative than logical, the force of his prose dependent more on the dazzling insights that flow from unexpected juxtapositions than from a carefully reasoned argument. What he calls in the title of one of his chapters "the spatial sentence" is designed to arrest the smooth temporal flow of ordinary discursive prose.[17] Such sentences even suspend the triumphalist march of Hegelian dialectics, whose logic Jameson, in his more Lukácsian moods, embraces. Like Benjamin, Jameson exploits the explosive power of demolishing generic conventions and creating new

15 Walter Benjamin, "The Destructive Character," in *Reflections: Essays, Aphorisms, Autobiographical Writings*, ed. Peter Demetz, trans. E. F. N. Jephcott (New York: Schocken, 1986); Walter Benjamin, *One-Way Street*, in *One-Way Street and Other Writings*, trans. J. A. Underwood (London: Penguin, 2009), p. 55. See Irving Wohlfahrt, "No-Man's-Land: On Walter Benjamin's 'Destructive Character,' " *Diacritics* 8: 2 (1978), pp. 47–65.

16 See, for example, Stephen Helmling, *The Success and Failure of Fredric Jameson: Writing, the Sublime, and the Dialectic of Critique* (Albany: SUNY Press, 2000). In 1997, Jameson was "awarded" the first prize in the New Zealand University of Canterbury's "World's Worst Writing Contest," a dubious honor endorsed by the novelist David Foster Wallace in his essay "Authority and American Usage," in *Consider the Lobster and Other Essays* (New York: Little, Brown, 2005), p. 115.

17 Jameson notes that the theses presented in Benjamin's essay titled "The Work of Art in the Age of Mechanical Reproducibility" are not discursive or "steps in a logical argument or demonstration, but rather moments of historical consequence that fan out in some well-nigh synchronic or structural fashion." *The Benjamin Files*, p. 192. That he himself may feel some frustration at the results is indicated by the slight note of irritation he permits himself at the close of the chapter he devotes to it, which ends by remarking on "the essay's incorrigible lack of focus" (p. 219).

constellations out of the ruins. In fact, in *The Benjamin Files*, he goes so far as to contend that Benjamin's *The Origin of German Tragic Drama* suffered from being forced into the form of a scholarly treatise, and he tries to reread it via "dialectical images" or "thought-pictures," which emerge only when the constraints of academic prose are destroyed.

The insights generated by this approach are substantial, but the effort to keep up with the relentless pace of their revelation may strain the patience of Jameson's readers. His prose can at times seem like the transcript of a fever dream, invested with emotion, dazzling in its range of reference, but frustratingly interior to the mind of the dreamer.[18] A quarter-century ago, in a prematurely titled assessment of Jameson's career called "Late Jameson," Geoffrey Galt Harpham invoked James Joyce to describe Jameson's *Seeds of Time*, much of which "reads like a 'Jameson's Wake,' an unfiltered dream-monologue composed of endless sentences in which all manner of odd or unsorted things float around, occasionally bobbing to the surface."[19] The same can be said of parts of *The Benjamin Files*, where Jameson blithely inserts cryptic free associations he has no time or inclination to explain, for example: "drawing on the anthropological materials collected and named by *le président* de Brosses" (p. 152); "the essay itself will no doubt disappoint Proustians, especially recent converts" (p. 125); "it serves little purpose to rehearse the Badolian question" (p. 167).[20] It is perhaps also the feverish pace of his presentation that allows him to be fuzzy with a few of his facts: the publication of Georges Sorel's *Reflections on Violence* is misdated as

---

18 In *The Benjamin Files*, Jameson himself expresses reservations about the metaphor of dreaming, which he associates with phantasmagoria. He worries that it "presupposes a different realm into which we can wake up. Neither of these formulations seems very apt, either for capitalism or for the Paris of the Second Empire" (p. 154). The motif of dreaming and waking from dreams, collective as well as individual, in Benjamin has been widely remarked, for example, by Susan Buck-Morss. See her *The Dialectics of Seeing: Walter Benjamin and the Arcades Project* (Cambridge, MA: MIT Press, 1989) and *Dreamworld and Catastrophe: The Passing of Mass Utopia in East and West* (Cambridge, MA: MIT Press, 2000).

19 Geoffrey Galt Harpham, "Late Jameson," in *Shadows of Ethics: Criticism and the Just Society* (Durham, NC: Duke University Press, 1999), p. 176. The essay originally appeared in *Salmagundi* in 1996.

20 It turns out that Charles de Brosses, the eighteenth-century originator of the discourse about fetishes that influenced Marx, was president of the parliament of Dijon, and "Badolian" is the adjectival form now used to refer to the contemporary French Marxist Alain Badiou. I have no clue who the recent Proustian converts are.

1904 instead of 1908 (p. 140); Louis Daguerre is identified as the "panorama's inventor" (p. 5), when it was in fact invented two generations earlier and Daguerre was responsible for the diorama instead; and the origins of Benjamin's theory of mimetic similitudes is said, with no supporting evidence, "probably to be found in Rosenzweig" (p. 196).[21]

Unfortunately, Jameson, whose *Marxism and Form* contained a trenchant footnote on Theodor W. Adorno's dialectical use of the footnote form,[22] restricts his usage of footnotes here to a scant handful of nonsubstantive source references. Perhaps to make up for their absence, he introduces at random moments in his text schematic diagrams representing the force-field of different elements that make up constellations in Benjamin's thought.[23] These are, however, never sufficiently explicated or integrated into his argument, and sometimes the choice and labeling of their elements seem confusing. Why, for example, is "Event" in one of them parenthetically exemplified by "Thirty Years War, Weimar" (p. 73), neither of which was an event in any meaningful sense of the term? Despite their superficial resemblance to Benjamin's synchronic "dialectical images" or "dialectic at a standstill," they seem more like residues of the Althusserian structuralist Marxism through which Jameson once passed.

Nonetheless, despite these limitations, *The Benjamin Files* abundantly demonstrates that writing about Benjamin means taking risks to avoid the reduction and taming of his ideas through conventional paraphrastic synopsis. Inevitably, there are trade-offs that come with this decision.

21 For a detailed comparison, see Stéphane Moses, "Walter Benjamin and Franz Rosenzweig," in Smith, *Benjamin: Philosophy, Aesthetics, History*, pp. 228–46. He points out that a fundamental difference between them is "that the communicative function of language, which for Benjamin represents the main symptom of its degeneration, is for Rosenzweig identical with its quality of revelation" (p. 238).

22 Footnotes can be a way "living thought" challenges the reifications of "systematic philosophizing and the empirical study of concrete phenomena" (Fredric Jameson, "T. W. Adorno; or, Historical Tropes," in *Marxism and Form*, p. 9 n2). In *The Benjamin Files*, footnotes are rarely employed even to clarify Jameson's sources. At one point, he tells the reader, "I have just read the review of a book which purports to draw attention to the role of time itself in gastronomy" (p. 184), but he neglects to provide a citation.

23 Jameson often expresses doubt about the ideological role of visuality in contemporary culture, but diagrams have their own intrinsic quasi-visual logic. See John Bender and Michael Marrinan, *The Culture of Diagram* (Stanford, CA: Stanford University Press, 2010).

If Jameson practices a "politics of style," it is an uncompromisingly elitist one, requiring the reader to work hard to follow a train of thought that is often elusive and lacking in clear guideposts. Despite the admiration Jameson expresses for Bertolt Brecht's didactic intentions, *The Benjamin Files* is anything but a critical *Lehrstück* that patiently walks through obscure ideas to educate a popular audience.

For seasoned readers of Benjamin, however, Jameson provides ample stimulation. He wisely avoids a premature reconciliation and synthesis of the opposite theoretical extremes whose very incompatibility Benjamin defiantly wielded as a weapon in his struggle to think differently.[24] As a result, he can unflinchingly address Benjamin's audacious, if often puzzling, juxtaposition of theological ideas with historical materialism, which has occasioned so much controversy over the years, beginning in his own day.[25] Brecht, as is often remarked, was always mystified by his friend's attraction to religious ideas, while Gershom Scholem encouraged it, and Max Horkheimer and Adorno (contrary to Benjamin's fears) cautiously accepted it.[26] Jameson, who clearly sides with Brecht over Benjamin's other friends in most matters, nonetheless tries hard to take seriously the impact of what he calls Benjamin's "theological code," which he rightly distinguishes from a genuine

---

24   It has often been noticed that this pattern was reflected in his personal relations as well, a parallel that he himself acknowledged in a telling letter to Gretel Adorno, who had complained of the dangers in his friendship with Bertolt Brecht: "You of all people are by no means unaware that my life, like my thinking, is characterized by extremes. The breadth it thus asserts, the freedom to juxtapose objects and thoughts that seemed irreconcilable take shape only in the face of danger. A danger that is generally obvious also to my friends only in the guise of said 'dangerous' relationships." Benjamin to Gretel Adorno, early June 1934, in *Correspondence, 1930–1940*, ed. Henri Lonitz and Christoph Gödde, trans. Wieland Hoban (Malden, MA: Polity, 2008), p. 105.

25   For recent examples, see *Walter Benjamin and Theology*, ed. Colby Dickinson and Stéphane Symons (New York: Fordham University Press, 2016) and Peter E. Gordon, *Migrants in the Profane: Critical Theory and the Question of Secularization* (New Haven, CT: Yale University Press, 2020).

26   Scholem wrote to Benjamin in March 1938 that Adorno had assured him that Horkheimer "holds you in the *highest* regard, *but that he is entirely clear that, where you are concerned*, one is dealing with a *mystic* . . . They seem to have long been aware of much of what you consider secret and don't wish to have brought up, and *nonetheless* are still placing their hopes on you." Scholem to Benjamin, March 25, 1938, in *The Correspondence of Walter Benjamin and Gershom Scholem, 1932–1940*, ed. Gershom Scholem, trans. Gary Smith and Andre LeFevere (Cambridge, MA: Harvard University Press, 1989), p. 215.

religious "belief" (pp. 10, 231).[27] It had its uses for Benjamin, he contends, "not only because it develops collective categories unavailable in the purely empirical 'bad infinities' of modern political science or in the still purely individualizing 'values' of modern ethics or legality; but rather because theological categories give us access to historical and essentially narrative modes of thinking about mass realities" (p. 229). Even more important, he suggests, is that it helped Benjamin overcome his nostalgia and look forward rather than backward. "Theology," according to Jameson, "reserves a uniquely specific virtue for the domain of the future: it is called hope, and hope is very much a Benjaminian preoccupation from the beginnings of his career to its premature end" (p. 240).

What precisely, Jameson asks, constitutes the object of hope expressed in the idiom of theology? Rather than merely the alleviation of human suffering, the lessening of the exploitation of nature or a more just and equitable society, it harbors no less a maximalist aspiration than something it calls "redemption."[28] According to Jameson, redemption must

---

27   This is what Jameson means when he says that when Benjamin left his childhood and family behind, he also abandoned Judaism (*The Benjamin Files*, p. 129). Although correct in terms of participation in a community of orthopraxis, this bald statement may underestimate Benjamin's continued "Marrano" identity and identification with the religion into which he was born. See Agata Bielik-Robson, *Jewish Cryptotheologies of Late Modernity: Philosophical Marranos* (New York: Routledge, 2014), chapters 3 and 7. Another interpretation suggests that his allegiance was actually to the antinomian heresies generated by the Sabbatai Zevi. See Jeffrey Mehlman, *Benjamin for Children: An Essay on His Radio Years* (Chicago: University of Chicago Press, 1993), pp. 40-7. One might also ask the question, what does it mean to draw on theological ideas without believing in God (or being situated in a specific tradition of worshipping God)? Can one be a biologist without believing in "life" or a psychologist without accepting the idea of the "psyche"? Benjamin, for all his stress on the crisis of experience, never seems to have experienced believing in God or suffered when he lost that belief.

28   Benjamin's introduction of "redemption" into the vocabulary of Critical Theory is apparent in Adorno's later evocation of it. It appeared not merely in the famous final aphorism of *Minima Moralia* but also in *Negative Dialectics*, trans. E. B. Ashton (New York: Seabury, 1973), where he wrote, "If the possibility, however feeble and distant, of redemption in existence is cut off altogether, the human spirit would become an illusion, and the finite, conditioned, merely existing subject would eventually be deified as carrier of the spirit" (p. 400). Despite an oblique reference to *restitutio in integrum* in a discussion of epistemology (*Negative Dialectics*, p. 47), a variation of the *restitutio ad integrum* that Benjamin identifies with apocatastasis, Adorno did not spell out what the term might mean and seems to have accepted Horkheimer's qualms about the transfiguration of past suffering.

"be understood in a collective rather than in an individual way. It governs Benjamin's thinking, if not of history as a whole, then at least of the past and the dead: it functions for him as a debt and an obligation and is assimilated for him to communist and revolutionary ideals" (p. 12). By embracing it, Benjamin signaled his resistance to the wan compromises of secular realism, which led, inter alia, to the toothless politics of the social democratic tradition. What, however, did redemption really mean for Benjamin? The answer, Jameson suggests, lies with an obscure theological concept, which Benjamin invoked at only a few key points in his oeuvre: *apocatastasis*.[29]

The concept is first introduced in *The Benjamin Files*, abruptly and with no explanation, in Jameson's gloss on Benjamin's endorsement of Auguste Blanqui's "substitution of a political for a historical view of the past" (p. 147). In Jameson's brisk interpretation of this formulation, " 'political' means history in a different sense, the discontinuous history of the great uprisings, of the experience of defeat no less than the overthrow of the masters, the irresistible right to revolt, apocatastasis" (pp. 147–8). In the concept's second appearance, he claims that the form of the stories told by writers like Nikolai Leskov, whose disappearance from the modern world Benjamin lamented, "cunningly conceals within its structure that secret message of *apokatastasis*,[30] which is for Benjamin the redemption of history" (p. 175). Jameson waits, however, until near the end of the book to define for the reader "that breathtaking orthodox belief called apocatastasis, in which, after the trumpet of the Last Judgment, all of the dead of human history, sinners as well as saved without exception, will rise from the grave all equally redeemed, in some final and definitive bodily resurrection" (p. 231). This blanket

---

29   Benjamin invoked it, for example, in "The Storyteller" when he discussed Leskov's debt to Origen; see "The Storyteller," in Arendt, *Illuminations*, p. 103. It also appears in Convolute N of the *Arcades Project* (see Benjamin, "N [Re the Theory of Knowledge, Theory of Progress]," p. 46) and in one of his discussions of Surrealism, which he credited with "the will to apocatastasis . . . , the resolve to gather again, in revolutionary action and in revolutionary thinking, precisely the elements of the 'too early' and the 'too late' or the first beginning and the final decay." Walter Benjamin, *The Arcades Project*, trans. Howard Eiland and Kevin McLaughlin (Cambridge, MA: Harvard University Press, 1999), p. 698.

30   The English rendering of the word is sometimes spelled with a "c" and sometimes with a "k," and Jameson uses both.

amnesty, he concludes, is Benjamin's version of "universal history" (p. 239).[31]

What are we to make of these bold claims about apocatastasis as the telos of Benjaminian hope and the basis of his messianic reading of universal history, claims from which Jameson never visibly distances himself?[32] The word is derived from the Greek verb *apokathistemi*, which means "to restore" to wholeness or, in the Latin translation cited by Benjamin in his 1921 "Theological-Political Fragment," *restitutio ad integrum*.[33] While scholars have traced it back to Zoroastrian and Stoic sources, and some commentators have argued for its similarity to the Jewish idea of *tikkun olam*,[34] it emerged in Christianity only with the second-century Church Father Origen of Alexandria. Benjamin, Michael W. Jennings has noted, first learned about him by reading the theologian Adolf Harnack's *History of Dogma* at the end of the First World War.[35] Although defended by the influential fourth-century "Cappadocian Father" Gregory of Nyssa and inspiring later millennial groups like the Anabaptists, Moravian Brethren and Christadelphians, apocatastasis was roundly condemned by Augustine, who worried that it would undermine the power of God's grace in discriminating between

---

31 In Convolute N, Benjamin argued that "the authentic concept of universal history is a messianic one" ("N [Re the Theory of Knowledge, Theory of Progress]," 80). He contrasted it with a merely additive notion of universal history, which is based on the historicist notion of one thing after another.

32 For other discussions, see Michael W. Jennings, "The Will to Apokatastasis: Media, Experience, and Eschatology in Walter Benjamin's Late Theological Politics," in Dickinson and Symons, *Walter Benjamin and Theology*, pp. 93–110; Fabrizio Desideri, "Intermittency: The Differential of Time and the Integral of Space. The Intensive Spatiality of the Monad, the Apokatastasis and the Messianic World in Benjamin's Latest Thinking," *Aisthesis* 9: 1 (2016), pp. 177–87; and Michael Löwy, *Fire Alarm: Reading Walter Benjamin's "On the Concept of History,"* trans. Chris Turner (London: Verso, 2005), pp. 35–6.

33 Walter Benjamin, "Theological-Political Fragment," in *Walter Benjamin: Selected Writings*, vol. 3, *1935–1938*, ed. Howard Eiland and Michael W. Jennings (Cambridge, MA: Harvard University Press, 2006), p. 306. The phrase can be found in Acts 3:21 in the New Testament.

34 Löwy cited a comparison made by Scholem in 1932 (*Fire Alarm*, p. 35), but Andrew Benjamin warns against assimilating one to the other. See his "Time and Task: Benjamin and Heidegger Showing the Present," in *Walter Benjamin's Philosophy: Destruction and Experience*, ed. Andrew Benjamin and Peter Osborne (London: Routledge, 1994), p. 233.

35 Jennings, "The Will to Apokatastasis," p. 102.

damned and saved.[36] Origen's teachings were in fact declared heretical in the sixth century, and Christian Universalism, as the hope of redemption for all became known, remained a marginal doctrine in the Western church.[37]

Whether or not it deserved that fate we will leave to the theologians. But it is necessary to ponder its implications for Benjamin's messianic notion of "universal history," which Jameson believes can have a secular impact as well. One objection, which Jameson notes was raised by Horkheimer, concerns the fantasy that a future redemption can somehow make up for past injustices, which are irreparable. Jameson does not take this qualm seriously, however, as shown by his sarcastic (mis)characterization of Horkheimer as a "wise orthodox Marxist" who asks the question "in the tolerant spirit of an adult correcting a naïve and enthusiastic adolescent" (p. 231). But Horkheimer had a point in worrying that Benjamin failed to consider the possibility that belief in redemption for all can imply a kind of temporalized theodicy in which divine forgiveness trivializes actual past suffering.[38] And what is no less problematic, it flattens out the distinction between oppressor and oppressed.[39] For a blanket amnesty means that not only the forgotten victims of history will be

---

36   See Ilaria L. E. Ramelli, "Origen in Augustine: A Paradoxical Reception," *Numen* 60: 2–3 (2013), pp. 280–307.

37   It was marginal in Western Christianity but had more success in the Eastern Orthodox Christianity that influenced Russian writers like Leskov.

38   Herbert Marcuse made the same point at the end of *Eros and Civilization: A Philosophical Inquiry into Freud* (Boston: Beacon, 1955), where he somberly wrote: "Even the ultimate advent of freedom cannot redeem those who died in pain. It is the remembrance of them, and the accumulated guilt of mankind against its victims, that darken the prospect of a civilization without repression" (p. 216).

39   Benjamin's response to Horkheimer's criticism appeared in Convolute N in the *Arcades Project*: "The corrective to this line of thought lies in the reflection that history is not just a science but also a form of memoration (*eine Form des Eingedenkens*). What science has 'established,' memoration can modify. Memoration can make the incomplete (happiness) into something complete, and the complete (suffering) into something incomplete. That is theology; but in memoration we discover the experience (*Erfahrung*) that forbids us to conceive of history as thoroughly a-theological, even though we barely dare not attempt to write it according to literally theological concepts" ("N [Re the Theory of Knowledge, Theory of Progress]," p. 61). There is a problematic transfer here of God's merciful power in the Last Judgment to bestow universal redemption on everyone to the act of "memoration" granted to some fantasized last historian, who can also miraculously turn the partial happiness and complete suffering of past people into their opposites.

recognized and saved, but so too will the villains. One wonders if it really matters that "there is no document of civilization which is not at the same time a document of barbarism,"[40] if the civilized and the barbarians alike will be resurrected in glory at the end of time.

There is, in addition, an even more troubling implication, which emerges in connection with one of Jameson's most provocative contentions. It appears in his discussion of Benjamin's celebrated 1916 essay "On Language as Such and the Language of Man." The Adamic language before the Fall (and before Babel), according to Jameson's reading of Benjamin, is not yet a language of human judgment in which abstract moral standards are imposed on an imperfect world. It is connected instead to dialectical reason "(and, in contemporary terms, to the properly historical, which excludes ethics and moralizing and only grasps necessity). The moralizing judgment of things as good or evil is thus a degradation imposed on us by a fallen language" (p. 53).[41] The dialectical materialist, Jameson tells us, "must always find a position above mere judgment in history itself and in the historical necessity of changes" (p. 194). Apocatastasis thus also means restoring the Adamic language "as such" spoken in the Garden of Eden before the Fall and the loss of innocence that led to the imperfect expedient of moral judgments made by fallible humans on the basis of abstract rules or utilitarian consequences.

Jameson's contrast here between "the properly historical" and mere ethics and morality has a long pedigree in the Marxist tradition.[42] It allowed Lukács to overcome the hesitations he had expressed in his 1918 essay "Bolshevism as a Moral Problem" and join the Communist Party, a choice he then defended in terms of a wager on history in his essay of the following year titled "Tactics and Ethics."[43] It motivated Brecht to

---

40   Benjamin, "Theses on the Philosophy of History," in *Illuminations*, p. 256.

41   Jameson repeats the same point in his discussion of Benjamin's essay "Fate and Character" when he celebrates its "decisive separation of the notion of fate from ethics, from notions of guilt and innocence, and the 'moral accent' or what in the 1916 language he calls judgment." *The Benjamin Files*, p. 82.

42   In the case of Benjamin, however, it is not always clear that he landed squarely on the same side of this divide. Thus, in *One-Way Street*, where he argued in favor of partisanship over objectivity, he also asserted that "criticism is a moral issue" (p. 71).

43   Georg Lukács, "Bolshevism as a Moral Problem," trans. Judith Marcus Tar, *Social Research* 44: 3 (1977), pp. 416–24; Georg Lukács, "Tactics and Ethics," in *Tactics and Ethics, 1919–1929: The Questions of Parliamentarianism and Other Essays*, trans. Michael McColgan (London: Verso, 2014), pp. 3–11.

assert in his 1930 *Lehrstück* titled *Die Maßnahme* that "who fights for Communism must be able to fight and not to fight, to say the truth and not to say the truth, to render and to deny a service, to keep a promise and to break a promise, to go into danger and to avoid danger, to be known and to be unknown. Who fights for Communism has of all the virtues only one: that he fights for Communism."[44] It inspired Maurice Merleau-Ponty to scorn moralizing "bourgeois humanism" and countenance emancipatory violence in the name of a future socialist society in *Humanism and Terror* in 1947.[45]

In all of these cases, absolution is granted to those who transgress against allegedly transcendent moral standards in the service of a final historical outcome that will justify the dirtying of their hands.[46] Moral judgments based on abstract deontological rules—always tell the truth, always keep promises, et cetera—are like the corrupt words of fallen men, which will be overcome with redemption and the restoration of universal innocence. This does not mean, Jameson hastens to add, adopting a social Darwinist logic in which the victors can claim that they were the fittest to survive. This would be a "bad universal history" that would "lump all the nameless dead together in a single narrative, whose protagonists are the victors" (p. 237). Instead, apocatastasis suggests a benign "universal history" that ends with the social equivalent of religious redemption for the vanquished as well, or in Jameson's terms, a communist utopia in which no sin will turn out to be too grave to be forgiven and no sinner too evil to be saved.

In addition to the Adamic language "as such" spoken before the Fall, something else will be restored in Benjamin's vision of a redeemed world, which Jameson flags at a number of places in his book: the lost

---

44 Bertolt Brecht, *The Measures Taken* (1930), in *The Measures Taken and Other Lehrstücke*, trans. Carl R. Mueller (New York: Bloomsbury, 2001), p. 13.

45 Maurice Merleau-Ponty, *Humanism and Terror: An Essay on the Communist Problem*, trans. John O'Neill (Boston: Beacon, 1990).

46 Less euphemistically, it will justify violent means to bring about a desired end. Noting Benjamin's association of revolutionary with divine violence, Jameson writes, "Violence becomes the very condition of possibility of the Now-time, the 'now of recognizability' in which Sorel's myth of the general strike, God's vengeance on tyrants and archaic forces, and all the revolutions of human history, come together in an energizing and multidimensional 'dialectical image.' " *The Benjamin Files*, p. 143.

harmonies of the ancient cosmos.[47] For Benjamin, he writes, "the archaic comes in two forms—the bad chaos of myth and the good harmony of the cosmos and its similitudes" (p. 209). Jameson seizes on Benjamin's endorsement of the latter as a way to move beyond the excessively theological baggage accompanying any talk of original sin derived from munching on forbidden fruit in the Garden, which he wants to reinterpret—albeit very broadly—in historical terms.[48] The Fall, Jameson argues, is best understood metaphorically as "an event" that "characterize[s] the transition from some earlier unfallen cosmos of correspondences and similitudes to our own current world of slow deterioration" (p. 53).

Benjamin himself had located the transition in the early modern period, arguing that "nothing so distinguishes ancient from modern man as the former's submission to a cosmic experience of which the latter is scarcely aware. The decline of that experience begins with the flowering of astronomy at the start of the modern period."[49] He then added that the relationship the ancients had with the cosmos was "intoxication . . . the sole experience in which we grasp the utterly immediate and the utterly remote, and never the one without the other. That means, however, that communicating ecstatically with the cosmos is something man can only do communally. Modern man is in danger of mistakenly dismissing such an experience as trivial, dispensable, and leaving it to the individual—a rush of enthusiasm on fine, starry nights."[50] Only the

---

47 There is another aspect of ancient cosmological thinking, which emphasizes the cyclical return of harmonic correspondences over time. In Origen, as Jennings has pointed out, the idea of apocatastasis owed much to ancient thinkers: "A cosmological understanding of apokatastasis is typical of Platonism, Stoicism, and Gnosticism; all these share a belief in the rigorous *alternation* of ages of cosmic culmination and cosmic restitution." "The Will to Apokatastasis," p. 102. Benjamin's belief in the necessity of destruction and reconstellation shows his debt to this way of thinking, although he resisted the idea of permanent cycles. For a discussion of the subtle differences between ancient notions of eternal return and Benjamin's alternative, see Gilad Sharvit, *Dynamic Repetition: History and Messianism in Modern Jewish Thought* (Waltham, Mass.: Brandeis University Press, 2022).

48 At one point, to be sure, Jameson allows himself to say that Benjamin's ideal version of experience "finds its origins in the great cosmos of similitudes that forms the Edenic landscape of which the mythic is little more than the toxic regression in a ravaged modernity" (*The Benjamin Files*, p. 216), which conflates the two.

49 Benjamin, *One-Way Street*, p. 113.

50 Ibid.

occasional poet like Baudelaire—Jameson calls him Benjamin's "cosmological meteorologist" (p. 83)—protested against what we have lost, and only dubious occult practices like astrology and graphology preserve a faint memory of the similitudes that once tied human fate to the cosmic order.

Jameson is right to stress Benjamin's yearning for the restoration of a world of cosmic correspondences, but he fails to question Benjamin's vague timing of its loss or probe deeply into the origins and implications of the idea itself. One possible source is what anthropologists since Sir James Frazer have called "sympathetic magic" based on "the law of similarity" in which "*like produces like*, effect resembling cause."[51] The anthropologist Michael Taussig has argued that Benjamin's idea of mimesis is best understood in these terms.[52] A more likely origin would be Plato's *Timaeus*, which tells the story of how cosmic order emerged out of chaos and spawned a rich tradition of thinking about celestial harmonies and the Great Chain of Being that ultimately had an impact on medieval Christian thought. Despite Benjamin's focus on "the ancients" alone, the survival of their idea of cosmic order during the High Middle Ages provides the real backdrop for the transition that he laments.

As Hans Blumenberg has described it,[53] when the early Christian expectations of an imminent Second Coming were disappointed, it was no longer appropriate to continue an essentially gnostic denigration of creation as inherently corrupt. Instead, a world-affirming theology needed to incorporate a more stable notion of a secure, rule-bound cosmos, which was then provided by incorporating Greek philosophy into theology.[54] The Platonic cosmogenesis fostered the belief that all that existed had

51   Sir James George Frazer, *The New Golden Bough*, ed. Theodor H. Gaster (New York: Doubleday, 1959), p. 7.

52   Michael Taussig, *Mimesis and Alterity: A Particular History of the Senses* (New York: Routledge, 1993). For a discussion of the links between Frazer and Benjamin, see Patrice Ladwig, "Mimetic Theories, Representation, and 'Savages': Critiques of the Enlightenment and Modernity through the Lens of Primitive Mimesis," in *The Transformative Power of the Copy: A Transcultural and Interdisciplinary Approach*, ed. Corinna Forberg and Philipp W. Stockhammer (Heidelberg: Heidelberg University Publishing, 2017), pp. 37–66.

53   Hans Blumenberg, *The Legitimacy of the Modern Age*, trans. Robert M. Wallace (Cambridge, MA: MIT Press, 1983), part 2.

54   The dominant Greek philosopher for the Scholastics was, of course, Aristotle, although Neoplatonism, from the time of Plotinus on, also had an influence. There were, it should also be noted, ancient Greek proto-nominalists—for example, atomists like

emanated from God's essential being rather than being created separately from him. God's created cosmos, it was assumed, operates according to the rules of reason, intelligibility and harmony. Created, as they were, in the image of God, humans possess the ability to contemplate the heavens and read the cosmos as if it were a legible book.[55]

Although Benjamin was right to understand the modern astronomical observation of an infinite, dynamic universe as inimical to the ancient idea of contemplating an unchanging world and the ordered firmament above it,[56] he was wrong to blame the latter's collapse entirely on the rise of the former. Instead, the challenge occurred much earlier within Christian theology itself with the dawning realization that the doctrine of divine omnipotence derived from the creationist God of the Hebrew Bible was at odds with the constraints of an eternal, rational cosmic order.[57] If God's will was absolute and miracles could undo the order of nature he had once ordained, contingency replaced necessity and the ontological ground of real universals was uncertain. The theological rebellion within Scholasticism that registered this shift emerged among Franciscans like William of Ockham in the fourteenth century and inspired what became known as nominalism. Already called the *via moderna* in its own time, it played a now widely appreciated role in spawning what we like to think of as modernity.[58]

Leucippus and Democritus as well cynics like Antisthenes—but they were not widely appreciated until later.

55   Benjamin's abiding sympathy for this metaphor is shown in Convolute N, where he wrote that "the phrase 'the book of nature' indicates that we can read reality like a text. That will be the approach here to the reality of the nineteenth century. We open the book of past events." "N [Re the Theory of Knowledge, Theory of Progress]," p. 52.

56   The classic account is Alexander Koyré, *From the Closed World to the Infinite Universe* (Baltimore: Johns Hopkins University Press, 1957).

57   See Tamar Rudavsky, ed., *Divine Omniscience and Omnipotence in Medieval Philosophy: Islamic, Jewish and Christian Perspectives* (Dordrecht: Springer, 1985).

58   In addition to Blumenberg, *The Legitimacy of the Modern Age*, see Michael Allen Gillespie, *The Theological Origins of Modernity* (Chicago: University of Chicago Press, 2008). Blumenberg also spells out in great detail the long theological and philosophical preparation for the astronomical revolution in *The Genesis of the Copernican World*, trans. Robert M. Wallace (Cambridge, MA: MIT Press, 1987). There was, to be sure, a revival of interest in cosmic correspondences during the Renaissance with the upsurge of interest on the part of intellectuals like Marsilio Ficino and Giovanni Pico della Mirandola in Neoplatonism, which kept astrology, geomancy, necromancy and other forms of occult divination alive. But it did not flourish for long after the Scientific Revolution began in earnest.

Benjamin never seems to have found Ockham and his progeny worth taking seriously.[59] In his own appropriation of medieval thought, perhaps most extensively elaborated in the discussion of scriptural hermeneutics in *The Political Unconscious,* Jameson has also focused on symbolic levels of meaning that are more than just conventional impositions on a contingent world.[60] He has always been wary of nominalism, whose individualist and positivist legacy he still sees as pernicious in our own day. It expresses, he argued in his book on Adorno, "not merely a form of resistance to the bad Universal, but also a dilemma and a generalized historical situation, a crisis."[61] In his book on postmodernism, he claimed that it underpins the elevation of system-maintaining immanence over system-challenging transcendence.[62] So it is not surprising to see him warm to Benjamin's evocation of the pre-nominalist "good harmony of the cosmos and its similitudes" as a reminder of what we have lost and what might be regained once redemption—or at least its secular equivalent—is achieved.

However, Jameson never really confronts the theoretical reservations, as well as mounting empirical evidence, that led to the "crisis" and subsequent collapse of the ancient—and Scholastic—ideal of a "good harmony." Nor does he ponder the ambiguous implications of believing in benign similitudes between the heavenly spheres and the sublunary world, which could easily justify the prevailing political and social order as a reflection of eternal nature expressed in the Great Chain of Being. The ideal "cosmopolis," in which the harmonic order of the heavens was mirrored in the mundane world, demonstrated that "political theology"

---

59 Benjamin had, however, been interested in the earlier Scholastic philosopher Duns Scotus's linguistic theories, even considering them as a topic for his *Habilitationsschrift.* See Peter Fenves, *The Messianic Reduction: Walter Benjamin and the Shape of Time* (Stanford, CA: Stanford University Press, 2011), 55–9. It might be argued that Benjamin's interest in Adamic names shows his debt to an alternative tradition of nominalism, which might be called "Jewish" or "magical." I leave the development of this argument for a later date.

60 Fredric Jameson, *The Political Unconscious: Narrative as a Socially Symbolic Act* (Ithaca, NY: Cornell University Press, 1981), p. 31. For a discussion of this issue, see Andrew Cole, *The Birth of Theory* (Chicago: University of Chicago Press, 2014), pp. 126–32.

61 Fredric Jameson, *Late Marxism: Adorno, or, The Persistence of the Dialectic* (London: Verso, 1990), p. 164.

62 Fredric Jameson, *Postmodernism: or, The Cultural Logic of Late Capitalism* (Durham, NC: Duke University Press, 1991), p. 250.

could serve at times to legitimate the status quo.[63] Nominalism, in contrast, opened up a world of contingency and possibility in which human assertion had an opportunity to make rather than merely contemplate the world.

Tacitly, Jameson does acknowledge that restoring our faith in an actual harmonic cosmos—even one that downplays rational order in favor of ecstatic intoxication—might be insufficient as a goal of Marxist redemption. Thus, at one point in his analysis of Benjamin's enthusiasm for Auguste Blanqui's cosmological fantasy *L'Éternité par les astres*, he remarks that "true ontology is the effort to reach an as-yet-nonexistent ontology, the one we can still only imagine" (p. 28).[64] Determined to avoid his earlier mistake of attributing to Benjamin too much melancholic nostalgia for a lost world, Jameson seeks to unleash those anticipatory impulses that a "time traveler from some messianic future" would bring with him. He even backtracks a bit on the question of Benjamin's enthusiasm for the world of cosmic correspondences, admitting that "it is not certain that he thinks we can return to it or that he even wants to do so" (p. 220). Despite Benjamin's well-known disdain for conventional narrativizations of history as a tale of inexorable progress, Jameson points to indications that he believed it was still possible to use the adjective "advanced" to describe technical and aesthetic production.[65]

The directional temporality implied by this usage is made even more explicit in the passage from Benjamin's "Central Park," from his unfinished *Arcades Project*, with which Jameson opens *The Benjamin Files*: "For the dialectician, what matters is having the wind of world history in one's sails. For him, thinking means setting the sails. What is important is *how* they are set. Words are for him merely the sails. The way they

---

63 For a discussion of this effect, see Stephen Toulmin, *Cosmopolis: The Hidden Agenda of Modernity* (Chicago: University of Chicago Press, 1990). The adjective "cosmopolitan" has a somewhat different meaning, harkening back to the ancient idea of being a "world citizen."

64 Benjamin read Blanqui's fantasy as an example of the obsession with eternal recurrence in the nineteenth century, also expressed by Baudelaire and Nietzsche. Although it resonated with his critique of progress, Benjamin thought it problematically reified the dialectic of defeat as a permanent feature of all possible worlds. Whether or not Benjamin fully understood the text has become a source of some controversy.

65 Jameson identifies the criterion of advancement with Benjamin's overcoming of traditional aesthetic categories, which he shared with Breton and the Surrealists. *The Benjamin Files*, p. 213.

are set turns them into concepts."[66] A great deal can be said about the vivid metaphor of "the wind of world history," but it is necessary before anything else to contrast it with that other wind portrayed in Benjamin's celebrated reading of Paul Klee's painting *Angelus Novus* in his "Theses on the Philosophy of History." There, a storm wind, said to blow from Paradise, hurls the Angel against his will into the future. Looking back at the past, he sees a "single catastrophe which keeps piling wreckage upon wreckage." Its violence prevents him from folding his wings, collecting himself and performing his assigned mission: to "awaken the dead, and make whole what has been smashed."[67] That is, a fierce head-wind foils his performing the redemptive task of apocatastasis, which Benjamin identified with messianic hope. This is why he will disparagingly call the storm "progress," belief in which is the enemy of a redemptive notion of universal history.

The "wind of world history," in contrast, seems to be blowing in a very different direction. Its source is uncertain—no mention of Paradise here—but it may nonetheless help us reach its redemptive telos. Even if Bob Dylan may assure us that we do not need a weatherman to know which way the wind blows, it is useful to have a few dialecticians on hand to help steer us towards home. Their most fundamental article of faith is that the wind ultimately blows as a unified force and in one direction. For, as Jameson argued in *The Political Unconscious*, we can regain the urgency of individual histories only by situating them "within the unity of a single great collective story; only if, in however disguised and symbolic a form, they are seen as sharing a single fundamental theme— for Marxism, the collective struggle to wrest a realm of Freedom from a realm of Necessity."[68]

---

66   Walter Benjamin, "Central Park," in *Selected Writings*, vol. 4, *1938–1940*, ed. Howard Eiland and Michael W. Jennings, trans. E. F. N. Jephcott and others (Cambridge, MA: Harvard University Press, 2003), p. 176, quoted in Jameson, *The Benjamin Files*, p. 1.

67   Benjamin, "Theses on the Philosophy of History," p. 259. Why the storm is said to be blowing from Paradise is not readily apparent. Perhaps Benjamin meant that it is coming from the Garden of Eden, from which Adam and Eve were expelled after their transgression, causing the ongoing catastrophe that piles up at the Angel's feet. In Convolute N, he had already urged that "the concept of progress should be grounded in the idea of catastrophe. That things 'just keep going on' *is* the catastrophe." "N [Re the Theory of Knowledge, Theory of Progress]," p. 64.

68   Jameson, *The Political Unconscious*, p. 19.

The problem is, of course, that rather than blown by a strong, consistent wind towards any one destination, world history, *pace* both Benjamin and Jameson, may well seem more like a shuttlecock tossed every which way in a tempest. In violent storms, after all, gusts can shift wildly and blow from many different directions, so even the best dialecticians can lose their way. "How to tell time, to feel the direction of the winds of history, in such a multiverse?" (p. 211), Jameson allows himself to wonder.[69] In fact, the very idea of a coherent "world history" understood as a collective metanarrative written from the vantage point of a singular protagonist, humankind, may well be a dubious conceit.[70] Benjamin acknowledged as much when he stressed the need for historians to disrupt given narratives, destroy received accounts of the past, and re-constellate the debris left over. "Historical materialism," he insisted, "strives neither for a homogeneous nor for a continuous presentation of history."[71]

There is also the further complication that, in addition to whatever wind may be metaphorically buffeting human history, there are also the natural winds whose effects in the looming era of extreme climate crisis are anything but reassuring. Ever more violent hurricanes and tornadoes, polar vortices, firestorms and the like remind us that nature, rather than "approaching extinction,"[72] as Benjamin may have once worried, is

---

69   Jameson is using the term "multiverse" here not to mean Blanqui's cosmological fantasy of an infinite number of universes but to say simply that different places on this earth were experiencing in Benjamin's time different temporalities, or what Ernst Bloch would have called "nonsynchronicity."

70   One of the obvious dangers accompanying any attempt to write a singular narrative of the species as a totality is that it can easily elevate a partial perspective into a representative of the whole. Thus, Hegel's Eurocentric conviction that the reformed Prussian state was at the cutting edge of world history looks very parochial from, say, the perspective of an aboriginal person in the Australian outback, a peasant toiling in the fields of China or India, or an Inuit person living above the Arctic Circle. Once you get past the old prejudice that some people have a history and others do not, it is very hard to locate the putative protagonist of the story.

71   Benjamin, "N [Re the Theory of Knowledge, Theory of Progress]," p. 60. One wonders how this comports with Jameson's contention that Benjamin "had an unshakeable commitment to the conviction that the present, and history itself, has a logic." *The Benjamin Files*, p. 138. What kind of logic combines a belief that progress is catastrophe, interruption and destruction are salvific, new constellations of present and past are necessary, and all we have is theologically grounded hope that we will somehow be redeemed in the end?

72   The phrase is evoked by Jameson in his discussion of Adorno's remarks on "natural beauty." *The Benjamin Files*, p. 187. *The Benjamin Files* also has a chapter titled

reasserting itself with a vengeance against the hubris of human mastery. The chilling prediction of Roger Caillois, Benjamin's friend at the Collège de Sociologie in Paris, in a 1937 talk called "The Winter Wind" seems more resonant than ever, especially if we apply it to the entanglement of human with natural history:

> This is no longer clement weather. There is a rising wind of subversion in the world now, a cold wind, harsh, arctic, one of those winds that is murderous and so salubrious, one that kills the fragile, the sickly, and the birds, *one that does not let them get through the winter*. And so a silent, slow irreversible cleansing takes place in nature, like a death tide that rises imperceptibly.[73]

With all of these obstacles, to make the idea of a benign universal world history meaningful, we have to face the paradoxical fact that it does not actually exist, or at least, to borrow the terminology of Ernst Bloch, "not yet." It will only come into being at that remarkable moment of redemptive reckoning and universal amnesty called apocatastasis, which is why Benjamin admits it is a "messianic" hope. In a way, it bears comparison with the Adamic "language as such" that will also be restored at the end of time. As Peter Fenves has noted in an insightful reading of one of Benjamin's earliest ruminations on history, "The diversity of historical chronologies is comparable to the dispersion of languages after the collapse of the Tower of Babel."[74] World history "as such" may, in other words, be little more than an ideal construction of a possible unity at odds with the competing histories of actual men and women, which

---

"Nature Weeps," which does not, however, develop what that anthropomorphic metaphor might have meant for Benjamin.

73   Roger Caillois, "The Winter Wind," in *The College of Sociology (1937–39)*, ed. Denis Hollier, trans. Betsy Wing (Minneapolis: University of Minnesota Press, 1988), p. 42. The disturbing aspect of this talk is Caillois's callous celebration of the "salubrious" effects of this thinning out of the herd, leaving only the strongest to survive until the spring returns. Although one might assimilate this attitude to Benjamin's belief that destruction is necessary before redemption, it contradicts his hostility to the social Darwinist belief that history belongs to the victors.

74   Fenves, *The Messianic Reduction*, p. 121. If we take the parallel seriously, it suggests that, before the Fall, it would have been possible to speak of a unified "world history" that was then shattered. How, we might wonder, did it include all of those peoples whose origin myths were not derived from Genesis in the Hebrew Bible?

defy reduction to a common denominator.[75] Until the Last Judgment happens, however, all we can do is wager that one day it will and adjust our dialectical sails to catch a putatively homeward-bound wind that is paradoxically not yet actually blowing.

Jameson, for all his eagerness to take Benjamin's theological impulses seriously, sometimes betrays his uneasiness about their ultimate plausibility.[76] In his earlier book on Adorno, he had expressed some skepticism about "the mirage of Benjaminian mysticism" and "the archetypal motif of magical language: the act of naming, in which, not unexpectedly, Adam reappears to displace Plato."[77] Although Jameson more often here takes the side of Benjamin than that of Adorno, some of his resistance to magical thinking remains. He thus falls back in the end on another strategy to blunt the continuing catastrophic momentum of history: the role of *figurae* in challenging homogeneity, linearity and progressive development in our intercourse with the past and hope for the future. Here he draws on lessons he learned at the beginning of his career, when he studied with the great literary comparativist Erich Auerbach in graduate school at Yale, lessons he had already applied in earlier works like *The Political Unconscious*.[78]

Auerbach, as it turns out, was himself a friend of Benjamin's, and it appears that his 1929 study *Dante: Poet of the Secular World* helped inspire Benjamin's musings on similitudes and complex defense of allegory.[79] There has been a recent revival of interest in Auerbach's work on

---

75   Jameson admits that Benjamin realized that we have to distinguish between history as we imperfectly know it before redemption and "History itself, the real direction in which the wind of history is blowing in these 'final two seconds' at the close of world history's 'twenty-four-hour' day." *The Benjamin Files*, p. 235.

76   For example, at one point, he writes, "The evocation of a legendary event like 'the Fall' would seem to make some perfunctory acknowledgment of the presence of traditional theology unavoidable. I will attempt to elude even this concession, however, by anticipating a later discussion of Benjamin's idiosyncratic notion of history, to be characterized as a practice of 'periodization without transitions.' " *The Benjamin Files*, p. 53.

77   Jameson, *Late Marxism*, p. 55.

78   Jameson, *The Political Unconscious*, pp. 29–30.

79   Karlheinz Barck, "Walter Benjamin and Erich Auerbach: Fragments of a Correspondence," trans. Anthony Reynolds, *Diacritics* 22: 3/4 (1992), pp. 81–3. For a comparison of allegory in Dante and Benjamin, see Ethan Knapp, "Benjamin, Dante, and the Modernity of the Middle Ages; or, Allegory as Urban Constellation," *Chaucer Review* 48: 4 (2014), pp. 524–41. Jameson had already recognized the relevance of the

figura, and it would be impossible to sort out all the issues it has raised now.[80] Suffice it to say that it focused on the importance of two moments or events in history being understood in terms of prefiguration and realization, the classic example in Christianity being the way in which incidents and figures in the Hebrew Bible—renamed the Old Testament—were understood as anticipating those in the New Testament. Tertullian, for example, claimed that the Joshua of the Book of Numbers prefigures Jesus, "a figure of him who was to be" (*figuram futurorum*). Originally signifying, inter alia, "shape," "form," "picture," "statue," "plan" and "figure of speech," the Latin word *figura* ultimately gained the typological meaning that made it so charged a feature of Christian sacred history. Understood to have ontological weight, *figurae* were thus more than mere tools of prophetic rhetoric.

For Jameson, "the very heart of what is profound and original in Benjamin's work" is "the relationship between narrativity and the raw material of social life, the figurability and representability of history itself" (p. 161). The reason Benjamin was so taken with the traditional story or tale as opposed to the modern novel is that the former allows, even encourages, retelling, whereas the latter makes it impossible.[81] The conventional comparison made between historical narration and the classical realist novel is thus deeply problematic, at least insofar as a more redemptive version of history is concerned.[82] But so too is a static

comparison when he wrote, "Benjamin's thought is best grasped as an allegorical one, as a set of parallel, discontinuous levels of mediation which are not without resemblance to that ultimate model of allegorical composition described by Dante." "Walter Benjamin; or, Nostalgia," in *Marxism and Form*, p. 60.

80   See, for example, James I. Porter, "Disfigurations: Erich Auerbach's Theory of *Figura*," *Critical Inquiry* 44: 1 (2017), pp. 80–113. Other scholars, most notably Jane Newman and Victoria Kahn, have also revived interest in Auerbach's work on allegory and *figura*.

81   Jameson also argues that for Benjamin, the context of the tale includes "that whole cosmos unified by its analogies . . . , a world organized outside worldly categories either by God's plan or natural law." *The Benjamin Files*, p. 168.

82   Perhaps the first major challenge to the comparison came in Hayden White's provocative 1966 essay titled "The Burden of History," which was reprinted in *Tropics of Discourse: Essays in Cultural Criticism* (Baltimore: Johns Hopkins University Press, 1978), pp. 27–50; in it, he argued for the incorporation of modernist aesthetic techniques in historical narration. He returned to the subject in "Modernism and the Sense of History," *Journal of Art Historiography* 15 (December 2016), pp. 1–15, where he drew on Jameson's *A Singular Modernity: Essay on the Ontology of the Present* (London: Verso, 2002). Jameson, for his part, wrote a long and critically appreciative review of White's

or cyclical notion of recurrent types, which Jameson had already criticized in *Marxism and Form* as "always the sign of historical thinking arrested halfway, a thought which, on the road to concrete history, takes fright and attempts to convert its insights into eternal essences."[83] What Auerbach's theory provided, in contrast, was a sense of repetition with a difference, and not just another version of Nietzsche's "eternal recurrence." Benjamin's notion of "dialectic at a standstill" also involves "a similitude between at least two moments of history" (p. 222), but not a simple identity. It suggests instead a completion of the first moment, a moment that was marked by failure, by the second. "This is, then, the ultimate meaning of Benjamin's enigmatic 'dialectical image' . . . This duality is a form of allegorical figuration and . . . the moment of the past, the historical monad, is, in its very failure, an incompleteness and a prefiguration of a realization to come" (p. 232).

Jameson is not alone among contemporary Marxists in mobilizing the power of figural repetition with a difference. It is also a feature of the attempt by Alain Badiou to urge what he calls "fidelity to the Event," based on the belief that what may have seemed like a defeat in the revolutionary struggle is only the first iteration of what might later be successful.[84] Jameson composed an appreciation of Badiou in 2016, in which he noted his claim that the Event does not exist in the present (the realm of static Being), but rather it exists in the "no longer" and "not yet" of a figural temporality. Or more precisely, its time is that of the future anterior (sometimes called the future perfect), the time of what will come to be a completed past in what will be the future. It is, as Jameson has also tellingly admitted, one in which the masses do not play a role as an agent of historical change:

Metahistory: The Historical Imagination in Nineteenth-Century Europe (Baltimore: Johns Hopkins University Press, 1973) in "Figural Relativism, or the Poetics of Historiography," *Diacritics* 6: 1 (1976), pp. 2–9, where he warned against a cyclical notion of historical types.

83   Jameson, "Marcuse and Schiller," in *Marxism and Form*, pp. 93–4.

84   See, for example, Alain Badiou, *Philosophy and the Event*, trans. Louise Burchill (Malden, MA: Polity, 2013). On the recent French discourse of "the event," see Martin Jay, "Historicism and the Event," in *Against the Grain: Jewish Intellectuals in Hard Times*, ed. Ezra Mendelsohn, Stefani Hoffman and Richard I. Cohen (New York: Berghahn Books, 2014), pp. 143–67. For a more general treatment, see Robin Wagner-Pacifici, *What Is an Event?* (Chicago: University of Chicago Press, 2017).

Their presence is also detected after the fact, in the ruins of 1848 or 1917: collectivity cannot constitute an *actant* in this narrative sense. Yet these convulsive events themselves can somehow be reawakened in the present, in what sounds like a fraternal echo of Benjamin's energetic formulation: "To Robespierre ancient Rome was a past charged with the time of the now [*Jetztzeit*] which he blasted out of the continuum of history." This "tiger's leap into the past" of Benjamin is surely an excellent interpretation of what Badiou means by "fidelity" to the Event.[85]

This admission raises a very sensitive question about the relationship between Benjamin's imaginative attempt to juxtapose theology with historical materialism: what are its political implications, if any? It is sobering to remember that the rhetoric of "redemption" has not always been adopted in the service of progressive causes; it was, for example, the rallying cry of aggrieved Southerners in the fight against Reconstruction after the American Civil War. Jennings has noted that "in *The Arcades Project*, Benjamin speaks of the 'will to apokatastasis' as the resolve to gather again, in revolutionary action and in revolutionary thinking, precisely the elements of the 'too early' and the 'too late' of 'the first beginning and the final decay' . . . The will to apokatastasis is in this sense the political will, the will to bring an end to what is in the hope that, in a cosmological turn, something better might succeed it."[86] Jameson endorses this estimation of the hortatory message brought back by Benjamin in his guise as a "time traveler from some messianic future."

But is it a message that is likely to be heard and acted on, and by whom?[87] Whose political engagement, we might wonder, will be galvanized by the goal of returning to an ancient ideal of cosmic harmony, in which our fate is coordinated with celestial gyrations? Whose

---

85 Fredric Jameson, "Badiou and the French Tradition," *New Left Review* 2: 102 (November/December 2016), p. 109.

86 Jennings, "The Will to Apokatastasis," p. 98.

87 Jameson, to be sure, has never been keen to count on the leading role of praxis in his interpretation of Marxism. Thus, in *The Political Unconscious* he wrote that "history is what hurts, it is what refuses desire and sets inexorable limits to individual as well as collective praxis, which its 'ruses' turn into grisly and ironic reversals of their overt intention" (p. 102).

revolutionary zeal will be quickened by dreams of restoring an Adamic "language as such" beyond the Babel of different tongues? Whose hunger for social justice will be whetted by a desire for an apocatastasis in which oppressor and oppressed alike are granted salvation by an indifferently merciful God? Whose organizing talents will be mobilized by the dream of salvation for all, when, at least in the United States, we cannot even build a consensus for health care for all? In short, can we really hold out hope for a benign version of universal history in which a mighty wind will finally be blowing in the right direction, allowing us to hoist our sails and reach the promised land?

Benjamin's maximalist agenda, it might be conjectured, reflects what might be called "left mania" more than "left melancholia." That is, the version of messianic hope he took from his eclectic theological sources is so exorbitant in its goals that it suggests a refusal or inability to acknowledge the limits of reality. Melancholy and mania, as Freud famously argued, may well be two sides of the same coin, as experienced in bipolar manic-depressive disorders.[88] Both are contrasted with proper mourning in which a lost object is acknowledged as such and grief at its disappearance softens into somber acceptance of what has been lost. Benjamin, as I have argued elsewhere, was intransigently resistant to the consolations of mourning, especially when they demanded reconciliation with the status quo of a world that had produced the horrors of the First World War and seemed determined to restore all the conditions that had caused it in the first place.[89] He was determined to keep the wound unhealed until a genuine cure could be found, and he tirelessly sought any hint of what that might be in an astoundingly wide variety of places, ranging from theology, linguistics, philosophy and literature to the visual arts,

---

88   I hasten to add that I am not offering a psychological explanation of Benjamin's apocalyptic and messianic inclinations, which would fly in the face of Jameson's repeated warning against psychologization as a mark of bourgeois ideology. Nor do I want to invoke the condescending epithet "infantile disorder," which Lenin famously applied to "left-wing communists." Instead, I want to suggest a more collective phenomenon that links bitter disappointment with exorbitant hopes, a dialectic of defeat and intensified utopianism.

89   Martin Jay, "Against Consolation: Walter Benjamin and the Refusal to Mourn," in *Refractions of Violence* (New York: Routledge, 2003), pp. 11–24. See also my essay "The Apocalyptic Imagination and the Inability to Mourn," in *Force Fields: Between Intellectual History and Cultural Critique* (New York: Routledge, 1993).

modern technology and popular culture, not to mention graphology and hashish.

Among its many virtues, *The Benjamin Files* shows how compelling that quest can still be for someone with the steadfast commitment, capacious learning and imaginative capacity of a Fredric Jameson. But I have to confess that, despite all his heroic efforts to infuse historical materialism with the manic energies of Benjamin's "theological code," the odds seem to me overwhelmingly against its success. Kant's more modest attempt to write a universal history from a cosmopolitan point of view never realized, after all, the practical intent that motivated it, the achievement of perpetual peace among nations. It is hard to think that a universal history from a messianic point of view, whose redemptive ambitions are even higher, will be more successful. We are as likely to trade in our linguistic plurality for the *Ursprache* spoken in the Garden before the Fall as we are to forge our riot of different historical narratives into one coherent story, especially one in which even the vilest villains will be saved along with their victims. The "wind of history" may well turn out to be little more than what the nominalists like to call a *flatus vocis*.

Ironically, to return to our point of departure, Jameson's 1969 essay on Benjamin's nostalgia can perhaps best be understood not as the prefigural anticipation of *The Benjamin Files*, but rather as its completion. That is, for all of Jameson's ingenious efforts to wrest a utopian message from the wreckage of Benjamin's melancholic lament for a world we have lost, for all his insistence that the theological moment in Benjamin's constellation expresses hope for a redeemed future, for all his subtle distinction between Benjamin's critique of the ideology of progress and his admiration for what is genuinely "advanced," what emerges from his new book is still the priority of Benjamin's saturnine melancholia over his manic hopes.[90] If we are to take seriously the overturning of conventional historicist chronology, evolving and unidirectional, advocated by both Benjamin and Jameson, then why not turn the

---

90   It is hard not to conclude that Jameson is grasping at any straw available to show that manic hope is still alive when he suggests that, "as for the postindustrial, may it not be conjectured that hackers' work is also a handicraft and that it is not necessarily a pipe dream to remind ourselves of the Utopianism of the first users of the Internet, now captured by vast cartels and business conglomerates and yet still artistically subverted in undiscoverable nooks and crannies of the known universe?" *The Benjamin Files*, p. 217.

book of 2020 into the prefiguration of the essay of 1969? The result may be preposterous in the precise sense of that word, which means that what comes last is turned into what comes first. But it is certainly no less preposterous than believing that the wind of world history is, despite all indications to the contrary, blowing us towards the restoration of cosmic harmonies, an Adamic "language as such," and the universal salvation called apocatastasis.

7

Leib, Körper and the Body Politic

The previous chapter voiced reservations about certain of the more implausible goals of Walter Benjamin's utopian agenda and questioned their relevance for a progressive politics. This one, in contrast, finds unexpected political inspiration in the ruminations on the body in his "anthropological materialism." It does so through a detour that explores the significance of the distinction between Leib *and* Körper, *which had been first developed in the phenomenology and philosophical anthropology of Max Scheler, Edmund Husserl and Helmuth Plessner during the Weimar era and later.*

In the light of Max Horkheimer's early dismissal of philosophical anthropology and Adorno's frequent critiques of phenomenology, it may seem odd to enlist their services in setting the stage for Benjamin's argument.[1] Plessner's defense of artifice, protective distancing from nature, masks and

---

1 Max Horkheimer, "Remarks on Philosophical Anthropology" (1935), in Horkheimer, *Between Philosophy and Social Science: Selected Early Writings,* trans. G. Frederick Hunter, Matthew S. Kramer and John Torpey (Cambridge, MA: MIT Press, 1993); Theodor W. Adorno, *Against Epistemology: A Metacritique,* trans. Willis Domingo (Cambridge, MA: MIT Press, 1983). For considerations of their reservations about philosophical anthropology, see Dennis Johannßen, "Toward a Negative Anthropology: Critical Theory's Altercations with Philosophical Anthropology," *Anthropology and Materialism* 1 (2013), and "Humanism and Anthropology from Walter Benjamin to Ulrich Sonnemann," in *The Sage Handbook of Critical Theory,* eds. Werner Bonefeld, Chris O'Kane and Beverly Best (London: Sage, 2018); and Kylie Gilchrist, "We Cannot Say What the Human Is: The Problem of Anthropology in Adorno's Philosophy of Art," *New German Critique,* no. 142 (February 2021).

self-armoring has, after all, been compared to the machine-like "cool conduct" of the New Objectivity movement of the Weimar era, against which Critical Theory often railed.[2] And, despite the lingering effects of Marcuse's early training with Heidegger, it is often assumed that Critical Theory had little use for the ahistorical assumptions of a philosophy that sought to bracket the experienced world present to human consciousness in search of knowledge of abiding essences.

Recent commentators have, however, questioned the stark contrast between Critical Theory and both philosophical anthropology and phenomenology.[3] In addition, the friendly relations between Horkheimer, Adorno and Plessner, who even worked together when the Institute returned to Germany after the war, have also been acknowledged.[4] And so, too, have the lasting effects of Benjamin's own early interest in phenomenological methods and ideas.[5] In short, there is no reason to avoid turning to theorists like Plessner and Husserl (not to mention others like Merleau-Ponty, whose politics might make him a more natural collaborator) for ideas that enrich Critical Theory.

What makes reading the Leib/Körper distinction so fruitful is the work it does, filtered through Benjamin's allegorization of the body as disarticulated corpse, to challenge the vitalist notion of organic wholeness as the normative model of social and political "health." It alerts us to the dangers in marginalizing the passive body, the vulnerable body that suffers as well

2   Helmut Lethen, *Cool Conduct: The Culture of Distance in Weimar Germany*, trans. Don Reneau (Berkeley: University of California Press, 2002), pp. 52–67, 88–94.

3   See, for example, Alexei Procyshyn, "Phenomenology and Critical Theory," in *The Routledge Handbook of Phenomenology and Phenomenological Philosophy*, ed. Daniele De Santis, Burt C. Hopkins and Claudio Majolino (London: Routledge, 2020); and Carl Gelderloos, *Biological Modernism: The New Human in Weimar Culture* (Evanston, IL: Northwestern University Press, 2020), which directly challenges Lethen's reading of Plessner. For an earlier, nuanced consideration of philosophical anthropology and its implications for Critical Theory, see Axel Honneth and Hans Joas, *Social Action and Human Nature*, trans. Raymond Meyer (Cambridge: Cambridge University Press, 1988).

4   Monika Plessner, *Die Argonauten auf Long Island. Begegnungen mit Hannah Arendt, Theodor W. Adorno, Gersholm Scholem und anderen* (Hamburg: Rowohlt, 2015). Detlev Claussen's afterword to the volume details their collaborative interactions. For a sustained comparison of their positions, see Hans-Peter Krüger, *Homo Absconditus: Helmut Plessners Philosophische Anthropologie im Vergleich* (Berlin: De Gruyter, 2019), chapter 18.

5   See Peter Fenves, *The Messianic Reduction: Walter Benjamin and the Shape of Time* (Stanford, CA: Stanford University Press, 2011).

as acts, in our political imaginary. It helps us acknowledge our common fate with those who are not political agents or full participants in a national or popular drama of sovereign mastery. As such, it reminds us that fantasies of collective meta-subjects, able to "make history" in the way artists make works of art, are transfigurations of idealist metaphysics rather than materialist in the broad sense that situates humankind in the world of inanimate as well as animate matter.[6]

There can be few more persistent biases than our holistic preference for unity over disunity, integration over disintegration, harmony over discord and consensus over dissensus. Even when we value fragments or shards of what was once whole, we imbue them with the pathos of nostalgia and mourn their lost integrity. Whether understood in organic or mechanical terms, the complex entities we construe as immanently functional are normatively honored and their opposite stigmatized as pathological. When separation or differentiation occurs, we often label it alienation or estrangement and pine for its overcoming. When stark dualisms are posited—subject/object, mind/body, self/other, culture/nature, soul/flesh, form/content, to name only a few—we hasten to sublate or deconstruct them or search for a *tertium datur* that mediates the opposition. Aesthetic models of coherence, balance, organic unity and completion normally trump those that favor dissonance, disproportionality and open-endedness. Decadence is defined precisely by the lack of a triumphant cadence rounding off the end of a story or composition. In short, integration and totalization are identified with life well lived, and their loss with death, decay and entropy.

An obvious arena for the playing out of these fears and the strategies we employ to meet them is in our corporeal imaginaries. Here, the contrast is between bodies understood on the one hand as functionally organized, generative, securely boundaried and inviolable, and on the other as decaying, grotesque and vulnerable to external invasion.[7]

---

6 This essay began as a keynote address to the conference "Bodies of Power: Somaesthetics and Politics" at Florida Atlantic University in November 2021, organized by Richard Shusterman. It is also included in Valentina Antoniol and Stefano Marino, eds., *Existence, Politics, Somaesthetics: Comparative Perspectives on Foucault and Shusterman* (London: Bloomsbury, 2023).

7 There are, of course, occasional celebrants of what Deleuze and Guattari, adopting a phrase from Antonin Artaud, called "bodies without organs," whose

Although often expressed in the vocabulary of biology, with healthy and generative bodies counterposed to their sick, degenerative or moribund opposites, aesthetic models of wholeness and proportionality are no less prevalent.[8]

The political implications of this bias for corporeal wholeness have been widely appreciated. It was perhaps expressed most explicitly in the familiar metaphor of the body politic, whose long history begins with the ancient Greeks and reached its apogee in the Middle Ages with works like Al-Farabi's *The Perfect State* and John of Salisbury's *Policraticus*. Its metaphoric efficacy was based on the identification of political functionality with the image of corporeal health, robustness and beauty. But it could also be used to stigmatize allegedly pathogenic toxins in the body, which were identified with marginalized or abjected internal enemies or foreign intruders.[9] We all know the sinister outcomes of this kind of rhetorical transfer from the organic body to the political arena.

Rather than examining this familiar analogy, I want instead to interrogate the political implications of another way of conceptualizing the human body, one which avoids the simple alternative of healthy holistic integration or dysfunctional decay. I am speaking of a dichotomy that has come down to us from the philosophical, anthropological and phenomenological traditions in early twentieth-century Germany and France, which differentiates between the body as *Leib* and the body as *Körper*.[10] Broadly speaking, *Leib* signifies the body as subjectively, if

undifferentiated, ephemeral structures and permeable borders allow a de-territorialized, discontinuous flow of energetic forces. See Gilles Deleuze and Félix Guattari, *Anti-Oedipus: Capitalism and Schizophrenia*, trans. Mark Seem and Robert Hurley (London: Continuum, 2004); and *A Thousand Plateaus: Capitalism and Schizophrenia*, trans. Brian Massumi (Minneapolis: University of Minnesota Press, 2005).

8   Obvious examples are Leonardo da Vinci's famous drawing of the "Vitruvian Man" and Winckelmann's Hellenic ideal of noble simplicity and restraint, which could even transfigure Laocoön's body in obvious pain into a symbol of eternal, ideal beauty. Although there are, of course, other aesthetic ideals—think, for example, of the Japanese *wabi-sabi*, combining rustic simplicity with reverence for imperfection and the patina of aging—the bias for organic wholeness remains very powerful in our culture.

9   See the discussion in Jonathan Gil Harris, *Foreign Bodies and the Body Politic: Discourses of Social Pathology in Early Modern England* (Cambridge: Cambridge University Press, 1998).

10   As Hans-Peter Krüger has reminded me (personal communication, January 17, 2022), the distinction had already been noted by many other German philosophers from Herder, Fichte, Hegel, Feuerbach and Marx to Dilthey and Nietzsche.

often pre-reflexively, experienced, infused with operative intentionality and active purpose, whereas *Körper* suggests the body experienced as an extended object in the world, inert and passive, open to the intentions of others as well as one's own. Significantly, the two different nouns for body are always accompanied by distinct verbs: *Leibsein* and *Körperhaben*, which translate as "to be a body" and "to have a body." These suggest the active quality of the human experience of corporeality, which distinguishes our bodies from the inert objects of inorganic nature. Defying easy reconciliation in some higher dialectical third, the opposition avoids the often sentimental pathos of holistic totalization. And it offers us more conceptual clarity and less normative bias than the opposite extremes of corporeal organization and entropic decay. Instead, it suggests we understand the body neither as a functional organized totality nor a degenerative version thereof, but rather as an active participant in an ongoing process that always involves two experiential modalities. As such, it opens up new vistas on the relationship between bodies and what we call politics, which I want to explore in this essay.

It is sometimes said that the distinction between *Leib* and *Körper* was introduced by the philosophical anthropologist Helmuth Plessner in 1923.[11] Others have noted its earlier appearance in a 1916 book by Max Scheler called *Formalism in Ethics and Non-Formal Ethics of Value.*[12] Whatever its precise origin, it was further developed by Edmund Husserl, Maurice Merleau-Ponty and others in the phenomenological tradition and ultimately found its way into the discourse of somaesthetics. There is, in fact, a special issue of the *Journal of Speculative Philosophy* in 2010, introduced by Richard Shusterman's "Soma and Psyche,"[13]

---

11   Helmuth Plessner with Frederick Jacob Buytendijk, "Die Deutung des mimischen Ausdrucks. Ein Beitrag zur Lehre vom Bewusstsein des anderen Ichs," in Plessner, *Gesammelte Schriften*, vol. 7, *Ausdruck und menschliche Natur*, ed. Günter Dux, Odo Marquard and Elisabeth Ströker (Frankfurt: Suhrkamp, 1982), pp. 67–129. For a discussion, see Hans-Peter Krüger, "Persons and Their Bodies: The *Körper/Leib* Distinction and Helmuth Plessner's Theories of Ex-centric Positionality and *Homo absconditus*," *Journal of Speculative Philosophy* 24: 3 (2010). For a wide-ranging selection of essays on Plessner's legacy, see Jos de Mul, ed., *Plessner's Philosophical Anthropology: Perspectives and Prospects* (Amsterdam: Amsterdam University Press, 2014).

12   Max Scheler, *Formalism in Ethics and Non-formal Ethics of Value*, trans. Manfred Frings and Robert Funk (Evanston, IL: Northwestern University Press, 1973), p. 399.

13   Richard Shusterman, "Soma and Psyche," *Journal of Speculative Philosophy* 24: 3 (2010).

which explores its costs and benefits in a lucid and thorough way. In a more recent essay on the distinction, Shusterman tells us that he introduced the term "soma" to overcome whatever dualistic implications might flow from contrasting *Leib* with *Körper,* and notes that Husserl himself often spoke of a united *Leibkörper.* Drawing in particular on Plessner's analysis of the imbrication of the two modes of experiencing our bodies, he concludes that "both spontaneous and reflective somatic consciousness (*Leibsein* and *Körperhaben*) are essential for a person's flourishing, for successful functioning, improved performance and developmental growth. Somaesthetics celebrates the value of both."[14]

While acknowledging the value of balancing the two for the personal goals Shusterman wants to promote, we should, however, hesitate before collapsing them too quickly into an integrated whole if we hope to use the distinction to help us think about politics. Let me quickly sketch what I take to be the main implications of the distinction before passing on to its relevance for political theory. Calling into question the religious dichotomy of soul and flesh and the Cartesian dualism of mind and matter, it alerts us to the entanglement of our experiences of subjectivity and objectivity, the body as perceiver and as the perceived. This oscillation is perhaps most famously exemplified by what Husserl called the "double sensation" experienced when one hand touches the other, whose importance Merleau-Ponty also often stressed. You can either focus on the sensations that represent the "objective" characteristics of the hand you are touching, like the texture of its skin or shape, or on the subjective "sensings" of the hand that is doing the touching.[15] These two sensations never fuse into one, but can wobble back and forth, as we alternatively attend to one or the other.

Rather than undialectically opposed or ontologically distinct, both are always relationally intertwined, embodying the logic of both/and rather than either/or. On first impression, *Leib* may seem equal to the

---

14 Richard Shusterman, "Body Consciousness and the Excentric Self: Between Plessner and Somaesthetics," *Pragmatism Today* 9: 1 (2018), p. 19.

15 Edmund Husserl, *Ideas Pertaining to a Pure Phenomenology and to a Phenomenological Philosophy*; Book Two: *Studies in the Phenomenology of Constitution,* in *Collected Works of Edmund Husserl,* vol. 3, trans. Richard Rojcewicz and André Schuwer (Dordrecht: Kluwer, 1989), pp. 152–3. For a useful summary, see Donn Welton, "Soft, Smooth Hands: Husserl's Phenomenology of the Lived Body," in Donn Welton, ed., *The Body* (Malden, MA: Blackwell, 1999), pp. 38–56.

subject, whose interior conscious intends its movements and experiences its feelings. But it is also capable of losing itself in its environment, when for example it has a rapturous experience of music. And it can extend empathetically to include the *Leibsein* of others. *Körper*, in contrast, is identified more with a perception of one's body as being a thing in the world. Or more precisely, as Husserl emphasized, it is manifest as an "imperfectly constituted thing" because it is only experienced perspectivally, in part and even misshapen by its limited availability to our senses.[16] Such a mediated awareness implies that prior to the experience of "having a body" is the reflexivity enabled by "being a body." At the same time, the latter is made possible only by the "lived body" always already being situated in the larger world of extended material objects. Unlike the "centric" positionality of an animal, who stands opposed to and distinct from its environment, humans are positioned "eccentrically," needing to transgress the boundary of biological or instinctual self-sufficiency to create the supplement we call culture. But in so doing, we never leave behind entirely our rootedness in the material world.

In other words, the two corporeal modes are recursively and equiprimordially entailed, each latent in or presupposed by the other. The oscillation between them prevents humans from ever becoming fully at one with themselves, overcoming all self-alienation to achieve perfect organic unity. Rather than closed or perfectible, we are always open, double, and imperfect. For Plessner, this is an understanding of humankind as a "*homo absconditus*," comparable in its unknowability to the "hidden God" in the book of Isaiah in the Hebrew Bible.[17] Even our senses conspire to prevent a positive image of human nature from cohering. Associated with a specific sensual experience, *Leib* is more haptic, while *Körper* is more visual, although only imperfectly because not all of my body is visible within my visual field. In a temporal register, the former is immersed in the qualitatively heterogeneous felt time of what Bergson would have called *durée* or duration, while the latter is located in the quantitatively homogeneous spatialized time of the external

---

16   Edmund Husserl, *Ideas Pertaining to a Pure Phenomenology and to a Phenomenological Philosophy: Studies in the Phenomenology of Constitution*, trans. Fred Kersten (Dordrecht/Boston: Kluwer, 1989), p. 167.

17   Krüger, *Homo Absconditus*, pp. 407–8.

world.[18] *Leib* can include the temporal dimension of living intensely in the present moment, although its feelings of desire and fear can move beyond it, whereas *Körper* registers the inexorable succession of past, present and future.

A great deal more can be said about the distinction, which produces what has been called "the body-body problem" as opposed to the "mind-body problem" that has vexed philosophy from its beginnings.[19] Addressing it would require putting a lot more pressure on such terms as "subjectivity," "intentionality," "perception," "spontaneity" and "temporality." We would have to explore, as well, the complicated dialectic of internal and external, involving introjection, projection and the various modalities of intersubjectivity, which would call into question the self-sufficiency of either version of body as an independent entity radically set apart from its environment. We would have to probe the ways in which the body as the generator of desire and the body as the locus of suffering imperfectly map on to the distinction. We would have to ponder the ways that technological mediations of bodily experience, extending from the earliest mirror to the most recent developments in photographic selfies or micro-cameras that allow us to gaze at the hidden recesses of our bodies, influence the historical mix between *Leib* and *Körper*, which is never a fixed proportion.

These would all be fruitful avenues to pursue in any consideration of the distinction's meaning for politics, but I want to examine something else: the implication of identifying *Leib*, as it often is, with the "lived body." Related to the verbs *leben* (to live) and *erleben* (to experience) and the adjectives *lebendig* (animated or lively) and *leibhaft* (in the flesh), it foregrounds the body's organic vitality. As such, it inevitably links *Körper*, at least as latent potentiality, with the dead body, in other words with human mortality and our inevitable premonition of it. It is this awareness that is often seen as one of the most salient traits that distinguishes humans from other animals. Here, in English if not in German, we cannot avoid hearing the echo of "corpse" in *Körper*, both rooted, as they are, in *corpus* the Latin word for body.[20] Significantly, in Descartes's

18   See Maren Wehrle, "Being a Body and Having a Body: The Twofold Temporality of Embodied Intentionality," *Phenomenology and the Cognitive Sciences* 19 (2020), pp. 299–521.

19   Welton, "Soft, Smooth Hands," p. 48.

20   In German, *Leiche* or *Leichnam* is used for a dead body, with the latter being a slightly more formal term. Their etymology is the High Middle German *lichname*.

Second Meditation, where the body is located in space as extended matter without the power of self-movement, it has been described as having all the characteristics of a corpse.[21] No matter how much we associate *Leib* with the subjectivity, purposiveness and spontaneity of life, it is always dependent on the objective materiality making it possible, a dependency perhaps best emblematized by our boney infrastructure, which survives our deaths as a skeleton. As one observer puts it, "a world of organic, autonomous powers circulate within my visceral depths. Their otherness haunts the 'I,' surfacing at times of illness or approaching death."[22] There is, in other words, in addition to the present-mindedness of "I *am* my body," the anticipatory presentiment of "I will no longer *have* a body."

In *The Birth of the Clinic*, Michel Foucault argued that only with the gaze of modern medicine was death displaced from the spiritual world and "*embodied* in the *living bodies* of individuals . . . Western man could constitute himself in his own eyes as an object of science, he grasped himself within his language, and gave himself, in himself and by himself, a discursive existence, only in the opening created by his own elimination . . . generally speaking, the experience of individuality in modern culture is bound up with death."[23] Whether or not the new attitude of modern medicine towards death was the initial source of our perception of the body as an individual object or merely an institutional and discursive articulation of prior experiences, Foucault's linkage of the objectification of the body with the mortality of the individual is very instructive. It tells us that thinking of the *Leib/Körper* distinction's meaning for politics will inevitably raise an especially vexing issue: how does the realm of human practices and institutions we have come to identify with the political confront the most basic of human concerns, which are literally matters of life and death?

Before venturing a few, inevitably inadequate thoughts on these most daunting of issues, I want to clear some preliminary ground by considering three of the more traditional ways in which vitality and mortality have been considered in relation to politics, both literally and

---

21 For a discussion, see Welton, "Soft, Smooth Hands," p. 54.

22 Leder, "Flesh and Blood," p. 205.

23 Michel Foucault, *The Birth of the Clinic: An Archaeology of Medical Perception*, trans. A. M. Sheridan (London: Tavistock, 1973), pp. 196–7.

metaphorically. The first is the tradition derived from what the cele-brated medieval historian Ernst Kantorowicz famously called "the king's two bodies";[24] the second, the Hegelian identification of death and nega-tion, itself a variant of a longer tradition of what might be called sacrifi-cial sublimation; and the third, what has been known as "biopolitics" and its apparent opposites, "necropolitics" or "thanatopolitics." After we have introduced these alternatives, we can focus on what I hope to show are the different political implications of the distinction between *Leib* and *Körper*.

Drawing on the religious distinction between the *corpus mysticum* of Christ and his creaturely body, the medieval theory of monarchy explored by Kantorowicz differentiated between the eternal life of the institution of kingship and the finite lives of the mortals who temporarily occupy the role of king. One descended from grace, the other from nature, but they mingled in Christ, the Eucharist and, most importantly from a political point of view, a sacred notion of royalty. The dual nature of monarchy, at once symbolic and literal, allowed continuity of the body politic beyond the deaths of individual rulers through what we might call a political theological transcendentalization of vitality, which was now only fleet-ingly identified with actual, finite human bodies. Although the religious roots of the distinction grew less explicit and the authority of monarchy itself was diminished after the rise of republican politics, the logic of the king's two bodies remained, as argued by observers such as Claude Lefort and Eric Santner,[25] in modern political notions of the people and the nation. That is, there is a comparable distinction between a transcendental popular sovereign, the symbolic community of citizens whose authority legitimates a political order, and the empirical people who metonymically claim to represent it, as well as between an allegedly eternal nation and those who assert the right to speak on its behalf.[26]

24 Ernst Kantorowicz, *The King's Two Bodies: A Study in Medieval Political Theology* (Princeton, NJ: Princeton University Press, 1957).

25 Claude Lefort, *Democracy and Political Theory*, trans. David Macey (Minneapolis: University of Minnesota Press, 1988); Eric L. Santner, *The Royal Remains: The People's Two Bodies and the Endgames of Sovereignty* (Chicago: University of Chicago Press, 2011). Santner argues that the symbolic dimension of the people's body is better understand as a "surplus of immanence," which he calls "the flesh," rather than transcendence.

26 The potential slippage between divine and secular versions of transcendental vitality was already noted by the eighth-century Anglo-Latin scholar Alcuin of York, but he warned against it: "Nor should we listen to those who say 'the voice of the people is

Life, we might say, is transcendentalized and projected onto an essentialized ideal, kingship or the people, which somehow survives the inevitable deaths of those who are its empirical instantiations. It may, in fact, become so identified with what transcends creaturely finitude that it is located entirely with the hereafter, which begins only with the shuffling off of our mortal coils. Whether or not it reaches that extreme, which renders mundane politics nugatory, it posits, to borrow Foucault's well-known characterization of Kant's distinction between the noumenal and phenomenal subject, a "transcendental-empirical doublet," in which a clear hierarchy of value is assumed. Only the individual soul may, to be sure, enjoy eternal life, but the supra-individual avatars of the *corpus mysticum* on earth are imbued with the same value.

As Derrida notes in an essay called "Faith and Knowledge," for religions, "life has absolute value only if it is worth more than life . . . respect for life in the discourses of religion as such concerns 'human life' only in so far as it bears witness, in some manner, to the infinite transcendence of that which is worth more than it (divinity, the sacrosanctness of law)." The alleged dignity of life, he continues, "can only subsist beyond the present living being."[27] As is sometimes argued in the case of the Apostle Paul, the elevation of spirit or *pneuma* over flesh or *soma,* the former supposedly universal, the latter merely particular, might have been the source of catholic—with a small "c"—inclusivity. But it could also have very fateful mundane consequences for those groups that were identified solely with somatic particularity, especially the Jews.[28] As I hope to show shortly, the political implications of the phenomenological distinction between *Leib* and *Körper,* which is

---

the voice of God' [*vox populi, vox dei,* which was an old Latin saying] for the turbulence of the mob is always close to insanity." Alexander Hamilton is often quoted as saying something similar: "The voice of the people has been said to be the voice of God; and, however generally this maxim has been quoted and believed, it is not true to fact. The people are turbulent and changing, they seldom judge or determine right."

27 Jacques Derrida, "Faith and Knowledge," in *Religion,* ed. Jacques Derrida and Gianni Vattimo (Stanford, CA: Stanford University Press, 1998), p. 51.

28 According the David Nirenberg, the medieval identification of Christianity with lively spirit and Judaism with base matter or lifeless legalism exemplified this danger, which has echoes in the work of such contemporary Marxists as Alain Badiou. See his "'Judaism' as Political Concept: Toward a Critique of Political Theology," *Representations* 128: 1 (November 2014), pp. 1–29.

inherently nonhierarchical, are very different for those outside the charmed circle of the spiritually vital.

If the king's two bodies tradition led to a hierarchically arranged transcendental/empirical doublet in which eternal life was identified with universal or at least collective spirit and death with the mortal individual's creaturely flesh, what might be called the Hegelian tradition of speculative idealism understood the relationship of vitality and mortality in a more dialectical manner. For Hegel, to condense a complicated argument, death was understood as a necessary negation in a process that ultimately led to the reconciliation of apparent opposites, what in the theological terms going back to Gnosticism is called a *pleroma*.[29] As many interpreters of Hegel, including Alexander Kojève and Georges Bataille, have noted, the logic of salutary negation was also that of sacrifice in which the death of the individual was functional in the service of the life of the whole. Death, in other words, is happily recuperated for Hegel in what Bataille called a closed or "restricted economy" rather than bursting its bounds and becoming part of a "general economy" based on excess, waste, expenditure (*dépense*) and the undermining of exchange.[30]

In simpler terms, the dialectical heroization of the individual who risks death in order to serve the collective good, whether it be the progress of history, the survival of the community or the fulfillment of God's will, has been a potent political ploy for a very long time. From Horace's famous exhortation in his ode to valor, "*Dulce et decorum est pro patria mori*" ("it is sweet and proper to die for one's country") through Patrick Henry's "Give me liberty or give me death" up until Che Guevara's "*patria o muerte*" ("fatherland or death"), what is conventionally called "the ultimate" or "supreme" sacrifice has turned death into a justifiable means to realize a higher goal. Not surprisingly, Horace's line is inscribed over the rear entrance to the Memorial Amphitheater at Arlington National Cemetery. Shrouded in the same aura of sanctity that surrounds religious martyrs since at least the days of the early Christians and is still invoked by some to justify suicide bombers in our

29   For a discussion from the perspective of Schelling's critique of Hegel, see Saitya Brata Das, "The Tragic Dissonance," *Analytica Hermeneutica* 5 (2013), pp. 1–33.

30   Georges Bataille, *The Accursed Share: An Essay on General Economy*, trans. Robert Hurley, vol. 1, *Consumption* (New York: Zone, 1991); vols. 2 and 3, *The History of Eroticism and Sovereignty* (New York: Zone, 1993).

own day, it draws on a kind of theodicy in which the apparent evil of a violent death—sometimes not only that of the martyr, but also his or her innocent victims—is justified by an alleged higher good.

There has, of course, often been pushback against the dubious consolation to the actual victims offered by this logic. The powerful antiwar poem "Dulce et Decorum Est," written by Wilfred Owen shortly before his own death in the final week of the First World War, damns Horace's motto as "an old Lie" told to "children ardent for some desperate glory."[31] The recent Cuban demonstrators against the current regime have adopted *patria y vida* ("fatherland and life"), the title of a popular hip-hop song, as their defiant slogan. Rather than sublimating individual deaths in a narrative of collective redemption, they protest against the logic of sacrificial martyrdom that provides a dubious solace for the premature termination of a particular life.

An even more radical repudiation of the functionalization of individual death in the service of a collective project grew out of a revision of Michel Foucault's analysis of modern biopolitics by an array of international theorists, most notably Giorgio Agamben, Roberto Esposito and Achille Mbembe. For Foucault, contemporary biopolitics, which was derived from an earlier development of "biopower," involved the exercise of political rationality or what he called "governmentality" by both state and non-state actors to foster the collective health and lives of the populations they control. Unlike the repressive and negative use of power directed at individuals by the traditional juridical and discursive mechanisms employed by sovereign states, it expresses itself in positive terms and focuses on the flourishing of the species body understood demographically.[32] Propagation, births, life expectancy, disease prevention and sometimes genetic purity are all subjected to regulatory

---

31 Wilfred Owen, "Dulce et Decorum Est," in *The Collective Poems of Wilfred Owen*, ed. C. Day Lewis (New York: New Directions, 1964), p. 55.

32 These concepts were sketchily introduced in work published during Foucault's lifetime only at the end of his first volume of *History of Sexuality*, vol. 1, *The Will to Knowledge*, trans. Robert Hurley (New York: Penguin, 1998), but were developed in his posthumously published lectures at the Collège de France, including "*Society Must Be Defended*": *Lectures at the Collège de France, 1975–1976*, trans. David Macey (New York: Picador, 2003); *Security, Territory, Population: Lectures at the Collège de France, 1977–1978*, trans. David Macey (New York: Picador, 2009); and *The Birth of Biopolitics: Lectures at the Collège de France, 1978–1979*, trans. David Macey (New York: Picador, 2010).

intervention and control, as well as the soft power of hegemonic manipulation based on ever more refined biometrical technologies. Whether in the service of Nazi "racial hygiene," the regulation of carcinogens like nicotine,[33] or, to adopt a more current example, of limiting pandemic infection by mandating vaccinations, the avowed goal of biopolitics is to foster the welfare of populations, not merely affirm the power of the sovereign. It is understood by Foucault, in conformity with his general attitude towards power, as productive and enabling rather than restrictive or constraining.

Foucault had distinguished between a classical version of sovereign biopower whose rationale was "to take life or let live" and a modern biopolitics based on "regularization," which consists in "making live and letting die."[34] Although drawing on Foucault's distinctions, Agamben, Esposito and Mbembe have been more interested in the active and darker agenda of what they called thanatopolitics or necropolitics, which deliberately sought death rather than merely passively let it happen.[35] Bracketing the nuances of their arguments, we can discern a common pattern in their explorations of the more sinister effects of the biopolitical agenda and the differentiated populations it targets. They contend that the mechanisms regulating and managing populations identified by Foucault were not as disentangled from the traditional constraining power of sovereignty as he had assumed. Agamben, in particular, identifies it with a kind of

---

33   Ironically, Nazi racial hygiene was expressed not only in the elimination of "inferior" humans, defined racially or in terms of their disabilities, but also by campaigns against smoking. See Robert N. Proctor, *The Nazi War on Cancer* (Princeton, NJ: Princeton University Press, 1999).

34   Michel Foucault, "Society Must Be Defended," p. 247.

35   Giorgio Agamben, *Homo Sacer: Sovereign Power and Bare Life*, trans. Daniel Heller-Roazen (Stanford, CA: Stanford University Press, 1998); Roberto Esposito, *Bios: Biopolitics and Philosophy*, trans. Timothy Campbell (Minneapolis: University of Minnesota Press, 2008); Achille Mbembe, *Necropolitics*, trans. Stephen Corcoran (Durham, NC: Duke University Press, 2019) and "Necropolitics," *Public Culture* 15: 1 (2002), pp. 11–40; see Stuart J. Murray, "Thanatopolitics: On the Use of Death for Mobilizing Political Life," *Polygraph* 18 (2006), pp. 191–215; and "Thanatopolitics: Reading in Agamben a Rejoinder to Biopolitical Life," *Communication and Critical/ Cultural Studies* 5: 2 (2008), pp. 203–7; and John Troyer, *Technologies of the Human Corpse* (Cambridge, MA: MIT Press, 2020). There are nuanced differences between the two terms—necropolitics, for example, focuses on the unstable condition between life and death suffered by colonized and enslaved people, rather than literal death—but, for our purposes, they are virtually synonymous.

permanent "state of exception," which Carl Schmitt had located only in those moments when the legitimacy of a legal order was undermined. Such a state, he contends, was realized in its most naked form in Nazi concentration camps, where humans were often reduced to the living dead, zombie-like *Muselmänner,* as they were called, before they were literally exterminated. Esposito resisted Agamben's overly broad conclusion that the camps represented a distillation of modernity as a whole, in which "bare life" was robbed of any meaningful dignity. But in his analysis of the role of political "auto-immunity," he also acknowledged the function to which certain segments of the population were condemned as toxic pathogens that had to be destroyed or expelled to maintain the health of the community as a whole.

In this analysis, death becomes more than a regrettable byproduct of defending the nation or the state against its enemies, which can then be heroically recuperated. Wars, genocides, forced migrations, artificially induced famines and the like are deliberate strategies for either actively eliminating populations or callously exposing them to likely death. Eugenics could often justify the ruthless "weeding out" of alleged inferior exemplars of the species. Even when efforts have been made to limit civilian casualties in war and make its violence more "humane," the euphemistic defense of their deaths as "collateral damage" speaks to the necessary role they play in thanatopolitics.[36] These are deaths that are not seen, to borrow the terminology of Judith Butler, as "grievable," unlike those of martyrs in the service of allegedly noble causes.[37] Agamben's *"homo sacer"*—translatable as "accursed man" as well as "sacred man"—was, according to Roman law, someone who can be killed by anyone, but who cannot be the subject of a human sacrifice during a religious ceremony.[38] His life—mere animal *zoe* in Aristotle's

---

36 See Samuel Moyn, *Humane: How the United States Abandoned Peace and Reinvented War* (New York: Farrar, Straus and Giroux, 2021). Although he does not explicitly draw on the theorists we are discussing, his analysis comports with theirs.

37 Judith Butler, *Precarious Life: The Powers of Mourning and Violence* (London: Verso, 2004), p. 32. For a discussion of her contribution to the discourse of thanatopolitics, see Penelope Deutscher, "The Precarious, the Immune, and the Thanatopolitical: Butler, Esposito and Agamben on Reproductive Biopolitics," in *Against Life,* ed. Alistair Hunt and Stephanie Youngblood (Evanston, IL: Northwestern University Press, 2016).

38 The concept has been the focus of considerable controversy. For a recent intervention, which includes consideration of many of the issues and cites the relevant

terminology, rather than full human *bios*—was so bare of social worth that only the intervention of a god could save him. Mbembe argues that well before the invention of concentration camps, enslavement and colonization subjugated stigmatized populations who were forced to hover precariously between life and death. They were excluded from the national or popular community whose symbolically transcendental life could be invoked to compensate for the mortality of the individuals who comprised it, condemned instead to live in a permanent state of exception. The logic of necropolitical abjection can be seen as well in the way other stigmatized groups, for example, gays during the AIDS panic, could be callously excluded from those whose deaths were worthy of being grieved by the community as a whole.[39]

Much more can be said about the implications of these three modes of political engagement with the complexities of human corporeality. Whereas the first two attempt to provide consolations for individual deaths through symbolic transcendence or a dialectical negation of the negation, the third bitterly condemns the ways biopower has served as an excuse for abjecting, indeed often literally eliminating, whole groups deemed pathological or toxic. It is easy to be wary of the first two and sympathize with the victims of the injustices denounced by the third. And yet even in the case of thanatopolitics or necropolitics, there are, I want to argue, certain reasons to be cautious. One was recently revealed in the highly problematic way Giorgio Agamben reacted to efforts to deal with the threat of Covid-19. Arguing in February 2020 that the pandemic was nothing but a hoax artificially created to generate panic and justify an increase in the malevolent power of the state, he magnified the suspicion that thanatopolitics is the hidden agenda of biopolitics into a paranoid rejection of emergency measures to mitigate the spread of the virus.[40] Epidemiology, indeed modern medicine as a whole, Agamben charged, is in the

---

literature, see Pierpaolo Antonelli, "Sacrificing *Homo Sacer*: René Girard Reads Giorgio Agamben," *Forum Philosophicum* 24: 1 (2019), pp. 145–82.

39   See Jin Haritaworn, Adi Kuntsman and Silvia Posocco, eds., *Queer Necropolitics* (London: Routledge, 2012).

40   Giorgio Agamben, "The Invention of an Epidemic," f-origin.hypotheses.org. For a critique, see Benjamin Bratton, *The Revenge of the Real: Politics for a Post-pandemic World* (London: Verso, 2021), chapter 16.

service of strengthening the militarization of society, accelerating its transformation into a concentration camp, and degrading humans to the status of animals.

Agamben's dubious response to the pandemic and conspiratorial attack on those who have sought to contain it should not, of course, be turned into an excuse for rejecting *tout court* the analysis of the dark side of biopolitics powerfully developed by Esposito, Mbembe and others. They have indeed made us all aware of how concern for the health of collective bodies can degenerate into a politics of stigmatization, abjection and sometimes outright elimination of certain classes of people deemed subhuman. Their lives have indeed been rendered "bare," bereft of meaning, dignity and recognition. It is only through their anonymous deaths, which allegedly enable the flourishing of those whose lives are considered valuable, that they gain any worth. We should feel justifiable solidarity with these victims of the darker side of biopolitics, past and present, and resolve to overcome the conditions and attitudes that threaten to create their counterparts in the future.

But it should also be acknowledged that the emphasis on thanato- or necropolitics may distort the ways in which questions of life and death can have political relevance. That is, because its exponents focus entirely on the injuries inflicted on those who are victimized by the dark side of biopolitics, those subjected to violence, suffering and the premature end of life, as well as the callous disregard of society for their misery, they rarely ponder the implications of universal human mortality. Stressing the consequences of the logic of a Schmittian state of exception, in which rules are suspended and death can be dispensed with impunity by authorities outside the law, they turn away from the existential truth that there is no alternative rule to which mortality is an exception, no escape from our shared finitude. Accordingly, they have little to tell us about how politics might respond to the profound challenges presented by this unforgiving reality.

The distinction between *Leib* and *Körper* may, however, allow us to address this issue in a more sober and straightforward way than these other approaches. Foregrounding, as it does, two dimensions of corporeality, it avoids the hierarchical distinction between idealized spirit and base materiality that allows the king's two bodies tradition, and its republican inheritors, to elevate the eternal life of the *corpus mysticum* over the finite mortality of those who temporarily occupy its symbolic position. Resisting the dialectical sublation of death as a negation ultimately negated in a redemptive totalization that turns individual loss into a noble sacrifice in the service of the whole, it acknowledges the unresolvable oscillation between two modes of corporeality, which reciprocally entail each other, but can never fully be integrated. And, by refusing to situate the threat of mortal danger exclusively in a state of exception in which the lives of some are assured by the deaths of others, it acknowledges that to be human, no matter the luck of your circumstances, is to experience both being a lived body and having one that is, as it were, on loan from the objectifying natural forces that will inevitably reclaim it.

How does this help us think about the realm of human endeavor we call politics? First, it makes us wary of those ideologies that justify current suffering, even unto death, through the service it allegedly provides for the survival of the nation, the people, or whatever idealized cause it identifies with eternal life. Here it joins with the critics of thanato- or necropolitics in warning us against the abjection of allegedly toxic pathogens in a healthy body politic. But it goes beyond them in also casting suspicion on the heroization of sacrifices made by members of the hegemonic group, whose immunization against death is being sought. We may, of course, choose to work on behalf of a cause larger than our own self-preservation, but we should avoid imbuing it with the dubious symbolic charge of biological vitality. Honoring the *Leib/Körper* distinction, in which neither is identified with a transcendent version of eternal life, prevents the illegitimate transfer of the necessary function of individual death in the continuing evolution of the biological species to its putative political or ideological surrogates. It makes us wary of the ways in which images of supposedly healthy or beautiful bodies have been allegorized into national or popular symbols of vitality, and often with implicit gender or racial biases to boot.

If acknowledging the equiprimordiality of the distinction helps us avoid the problematic identification of life with a symbolic eternal body, it also may help us confront the various ways in which modern societies grapple with the rule of universal death, rather than the grim exceptions on which thanato- and necropolitics focus. There is, of course, a vast literature addressing this issue, which has culminated in the magisterial "cultural history of mortal remains" called *The Work of the Dead*, which my Berkeley colleague Thomas Laqueur published in 2015.[41] Among this remarkable book's many services is alerting us to the myriad ways humans have resisted attempts, traceable as far back as the Greek philosopher Diogenes, to treat dead bodies as mere carrion, with no claim on our respect or devotion. Although there have been exceptions in which "bare death" is the mirror image of "bare life"—most explicitly, the concentration camps Agamben too hastily turns into a model of modernity in general—even modern secular cultures with diminished faith in a spiritual afterlife continue reverentially to bury the bodies or treat the ashes of the cremated with enormous symbolic respect. Or, at least, they do for those lucky enough to escape anonymous mass graves and pauper funerals.

I have nothing to add to Laqueur's exhaustively researched, imaginatively interpreted account of the cultural work the dead continue to do after they have crossed the threshold. Nor do I want to address the various ways in which modern cultures treat mortal remains and their commemoration, or cope with our fears of human finitude.[42] What I want instead to offer are a few speculations about the way acknowledging our still sentient bodies as *Körper*, vulnerable physical objects which are proleptically haunted by their destinies as corpses, may have political ramifications. Let me begin with a focused, albeit indirect example, the right of "habeas corpus," which goes back in the Anglo-American legal tradition before the Magna Carta, was codified in an act of Parliament in 1679 and then enshrined in Article 1, section 9 of the US Constitution. The term is from medieval Latin and literally means "let you have the body." It guarantees a court's ability to command the physical appearance of a person accused of a crime to determine whether or not his or her detention is lawful. Although the US Constitution does allow it to be suspended in emergencies caused by rebellion or invasion, an extraordinary power exercised only by President Lincoln during the

---

41   Thomas Laqueur, *The Work of the Dead: A Cultural History of Mortal Remains* (Princeton, NJ: Princeton University Press, 2015).

42   The flood of literatures on these issues is unabated. For two interesting recent contributions, which examine them from different perspectives, see Dina Khapaeva, *The Celebration of Death in Contemporary Culture* (Ann Arbor: University of Michigan Press, 2017); and Sam Han, *(Inter)facing Death: Life in Global Uncertainty* (London: Routledge, 2019).

Civil War, it has long remained a cornerstone of any human rights regime.

As the verb "habeas" suggests, this is a "corpus" understood in the objective sense of *Körperhaben* rather than the subjective sense of *Leibsein*, a passive, vulnerable body that needs to be safeguarded against unlawful detention, or even worse, the sufferings of deprivation and torture.[43] Although strictly speaking a legal rather than political right, it acknowledges the importance of protecting individual physical bodies as such, rather than as mere containers of the immortal souls or moral persons who inhabit them. Or, at least, it understands that the latter cannot exist without the former. As a result, it refuses to turn bodies into empty sites for the exercise of discursive and disciplinary power, inscribed through cultural constructions which are cultural all the way down, as was sometimes suggested by Foucault in his discussion of biopower.[44] For, by understanding bodies in their guise of *Körper*, proleptically haunted by their inevitable death, we acknowledge a natural limit to cultural constitution. Politics, for all its efforts to mobilize the human capacity to imbue actions with purpose and turn it into collective will-formation—what Hannah Arendt famously called "acting in concert"—should also honor that limit. Only by doing so can a case be made for the legitimacy of human rights, such as habeas corpus, that resist the absolute power of an idealized popular sovereign without constraints.

A comparable lesson follows from the way in which the concept of the people has been contrasted with that of the population, a distinction whose implications I have tried to spell out elsewhere.[45] Whereas the "population" implies the total number of persons inhabiting a specific location, the "people" can either signify what the Greeks called an "ethnos," an ethnically, nationally or even racially defined community or tribe, or a "demos," the citizens of a polity, who rule it in a democracy.

---

43 It can, of course, be employed ironically, as Hilary Mantel pointed out in naming the second of her trilogy of novels about Thomas Cromwell *Bring Up the Bodies*. Here, it referred to the command given to court officials to bring supposed traitors languishing in the Tower, who were regarded as guilty and thus already as good as dead, to face the court in Westminster for a sham trial.

44 For a critique of this position, see Judith Butler, "Foucault and the Paradox of Bodily Inscriptions," in Welton, ed., *The Body*.

45 Martin Jay, "We, the People, and Us, the Population," *Salmagundi*, no. 210/211 (Spring/Summer, 2021).

Although rarely acknowledged, the distinction roughly maps on to that between *Leib* and *Körper*. That is, the active, purposeful notion of a "people" involved in the determination of its own political destiny tacitly draws on the idea of the body as lived; in fact, it elevates it to the level of a collective actor, an organic body politic, with the goal of, at a minimum, survival and, at a maximum, self-flourishing. The "population," on the other hand, is an enlarged notion of the body as *Körper*, experienced as an extended object in the world, inert and passive, vulnerable to the control of others. It is the body that can be managed for benevolent ends by the administrators of biopolitics and for malevolent ones by rulers who practice thanato- or necropolitics.

Understanding a population as an analog of the body as *Körper* can also lead us to consider the individual bodies of which it is composed in the same way. Doing so will perhaps sensitize us to the precarity of their existence, which is often dependent on the benign use of the power granted to active citizens of a people as a *demos,* those who can exercise the privileges of bodies in the guise of *Leib.* That is, it can expand the sense of "I have a body" beyond the self to include the bodies of others, bodies whose fate we may well hold, as it were, in our hands. Active members of a national community or democratic citizenry have the power, and some would argue the obligation, to protect those who find themselves under their jurisdiction, to care for them rather than exploit them. The relevant alternative may not be between animal *zoe* and human *bios,* one infused with spiritual dignity and the other abjectly reduced to mere life, but rather between two equally valuable modes of human corporeality.[46] *Pace* Agamben, the bleak telos of the concentration camp need not turn every well-intentioned exercise of biopolitics into a sinister thanatopolitics. Get yourself vaccinated, dammit!

Second, because the *Leib/Körper* is not an either/or opposition, but a both/and dialectical imbrication, it reminds those of us who may be active citizens, privileged to call ourselves "the people," that we too share an inevitable fate as finite beings, with inert, physically vulnerable bodies, always in some sense objects in the hands of others. The

---

46 The inadequacy of the Aristotelian distinction is also addressed in Jacques Rancière's critique of Hannah Arendt's understanding of genuine politics being denied to those in the "mere life" category. For a discussion, which cites all the relevant literature, see Andrew Schaap, "Enacting the Right to Have Rights: Jacques Rancière's Critique of Hannah Arendt," *European Journal of Political Theory* 10: 1 (2011).

reciprocal entanglement of the two modes of corporeality means that we are never exclusively one or the other, and that any metaphor of a body politic must contain an acknowledgment of both. That is, the image of a healthy, organic, hierarchically organized vital body as the model for a political community like a state should be replaced with one that also includes the mortal body, the body that less actively lives than passively suffers, the body that inevitably anticipates its future as a corpse. Rather than seeking to avoid confronting this sober truth through all the mechanisms of denial and consolation so imaginatively invented by virtually all cultures since time immemorial, it might be wiser to face it head on and create a politics commensurate with our untotalized, unharmonized, negatively dialectical *Leibkörper*.

Lest this all seem too fuzzy or abstract, I want to finish with a brief glance at one attempt to think historically about the implications of the distinction for politics, which was made by Walter Benjamin in the scattered remarks about the body that can be found throughout his work. As with everything Benjamin wrote, it takes a great deal of hermeneutic acuity and persistence to wrest a coherent argument from his elusive oeuvre, but luckily several cogent efforts have focused on this precise issue. Rebecca Comay, Gerhard Richter and, perhaps most explicitly, Léa Barbisan, have painstakingly unpacked his ruminations on the *Leib/Körper* distinction and its implications for politics.[47] What has come to be called Benjamin's "anthropological materialism," a label that can be traced back to a letter Adorno wrote to him in September 1936,[48] drew on his early encounter with phenomenological theory and continued to inform his later engagement with Marxism. The body in various guises, literal and well as metaphorical, individual as well as collective, his own as well as that of others, is a central concern of *One-Way Street*, *The Origin of German Tragic Drama*, *Moscow Diary* and a number of the other works in which he attempts to compose a physiognomy of modern

---

47 Rebecca Comay, "Benjamin's Endgame," in *Walter Benjamin's Philosophy: Destruction and Experience*, ed. Andrew Benjamin and Peter Osborne (London: Clinamen, 1994); Gerhard Richter, *Walter Benjamin and the Corpus of Autobiography* (Detroit: Wayne State University Press, 2000); and Léa Barbisan, "Eccentric Bodies: From Phenomenology to Marxism—Walter Benjamin's Reflections on Embodiment," *Anthropology and Materialism*, Special Issue no. 1 (2017).

48 Adorno to Benjamin, September 6, 1936, in *Adorno/Benjamin Correspondence*, p. 193.

life. It runs like a red thread through his intricate thoughts on language, images, mimesis, allegory and memory, as well as politics.

Rejecting the vitalist organicism of *Lebensphilosophie* and the total-izing aesthetics of German idealism, Benjamin was alarmed by the ways in which fascism had mobilized the rhetoric of corporeal wholeness and health for sinister purposes. Instead, he sought to valorize the body in ruins, the fragmented, dismembered body, the body available for allego-rization in new combinations. Rather than the site of fully present lived experience, the site of subjective integration, the body he preferred was temporally out of joint, retaining memories of the past and proleptically haunted by—or better put, imbued with faint hopes for—the future. He shared Husserl's sense of the *Körper* as a partial, perspectivally perceived object, writing in a 1918 fragment called "Perception and Body," that "it is highly significant that our own body is in many ways inaccessible to us. We can see neither our face, nor our back, nor our entire head, the primary part of our body."[49] Contrary to Husserl, Scheler and the phenomenological tradition, Benjamin, according to Léa Barbisan, "stretches the relation between *Körper* and *Leib* until it breaks: the body becomes the place where alienness (the object, the world, the outside) penetrates the sphere of the self and deeply disturbs its structure."[50]

But rather than a wholly negative condition to be overcome, it needs to be accepted, even, odd as it may sound, nurtured. As Benjamin put it with his characteristic elusiveness in an unpublished fragment from 1922 or 1923 called "Outline of the Psychophysical Problem": "The content of a life depends on the extent to which the living person is able to define his nature corporeally. In the utter decay of corporeality, such as we are witnessing in the West at the present time, the last instrument of its renewal is the anguish of nature which can no longer be contained in life and flows out in wild torrents over the body. Nature itself is a totality, and the movement into the inscrutable depths of total vitality is fate." But the surrender to fate has its costs: "The representation of total vitality in life causes fate to end in madness. For all living reactivity is

---

49   Walter Benjamin, "Wahrnehmung und Leib," in *Gesammelte Schriften*, vol. 6, ed. Rolf Tiedemann and Hermann Schweppenhäuser (Frankfurt: Suhrkamp, 1991), p. 67; cited both in Richter, *Walter Benjamin and the Corpus of Autobiography*, p. 61, and Barbisan, "Eccentric Bodies," p. 3.

50   Barbisan, "Eccentric Bodies," pp. 3–4.

bound to differentiation, whose preeminent instrument is the body."[51] Significantly, the *Leib* connects man to humanity at large and its mundane history, into which it is absorbed without remainder, while the *Körper* connects man to God, because it is only through the resurrection of individual bodies that the unique worth of each of us, our differentiation from the rest of humankind, might ultimately be realized. For Benjamin—and here he is providing a surprisingly different reading from Kantorowicz and the king's (or people's) two bodies tradition—it is the mortal body, the corruptible body that must die, rather than the allegedly eternal mystical body, that is the real locus of a possible transcendence.

Benjamin's attentiveness to the relationship between the body as *Körper* and mortality is brought to the fore in his ruminations on the central role of death and the corpse in the German *Trauerspiel*, which refuses the consoling catharsis of traditional Greek tragedy and celebrates mortification instead. Rebecca Comay insightfully situates it in his rejection of the Hegelian model of remembrance as *Erinnerung*, in which alienation is overcome through reconciling sublation, in favor of an alternative he calls *Eindenken*. The former involves a *re*-membering, in which "recollection would be precisely the resurrection of the idealized, transfigured body, a body restored to its organic unity and spiritual integrity as a whole." The latter is instead a "re-*membering*" or "the incoherent, multiply situated reawakenings of shattered body parts re-encountering themselves in time and space."[52] This repetitive re-encountering is neither an idealized interiorization of death based on the rhetoric of sacrificial martyrdom nor its foreclosure as utterly outside the closed circle of life, but rather a riposte to both:

> What is ultimately subverted or exceeded is the very opposition (but therefore also the essential reconciliation) of life and death as the final

---

51   Walter Benjamin, "Outline of the Psychophysical Problem," in *Selected Writings*, vol. 1, *1913–1926*, ed. Marcus Bullock, and Michael W. Jennings (Cambridge, MA: Harvard University Press, 1996), p. 396.

52   Comay, "Benjamin's Endgame," p. 255. Benjamin thus opposes what I have called elsewhere his Frankfurt School colleague Herbert Marcuse's neo-Hegelian faith in "anamnestic totalization." See Martin Jay, *Marxism and Totality: The Adventures of a Concept from Lukács to Habermas* (Berkeley: University of California Press, 1984), chapter 7.

horizon of every narrative. Death neither terminates nor is redeemed by the life which it not only ends or "finishes" but in fact marks as radically "finite" and, as such, unfinished. Neither resurrection nor proper burial, neither a spiritualization of death nor its securing as life's antithesis, can now be thought.[53]

Comay may be too hasty here in denying Benjamin's attraction to the idea of resurrection, which we have seen him ponder in his "Outline of the Psychophysical Problem," and to which he will frequently return in extolling the theological belief in "apocatastasis," the ultimate redemption of everyone and everything in the Last Judgment.[54] But she is right to note that, until that end time comes, the body as *Körper* and as corpse serves for Benjamin to resist the consoling fiction of spiritual totalization and unalienated reconciliation. Benjamin's theological terminology here might seem very far away from politics, but it implies a politics that has several intriguing possible implications. First, it undermines the fantasy of a subject-centered politics in which the search for a collective agent able to fashion history intentionally is laid to rest, a fantasy that also has motivated Marxism in many of its more humanist guises. Second, it calls into question the identification of the individual subject with an autonomous ego, fully sovereign in its self-mastery. As Barbisan puts it,

Benjamin stresses the fundamental "eccentricity" of the human being's body, which undermines every attempt to conceive of the body as a closed entity centered on the "self." The body, split between the "lived body" (*Leib*) and the "thing-body" (*Körper*), torn between the *ego* and the world, disrupts the boundaries of the supposedly autonomous

---

53 Comay, "Benjamin's Endgame," p. 267.

54 Benjamin invokes it, for example, in "The Storyteller," in discussing Leskov's debt to Origen. *Illuminations: Essays and Reflections*, ed. Hannah Arendt, trans. Harry Zohn (New York: Schocken, 1969), p. 103; in Convolute N of the Arcades Project, in *Benjamin: Philosophy, Aesthetics, History*, ed. Gary Smith (Chicago: University of Chicago Press, 1989), p. 46; and in discussing Surrealism, which he credits with "the will to apocatastasis ... the resolve to gather again, in revolutionary action and in revolutionary thinking, precisely the elements of the 'too early' and the 'too late' or the first beginning and the final decay." Walter Benjamin, *Arcades Project*, trans. Howard Eiland and Kevin McLaughlin (Cambridge, MA: Harvard University Press, 1999), p. 698.

individual. Benjamin conceives of the revolutionary collective according to this unpresentable model: not as a collective subject but as a collective body—as a plastic entity whose political agency relies on its ability to virtually incorporate everyone and everything.[55]

Finally, by reminding us of the continuity of our bodies as *Körper* with the world of inanimate matter to which we will inevitably return, it diminishes our anthropocentric self-image as the most valuable embodiment of vitality, the crowning species of creation able to lord it over all others. Instead, it restores our link not only with the biosphere as a whole, but with the larger geosphere and hydrosphere that make it possible. Instead of framing the issue of life and death in the terms of the opposition between biopolitics and thanato- or necropolitics, it situates it in a more profound context in which the lament of suffering nature also finds a voice.

To make these ideas a bit more concrete, let me finish by evoking two recent movements, which have had an international impact beyond the boundaries of the America from which they emerged: Occupy and Black Lives Matter. Without venturing an analysis of their complexities or predicting how effective they will ultimately prove, let me point to three aspects of their practice that comport with our larger argument. Unlike many progressive movements in the past, they have never assumed the posture of organic totalization with a hierarchically defined structure and a vanguard leadership. Remaining stubbornly decentralized, locally focused and resolutely undisciplined, they have resisted the search for a historical agent capable of "making" history or relying on its putative representative to act in the name of the whole. In addition, they have adopted the tactic of masses of vulnerable bodies occupying or marching through spaces, rather than *soi-disant* meta-subjects actively attempting to seize power. As such, they tacitly make common cause with the legions of migrants and asylum seekers who also march and occupy spaces, asserting their rights as precarious members of a passive population rather than the active citizens of a people, understood either as a *demos* or *ethnos*.

These are all bodies, we might say, as much in the guise of *Körper* as *Leib*. There is, in fact, a robust literature that claims that the slogan

---

55 Barbisan, "Eccentric Bodies," p. 10.

"black lives matter" should be more precisely rendered as "black bodies matter."[56] While justifiably protesting against the thanato- or necro-political reduction of those bodies to mere vessels for what Agamben would call "bare life," they also defiantly assert the value of even the suffering, vulnerable, disposable bodies that are so reduced. Resisting the consolation that might follow the apotheosis of George Floyd into sacrificial martyr in a just cause, they ask us to face the blunt truth of his meaningless death. Refusing the premature closure provided by the healing process of mourning, they fight to keep the wound open, insisting, as did Walter Benjamin, that apparently interminable melancholy may in the long run prove more redemptive than a shallowly optimistic and hasty suturing of the wound.[57] Without embracing the hopelessness that paralyzes Afro-pessimists at their bleakest, they relocate what W. E. B. DuBois famously called the double consciousness of American Blacks, not in their two souls, but in their two bodies. And in so doing, they help us all understand that through our shared mortality and its anticipation in our experience as *Körper,* all bodies not only matter, but in the end *are* in a profound sense only the matter out of which they are made.

56   See, for example, Daina Ramey Berry, *The Price for Their Pound of Flesh: The Value of the Enslaved, from Womb to Grave, in the Building of the Nation* (Boston: Beacon, 2017). Googling "black bodies matter" reveals a wealth of other efforts to address this issue.

57   See Martin Jay, "Against Consolation: Walter Benjamin and the Refusal to Mourn," in *Refractions of Violence* (New York: Routledge, 2003).

8

Marx and Mendacity: Can There Be a Politics without Hypocrisy?

We are living, the Frankfurt School claimed in its darkest moods, in a Verblendungszusammenhang, a total system of delusion in which imma-nent critique is in danger of losing its leverage. Not only is the distinction between truth and ideology eroding, but so too is the ability to distinguish between truth-telling and lying. As Adorno put it in Minima Moralia, *"Among today's adept practitioners, the lie has long since lost its honest function of misrepresenting reality. Nobody believes anybody, everyone is in the know. Lies are told only to convey to someone that one has no need either of him or his good opinion. The lie, once a liberal means of commu-nication, has today become one of the techniques of insolence enabling each individual to spread around him the glacial atmosphere in whose shelter he can thrive."[1]*

Written during the Second World War, these sentiments may seem even more grimly apposite in our age of "alternative facts," "fake news," "truthi-ness" and the "big lie" of a stolen election. For those appalled by the attri-tion of truth-telling, it may well seem self-evident that the only alternative is a politics of ruthless honesty and utter transparency, in which hypocrisy of any kind is anathema. But, significantly, Adorno begins the aphorism that includes the remarks cited above on a cautionary note: "An appeal to truth is scarcely a prerogative of a society which dragoons its members to

---

1 Theodor W. Adorno, *Minima Moralia: Reflections from Damaged Life*, trans. E. F. N. Jephcott (London: NLB, 1973), p. 30.

own up the better to hunt them down. It ill befits universal untruth to insist on particular truth, while immediately converting it into its opposite."[2] That is, there are moments when the better option, despite the familiar Quaker dictum, is to speak lies, not truth, to power.

There may, in fact, be additional reasons why the demand for absolute veracity may be inherently problematic in that sphere of human affairs we call politics. In a book published in 2010 titled The Virtues of Mendacity: On Lying in Politics, I made an effort to explore their validity. Two years earlier, an invitation to a conference in Santiago, Chile, commemorating the 160th anniversary of Marx's Communist Manifesto allowed me to consider in particular Marx's position on truth and politics.[3] Here I relied, as I was to do in the book, on a number of the points made by Hannah Arendt in her suggestive, if not always fully consistent, essays "Truth in Politics" and "Lying in Politics."[4] One of the other speakers listed on the program was the eminent French Marxist philosopher Alain Badiou, who has defended what he called the "truth procedure" of politics against, among others, Arendt. Alas, he was unable to come, and so the debate I had hoped to generate never really materialized.

The stakes of such a debate would have been high, as they touch on the vexed issue of politics in Marxist theory and practice. One way that it has been understood is by honoring the imperative to integrate the two, so that radical theory always guides emancipatory politics. Badiou's defense of the Leninist model of a vanguard party as the best way to realize this goal was never, however, shared by members of the Frankfurt School, a few random comments notwithstanding.[5] Instead, they more frequently resorted to

---

2   Ibid.

3   The conference "A 160 años del Manifesto Communista nel pensamiento de Marx" was organized by Eduardo Sabrovsky at the Universidad Diego Portales in Santiago, Chile, in November 2008. This essay was first published in Analyse & Kritik: Zeitschrift für Sozialtheorie 37: 1–2 (2015).

4   Hannah Arendt, "Truth in Politics," in The Portable Hannah Arendt, ed. Peter Baehr (New York: Penguin, 2000); "Lying in Politics," in Crises of the Republic (New York: Houghton Mifflin Harcourt, 1972).

5   See, for example, the informal discussion Horkheimer and Adorno conducted in 1956, preserved in notes taken by Gretel Adorno and published as Theodor Adorno and Max Horkheimer, Towards a New Manifesto, trans. Rodney Livingstone (London: Verso, 2011). At one point, Horkheimer floats the possibility of "an appeal for the re-establishment of a socialist party," which Adorno follows by saying "with a strictly Leninist manifesto" (p. 94). But they then admit that there is no concrete social addressee comparable to those mid-nineteenth-century workers of the world Marx had urged to

what Habermas famously called "a strategy of hibernation," in which radical theory itself was deemed by default the only possible praxis until objective conditions changed.

Although they distinguished this position from apolitical resignation while defending the integrity of theory against its pragmatic instrumentalization,[6] it did not satisfy everyone. For in the interim, which is the world in which we live and, if we are lucky, will continue for a long time, the messiness of political practice cannot be avoided. Once we recognize that it cannot be equated with hypocrisy-penetrating truth procedures in which pluralism is sacrificed to the dictates of theoretician-kings, the task of addressing the ambiguous functions of political mendacity can begin. For although not everything is mere opinion, especially in discourses like science, which at their best are grounded in disinterested methods of inquiry, there are no comparable protocols that can sort out the riot of values, worldviews and narratives that compete in the political arena, where the quest for singular truth is more tyrannical than liberating. Although the essay focuses on Alain Badiou and Hannah Arendt, it implicitly offers an immanent critique of what has been called the first generation of the Frankfurt School's "political deficit." But it does so not with the intention of bemoaning their alleged failure to unite Critical Theory with radical politics, but rather to underscore their inattention to the ways in which democratic politics, with all of its imperfections, can flourish.

~

unite: "We do not live in a revolutionary situation, and actually things are worse than ever . . . Any appeal to form a left-wing socialist party," Adorno concludes, "is not on the agenda" (p. 107). Although a few commentators have tried to turn Adorno into a closet Leninist—Horkheimer would defeat even their most imaginative efforts—there is no evidence that he ever considered joining a communist party or was even a fellow traveler of one. After returning to Germany, he was a frequent and unrelenting critic of the GDR and of intellectuals like Lukács who supported the Soviet Union, although it is always possible to speculate that, despite his disdain for the authoritarianism of actually existing Leninist parties and regimes, he secretly supported an ideal version of them. But squaring such a politics with a negative dialectics devoted to the virtues of non-identity and idiosyncrasy is no easy task.

6　See Adorno's defiant essay "Resignation," *Telos*, no. 35, 1978. Written in 1968, when Adorno was taxed by militant German students for betraying the radical goals of Critical Theory, the essay was also a tacit riposte to the more engaged politics of Herbert Marcuse, who sympathized more with the New Left cause. See Theodor W. Adorno and Herbert Marcuse, "Correspondence on the German Student Movement," trans. Esther Leslie, *New Left Review* 1: 233 (January/February 1999).

In 1872, an anonymous attack was launched in the Berlin *Concordia: Zeitschrift für die Arbeiterfrage* against Karl Marx for having allegedly falsified a quotation from an 1863 parliamentary speech by Gladstone in his own Inaugural Address to the First International in 1864. The polemic was written, so it was later disclosed, by the eminent liberal political economist Lujo Brentano.[7] Marx vigorously defended himself in a response published later that year in *Der Volksstaat*, launching a bitter debate that would drag on for two decades, involving Marx's daughter Eleanor, an obscure Cambridge don named Sedley Taylor, and even Gladstone himself, who backed Brentano's version. Finally, Friedrich Engels summed it all up in 1891 in a long pamphlet with all the relevant materials reprinted called *In the Case of Brentano vs. Marx*.[8] I need not tell you whose side he took.

Who got the better of the argument may still be a matter of dispute, although the episode has faded almost entirely from memory and is rarely ever mentioned in the voluminous literature on Marx. I have no interest in reviving it now or trying to adjudicate the claims of either party. What is more important for our purposes is what it reveals of Marx's attitude towards the virtues of truth-telling, which was entirely conventional. That is, for Marx the charge of lying—Brentano called it his "dogged mendacity" in a later round of their exchange—was deeply insulting, and not only because of his personal reputation. It also cast aspersions on the integrity of the movement and cause for which he had devoted his considerable energies. Marx had, after all, excoriated capitalism precisely for its mystification of real social relations, its cloaking of exploitation in the veil of pseudo-equality, its fetishistic focus on parts instead of wholes. Although there is a crucial difference between the deliberate telling of falsehoods and the systemic deceptions produced by ideological mystification leading to "false consciousness," Marx clearly thought he had truth on his side in the exposure of both. While scorning the ahistorical, formal morality that led thinkers like Augustine, Montaigne or Kant to condemn lying categorically, no matter the consequences, Marx nonetheless was deeply invested in developing a theory

---

7   For a biography of Brentano, see James Sheehan, *The Career of Lujo Brentano: A Study of Liberalism and Social Reform in Imperial Germany* (Chicago: University of Chicago Press, 1966).

8   The entire dossier is available at marxists.anu.edu.au.

and nurturing a praxis that would be in the service of the truth and its telling.

Marx was, in fact, so keen on promoting the value of revealing the truth that in *The Communist Manifesto* he gave backhanded praise to the bourgeoisie for having done so inadvertently. That is, although they did not deliberately *say* the truth, they acted in such a way that it was exposed. "The bourgeoisie," he famously wrote, "has torn away from the family its sentimental veil, and has reduced the family relation to a mere money relation . . . man is at last compelled to face with sober senses, his real conditions of life, and his relations with his kind." Tellingly, in *The Manifesto*, he mocked the other German socialists who merely translate French materialist ideas into their still idealist vocabularies, despite the backward conditions in Germany. These were the so-called True Socialists, a term they applied to themselves, but which he used ironically. Although not mentioning them by name, Marx seems to have been talking about Moses Hess and other followers of Ludwig Feuerbach.[9] Their mistake was to locate the truth solely on the level of philosophical abstractions and ignore socioeconomic realities, which cannot yet sustain their utopian hopes. Because they failed to grasp the interaction of surface and depth, they ultimately were in the service of the status quo, which they paradoxically helped maintain by undialectically denouncing the bourgeoisie, the very class that was actually unveiling the deeper truths of capitalism by its economic activities. One meaning of the truth for Marx, then, was revealing what is really the case on all levels of the social whole, probing beneath the surface to show what is hidden by veils, making manifest to the senses what is intelligible to theory. And it is the bourgeoisie, odd as it may sound, which was accomplishing this task in practical rather than theoretical terms in the Europe of 1848.

There is, however, another sense of the idea of truth that Marx distinguished from the mere revelation of what is the case that allows even the bourgeoisie to be its agent. Here, the criterion is not adequacy to what exists, either on the deep or superficial level (or dialectically on both), but rather what can and should be the case in an emancipated or redeemed future. Here, truth is never solely a cognitive or descriptive

9   Warren Breckman, *Marx, the Young Hegelians, and the Origins of Radical Social Theory* (Cambridge: Cambridge University Press, 1999), pp. 196 and 204.

category, but also a normative one. Here the revealers and tellers of the truth are not the bourgeoisie, but the class that will supplant them, the proletariat. Subsequent Marxists well into the present day would repeat this claim, even if often relinquishing the accompanying argument about the class that is its material support. Thus, for example, Theodor W. Adorno would defend what he called "an emphatic" concept of truth and claim that "the idea of scientific truth cannot be split off from that of a true society."[10] Alain Badiou would argue in a similar vein, that "we shall call 'justice' that through which a philosophy designates the possible truth of politics."[11] A skeptical observer like Leszek Kołakowski could even claim that Marx was not really interested in the issue of truth in any traditional sense of the term, but rather only in efficaciously bringing about justice and emancipation: " 'false consciousness' is not regarded by Marx as 'error' in the cognitive sense, just as emancipation of consciousness is not a matter of rediscovering 'truth' in the ordinary sense . . . the difference between false and liberated consciousness is not between error and truth but is a functional difference related to the purpose served by thought in the collective life of mankind."[12] Thus the Marxist notion of ideology was not the same as the more capacious idea of error insofar as the former was not only wrong but also functioned explicitly to maintain the power of the dominant class and did so by concealing the contradictions that obtained in the objective world. Not all errors served this purpose.

The inevitable question that arises from this dual notion of non-ideological truth is as follows: "How can we move from one to the other?" How can truth claims about what is the case both in terms of surface and depth in the complex totality of the present be converted into truth claims about the emancipated, just, egalitarian and free society of the future? Can one easily combine a scientific or theoretical understanding of the present world with an activist and critical anticipation of a future

---

10 Theodor W. Adorno, "Introduction," in *The Positivist Dispute in German Sociology*, trans. Glyn Adey and David Frisby (London: Heinemann,1976), p. 27. The idea of an "emphatic" concept of truth drew on the Platonic notion of *em-phanein* or "entering into appearance." That is, it meant that what was potentially true had to be realized in actuality.

11 Alain Badiou, *Metapolitics*, trans. Jason Barker (London: Verso, 2005), p. 97.

12 Leszek Kołakowski, *Main Currents in Marxism*, vol.1, *The Founders*, trans. P. S. Falla (Oxford: Oxford University Press, 1978), pp. 174–5.

one? It may have been once possible to believe in a Hegelian Marxist version of history in which the emancipated future was latent in the unredeemed present as its determinate negation, a belief that underlay such early twentieth-century Marxist classics as Georg Lukács's *History and Class Consciousness* and Herbert Marcuse's *Reason and Revolution*. Their answer to the neo-Kantian Revisionism of Bernstein, who had radically separated facts from values, the "is" from the "ought," was faith in the totalizing power of the working class to overcome "the antinomies of bourgeois thought" through their revolutionary actions. But today, too much intervening history has happened to allow anyone but the most Pollyannish of Marxists to hold such a view.

In fact, it has been recognized by scholars of Marx's own development that after his initial optimism about the convergence of deep, theoretically available truths and the surface "facts" available to the senses, which reached its crescendo in *The Communist Manifesto* and *The Class Struggles in France* (1850), he too acknowledged a growing gap between the structural truths of capitalism with all of its contradictions and the consciousness of those who were assigned the task of bringing a new truth into the world. As Jerrold Seigel has put it in a section of his biography *Marx's Fate* tellingly called "Society Revealed—and Reveiled," "in *The Eighteenth Brumaire* the metaphors of revelation so triumphantly employed in *The Class Struggles* gave way to veils and masks . . . If *The Class Struggles* had been the history of a nation's increasingly clear revelation of its own inner character, *The Eighteenth Brumaire* presented the image of a country unable to free itself from delusion."[13] Beneath the false surface, to be sure, there still pulsated the class struggle, understood objectively, as well as the contradictions of the capitalist system, but their effects were no longer manifest to the senses of even those who most suffered from them. Subjective consciousness and objective reality were once again at odds. Theory and practice would go their separate ways, at least for a while, and the split between the truth of what was the case, no longer manifest on the surface level as Marx had thought when he wrote *The Communist Manifesto*, would be even more tenuously connected with the truth of an emancipated society of the future. Although Marx hoped they would ultimately reunite, as shown by his

---

13 Jerrold Seigel, *Marx's Fate: The Shape of a Life* (Princeton, NJ: Princeton University Press, 1978), p. 201–2.

evocation of Shakespeare's famous metaphor of the "old mole" of revolution resurfacing after its time underground to be greeted with the praise "well grubbed," there is no indication it will happen any time soon.

Still—and this is the main initial point I want to make—Marx was always beholden to the dual ideals of truth and truthfulness, both in theoretical and practical terms. That is, whether understood as a cognitive proposition about the realities of his day or a normative goal to be achieved in the emancipated society of the future, he valued truth above almost anything else. And, as his outrage over the accusations of Brentano and his supporters demonstrates, he valued no less his own reputation for truth-telling, for truthfulness as a personal badge of honor and a virtue in the struggle to change the world. What, I want to ask, were the consequences of his fierce advocacy of truth and truthfulness for politics? If ideology is somehow the same as "false consciousness," does that mean that any falsehood, deliberately told or not, must equally be condemned as politically regressive? What are the implications of promoting a rigorous politics of truth and truthfulness?

In answering these questions, it is necessary to acknowledge that a politics of truth and a politics of truthfulness should not be simply equated. In fact, as the case of Plato demonstrates, they may just as easily be distinct. That is, Plato had no doubts that his philosophy aimed at the truth, a singular and eternal truth, and that his version of the best political community depicted in *The Republic* and elsewhere was truly what he claimed it to be. But he was also willing to countenance in the rulers of that republic what he called a *gennaion pseudos*, which is normally translated as a "noble lie." In *The Republic* (414b–c), he discusses the myth of the metals originated by Hesiod, in which God had supposedly made the golden race to rule, men of silver to be soldiers and people of iron and bronze workers. For the sake of political stability based on allegedly natural hierarchies of talent and function, Plato allows the telling of such falsehoods—or, if *pseudon* is more liberally translated, fairy tales like those told to children, containing a kernel of symbolic truth—for the masses' own good. Not only is the lie thus told for a noble purpose, but it is also justifiable because it is told by a noble leader, well bred and of superior moral character. According to one commentator, "For Plato it is right for the ruler to tell the *gennaion pseudos* not because it is for the public good—even a crude utilitarian could do this—but rather because of the kind of individual the ruler is . . . they are truth-loving agents and possess noticeably superior intellectual and moral abilities to those of the general population."[14] In other words, the ultimate justification for benign lying is the trust that the ruled have in the virtue and rationality of their rulers, the Guardians of the Republic who have the common good in mind. Like the harmless myths told to children for educational purposes, lies are useful in manipulating the gullible masses to follow their best interests. Ultimately, they will thank the rulers who will reveal their ruse as a necessary expedient in an educational process. Although it is sometimes argued that because *The Republic* candidly reveals the need to tell "noble lies," Plato really intended to expose and diminish their power,[15] this result would follow only if those gullible masses actually read the text, not a likely prospect.

Later in *The Republic*, Plato reasserts the point that rulers will have to concoct "a throng of lies and deceptions for the benefit of the ruled," for example, encouraging marriage only among the elite in order to maximize the chance for the procreation of superior children for the state.[16] Although unfriendly to the "lies" of rhetoricians and artists, whose fictions distract humankind from the truth, Plato accepted the necessity of the political lie as a useful expedient—like the moderate use of poison to cure (a *pharmakon*)—in the effort to secure the just and virtuous republic among men. Or, more precisely, he accepted mendacity only from those who deserved to rule and explicitly denied it to their inferiors. Only experts, after all, know how to use a dose of poison to cure; others are likely to produce disastrous results. Plato, in short, supported a politics of truth, but not of truthfulness, a position that was revived with considerable effect in the past century by Leo Strauss and his neoconservative progeny.

In the Marxist tradition, it was also tacitly sanctioned by Lenin, who never agonized over the tactical use of mendacity to get an edge in a struggle he understood in terms of producing an ultimately just and

---

14   D. Dombrowski, "Plato's 'Noble' Lie," *History of Political Thought* 18: 4 (Winter 1997), p. 575.

15   For this claim, see Catherine and Michael Zuckert, *The Truth about Leo Strauss: Political Philosophy and American Democracy* (Chicago: University of Chicago Press, 2006), p. 131.

16   Plato, *The Republic*, 459c–460d.

emancipated society. As illustrated by the very name of Bolshevism, deception was a viable tool in that cause. As is well known, the name "Bolshevik" was adopted during a controversy within the Russian Social-Democratic Party in 1903. The word "Bolshevik" (from *bolshe*, meaning more) meant one of the majority, whereas "Menshevik" (from *menshe*, meaning less) denoted one of the minority. At the 1903 party convention, however, the majority of the delegates were later called "Mensheviks," while the minority arrogated for themselves the name "Bolsheviks." This reversal of meaning came about by accident when the Jewish Socialist Bund briefly left the hall, leaving the rump with Lenin's faction momentarily in control. This opportunity was enough for the minority permanently to seize the "Bolshevik" label, tacitly justified by the faith that in the future the truth would correspond to what was then not the case.

In contrast, modern descendants of the sophists decried by Plato as being against both truth and truthfulness, such as Hannah Arendt, have argued against the dangers of believing either could support a healthy version of politics. Let us pause with her argument before returning to the implications of Marx's politics of truth and truthfulness. Arendt was a committed pluralist, valorizing different opinions over coercive knowledge or theoretical certainty, especially in the realm of politics. She decried the authoritarian Platonic fantasy of an "ideocracy,"[17] ruled by the idea of the Good, in favor of an endless Socratic dialogue among contesting beliefs. "The search for truth in the *doxa*," she warned, "can lead to the catastrophic result that the *doxa* is altogether destroyed, or that what had appeared as revealed is an illusion . . . Truth therefore can destroy *doxa*; it can destroy the specific political reality of the citizen."[18] Whereas Plato believed in natural hierarchy, she was a fervent defender of the egalitarian premises of democracy produced in the artificial space of politics, a space between men called "the world," not inherent in them prior to the creation of that space. Whereas he argued that rulership was the essence of "the political," she replied that it was instead "action and speech." Privileging good governance, she argued, was a mistaken

---

17   Hannah Arendt, *The Promise of Politics*, ed. Jerome Kohn (New York: Schocken, 2005), p. 11.

18   Ibid., p. 25.

extrapolation from the private household to the public realm. And, while she preferred dialogic agonism to monologic uniformity, she believed, *pace* Carl Schmitt, that men "acting in concert"[19] could nonetheless overcome the eternal antagonism of "friend and foe," while never, to be sure, reaching a universal consensus abolishing all differences of opinion and value.

In *The Human Condition*, first published in 1958, Arendt commented on the effect of the loss of certainty about the truth in the modern age, which "ended in a new, entirely unprecedented zeal for truthfulness— as though man could afford to be a liar only so long as he was certain of the unchallengeable existence of truth and objective reality, which surely would survive and defeat all his lies."[20] "It certainly is quite striking," she continued in a footnote, "that not one of the major religions, with the exception of Zoroastrianism, has ever included lying as such among the mortal sins. Not only is there no commandment: Thou shalt not lie (for the commandment: Thou shalt not bear false witness against thy neighbor, is of course of a different nature), but it seems as though prior to puritan morality nobody ever considered lies to be serious offenses."[21] In *On Revolution*, which appeared in 1963, she discussed the role played by the campaign against hypocrisy during the French Revolution, whose target was the corruption of the ancien régime court: "It was the war against hypocrisy that transformed Robespierre's dictatorship into the Reign of Terror . . . if it became boundless, it did so only because the hunt for hypocrites is boundless by nature."[22] Although Arendt recognized the dangers of hypocrisy, she warned that the ruthless quest to purge it from the public realm, the insistence on tearing away all masks to reveal the "true self," had the effect of dissolving the distinction between the natural self and the public *persona*, a distinction—based on the theatrical tradition of

---

19   The phrase, she noted, was originally Edmund Burke's. Ibid., p. 127.

20   Arendt, *The Human Condition* (Garden City, NY: Doubleday, 1958), p. 253. In calling the zeal for truthfulness "unprecedented," she was clearly unaware of the tradition of the *parrhesiastes* later discussed by Foucault.

21   Ibid., p. 369. This is a very odd claim to make for someone who had written her 1929 dissertation on Augustine (*Love and Saint Augustine*, ed. by Joanna Vecchiarelli Scott and Judith Chelius Stark [Chicago: University of Chicago Press, 1996]), but it shows Arendt's general distrust of the deontological prohibition of lying under all circumstances.

22   Arendt, *On Revolution* (New York: Viking, 1965), p. 95.

dramatis personae—that had provided legal protections unwisely abandoned in the hunt for absolute transparency.[23]

The same suspicion of unqualified truthfulness animated her two later essays on the theme, "Truth in Politics" of 1967 and "Lying in Politics" of 1971.[24] The first of these begins with a "commonplace" assertion:

> No one has ever doubted that truth and politics are on rather bad terms with each other, and no one, as far as I know, has ever counted truthfulness among the political virtues. Lies have always been regarded as necessary and justifiable tools not only of the politician's or the demagogue's but also of the statesman's trade.[25]

The first justification for lying in politics Arendt considered is that which sees politics in terms of means and ends, the consequentialist position that has often been counterposed to a deontological one by, for example, Benjamin Constant in his debate with Kant.[26] From this point of view, it may seem that "lies, since they are often used as substitutes for more violent means, are apt to be considered relatively harmless tools in the arsenal of political action."[27] In other words, if survival is the goal, then lying might be justified. Arendt, however, quickly distanced herself from this position, noting that no society can last for long that lacks a reverence for the truth: "No permanence, no perseverance in existence, can even be conceived of without men willing to testify to what is and appears to them because it is."[28]

Following a brief discussion of the conflict between truth-telling and politics in Plato and Hobbes, Arendt distinguished rational truths—those of mathematics, science and philosophy—from factual truths, arguing that "although the politically most relevant truths are factual,

---

23   For a discussion of her ambivalence concerning masks and full unmasking, see Leora Bilsky, "Citizenship as Mask: Between the Imposter and the Refugee," *Constellations* 15: 1 (March 2008).

24   See note 4.

25   Arendt, "Truth in Politics," p. 545.

26   The relevant documents and commentaries on them can be found in Georg Geismann and Hariolf Oberer, *Kant: Das Recht der Lüge* (Würzburg: Königshausen and Neumann, 1986).

27   Arendt, "Truth in Politics," p. 546.

28   Ibid., p. 547.

the conflict between truth and politics was first discovered and articulated with respect to rational truth."[29] The Greeks, she argued, had been more concerned to contrast rational truth with either error or ignorance, in the case of science, or opinion and illusion, in the case of philosophy, than with outright lies. "Only with the rise of Puritan morality, coinciding with the rise of organized science, whose progress had to be assured on the firm ground of the absolute veracity and reliability of every scientist, were lies considered serious offenses."[30]

The crucial issue for the political realm is not that of rational truth, which is monologic and hostile to plurality, but factual truth, which involves other people and is dependent on testimonials and witnessing. Facts and opinions are thus both in the political realm. But, ultimately, there is a tension between them, for "all truths—not only the various kinds of rational truth but also factual truth—are opposed to opinion in their *mode of asserting validity*. Truth carries with it an element of coercion, and the frequently tyrannical tendencies so deplorably obvious among professional truthtellers may be caused less by a failing of character than by the strain of habitually living under a kind of compulsion."[31] Politics always keeps open the possibility of future persuasion, whereas truth demands to be recognized once and for all. Thus, "seen from the viewpoint of politics, truth has a despotic character,"[32] which makes both tyrants who see it as competition and governments based on consent uneasy about it. The reason truth is problematic for the latter, Arendt averred, is that factual truth, like rational truth, "peremptorily claims to be acknowledged and precludes debate, and debate constitutes the very essence of political life. The modes of thought and communication that deal with truth, if seen from the political perspective, are necessarily domineering; they don't take into account other people's opinions, and taking these into account is the hallmark of all strictly political thinking."[33] Although what Kant had called "enlarged mentality" meant that other opinions can be taken into account, the goal of a single truth is counter-political. Any attempt to discover and follow a singular ethical position will also spell disaster for politics. Democracy can only

29   Ibid., p. 549.
30   Ibid.
31   Ibid., p. 555.
32   Ibid.
33   Ibid., p. 556.

thrive, Arendt continued, when this quest is abandoned. Thus, although the Declaration of Independence spoke of "self-evident truths," it prefaced the assertion of their self-evidence by saying "*We hold* these truths to be self-evident," which implied that "equality, if it is to be politically relevant, is a matter of opinion, and not 'the truth.' "[34] Even Jefferson tacitly admitted that he was basing the Declaration on opinion, not truth.

There is also a positive implication that one can draw from the role of mendacity in politics, which is connected to the fundamental principle of "the political" for Arendt: the power to act, to interrupt the apparent causality of fate and start a new chain of consequences, a new narrative of meaning. Lying, she argued, "is clearly an attempt to change the record, and as such it is a form of *action* . . . While the liar is a man of action, the truthteller, whether he tells rational or factual truth, most emphatically is not."[35] Whereas the truthteller often tries to accommodate the cause of truth to the interests of the collective, "the liar, on the contrary, needs no such doubtful accommodation to appear on the political scene; he has the great advantage that he always is, so to speak, already in the midst of it. He is an actor by nature; he says what is not so because he wants things to be different from what they are—that is, he wants to change the world."[36] Truth-telling is thus in a fundamental sense conservative, preserving what is the case, except in those instances—and here totalitarian polities are implied—when daily life is as a whole a lie.

There is, however, an important distinction between traditional political lies, told by diplomats and statesmen, and modern ones, most explicitly employed by totalitarian regimes. Whereas the former involved secrets or intentions, "modern political lies deal efficiently with things that are not secrets at all but are known to practically everybody. This is obvious in the case of rewriting contemporary history under the eyes of those who witnessed it, but it is equally true in image-making of all sorts."[37] Because the modern lie harbors a certain violence, it has a powerful destructive force: "The difference between the traditional lie

---

34   Ibid., p. 560.
35   Ibid., p. 563 (italics in original).
36   Ibid.
37   Ibid., p. 564.

and the modern lie will more often than not amount to the difference between hiding and destroying."[38] The latter—and here Arendt was talking about the "Big Lie" of totalitarianism—threatens to become an entirely new "reality," which often fools the teller himself. In fact, self-deception, she argued, is fundamental to the modern lie, in which even the liar is caught up in the falsehood. Although the spread of global communication networks makes it hard to sustain the "Big Lie" for very long, there is a danger in our losing our bearings in a reality whose ground is not easy to ascertain.

There is, however, so Arendt continued, a basic difference about lies concerning the past and those that involve the future. Only the latter can be genuinely changed by lies: "Not the past—and all factual truth, of course, concerns the past—or the present, insofar as it is the outcome of the past, but the future is open to action."[39] Such action can only take place against the relatively stable background of a past that is stubbornly factual. But, ultimately, there is a conflict between the imperative to tell the truth and the realm of politics, because the former is monologic rather than dialogic: "Outstanding among the existential modes of truth-telling are the solitude of the philosopher, the isolation of the scientist and the artist, the impartiality of the historian and the judge, and the independence of the fact-finder, the witness, and the reporter."[40] Although there are public institutions, like the judiciary and the university, whose telos is the truth and whose impartial findings impinge on the public realm, it is necessary to acknowledge that such a boundary does exist. If we examine politics only from the external perspective of truth-telling, Arendt warned, we will miss what makes politics so valuable in itself: "the joy and the gratification that arise out of *being* in company with our peers, out of acting together and appearing in public, out of inserting ourselves into the world by word and deed, thus acquiring and sustaining our personal identity and beginning something entirely new."[41] However much we may try to hold the realm of the political to the high moral standards of the truth-teller, however much we may want to resist the modern totalitarian destruction of even factual

---

38 Ibid., p. 565.
39 Ibid., p. 569.
40 Ibid., pp. 570–1.
41 Ibid., p. 574 (italics in original).

truth by the "Big Lie," "it is only by respecting its own borders that this realm, where we are free to act and to change, can remain intact, preserving its integrity and keeping its promises."[42] In short, while it would be disastrous to politicize everything, it would be no less a loss to human freedom to extirpate the uncertain realm of opinion, rhetoric, and, yes, mendacity that we call "the political."

The upshot of Arendt's complicated animadversions on lying in politics was that there were benign and injurious versions of it. When it was done by rulers who thought they were in command of a rational, absolute truth and were able to exercise their will over the contingent facts, it could lead to disaster. When it tried to create an entirely alternative world, it came up against the resistance of reality, especially that of past facts, and undermined the trust necessary to "act in concert." But when lying was a weapon in the endless struggle of plural opinions, in which there was no strong claim to a singular truth and rhetoric rather than calculation prevailed, Arendt praised it as an expression of imagination, action, even freedom to change the world. In the service of a counterfactual denial of what is, she speculated, it might point to an alternative world of what might be. Whereas the "Big Lie" was an expression of man in his guise as *homo faber*, the fabricator of a world that was like a finished object, more modest lies were the sign of man as free actor in which the world was still open to change.[43] As such, they were inextricably bound up with the essence of "the political," as Arendt defined it, the arena in which monologic truth and coercive reason were tyrannical intruders. In moderation and within the boundaries of "the political," mendacity was thus not, for Arendt, an unequivocal evil to be denounced. Indeed, as the case of the anti-hypocritical Robespierre and the Terror showed, the wholesale denunciation of it might well produce worse results than its opposite.

In so arguing, Arendt was setting herself not only against the Platonic defense of a politics of truth but not truthfulness, but also against Marx's

---

42 Ibid.

43 For an insightful discussion of this distinction in Arendt, see Vincenzo Sorrentino, *Il Potere Invisibile: Il Segreto e la Menzogna in Politica Contemporanea* (Molfetta: Dedalo, 1998), p. 115. For another treatment of the ways in which certain lies function to change the future in a positive way, see Benedict Carey, "I'm Not Lying, I'm Telling a Future Truth. Really," *New York Times*, May 6, 2008, p. D5. He argues that exaggerations in self-presentation are often indications of a plan for improving the self.

politics of truth and truthfulness. A spirited defense of his position against her argument was mounted in Alain Badiou's 1998 *Abregé de métapolitique* (English translation *Metapolitics*), to which I want to devote the remainder of this essay. Occasioned by the 1991 French translation of Arendt's lectures on Kant's political philosophy, edited by Myriam Revault d'Allonnes, Badiou's critique is directed against the claim that "politics is anything but a truth procedure."[44] In so believing, Arendt, he charges, is a modern-day sophist, ultimately dedicated to promoting conventional parliamentary politics. He vigorously rejects her contention that the quest for truth is coercive and shuts off debate, arguing instead that "a singular truth is always the result of a complex process in which debate is decisive. Science itself began—with mathematics—with the radical renunciation of every principle of authority."[45] There are, he argues, no special rights for falsity and lying. Although debate is essential to politics, Badiou continues, Arendt is wrong in her lectures on Kant to privilege post facto judgment on the part of the spectator rather than the active creativity of the participant. "Debate is political," he argues, "only to the extent that it crystallizes in a decision." Voting as a way to reach that decision, Badiou then claims, is insufficient, as majority opinion has very little to do with establishing the truth: "If our knowledge of planetary motion relied solely on suffrage as its protocol of legitimation, we would still inhabit a geocentric universe."[46] There is no simple passage from the subjectivity of judgment, however much based on the weighing of evidence and the application of reason, to the objectivity of the truth. There is no way to go from the diversity of opinion to a unified consensus about what is true. In fact, the very idea of a consensus is problematic, Badiou argues, because it is based on a flawed notion of communicability, which "suggests that the plurality of opinions is sufficiently wide-ranging to accommodate difference. And yet everyone knows from experience that this is inaccurate, and that there is no place for debating *genuinely* alternative opinions, which at best are subject to dispute."[47] This limited

---

44 Badiou, *Metapolitics*, p. 12. Arendt's posthumously published lectures appeared in English as *Lectures on Kant's Political Philosophy*, ed. Ronald Beiner (Chicago: University of Chicago Press, 1982).

45 Badiou, *Metapolitics*, p. 14.

46 Ibid., p. 15.

47 Ibid., p. 18 (italics in original).

version of politics works to exclude extreme positions from discussion, for instance (and these are his examples), anti-Semitism or Nazism. The result is a politics defined narrowly as "the name of those judgments which, regulated by the share of the common, resist evil, i.e. the destruction of this share."[48] In contrast, Badiou offers a politics that is never consensual, located in the actions of actors not the judgments of spectators, and singular rather than pluralist. Not surprisingly, he exalts figures like Saint-Just and Robespierre, the incorruptible purists who are anathema to the Arendt of *On Revolution*. "The essence of politics," he concludes, "is not the plurality of opinions. It is the prescription of a possibility in rupture with what exists."[49]

Whether Badiou's characterization of Arendt's position is valid is not the issue here, although it should be mentioned that she was a supporter—as is Badiou himself—of councils and not of parliaments, the primacy of parties or the ethical state; that she advocated action over spectatorship in all of her work prior to her last lectures on Kant; that she emphasized the importance of the radically new in politics through her category of "natality"; and that she never promoted universal rational consensus as even a counterfactual telos in the manner, say, of Habermas. To provide a more accurate reading of Arendt's argument is, however, a task for another time. Our focus instead is now on the question of the role of truthfulness and the quest for truth in the realm of the political. Badiou, whose position I take to be consistent with Marx's, and Arendt represent diametrically opposed positions. By stressing the roles of judgment, opinion and plurality, so Badiou charges, modern day sophists raise falsity above truth and deny politics its capacity to challenge the status quo. By seeking a singular, univocal truth, Arendt claims to the contrary, philosophers who want to overcome opinion and judgment end up imposing their theoretical utopias on the messiness of the world and become unwitting allies of political tyranny. For Badiou, politics involves purification, ridding the world of hypocrisy, ideology and corruption; for Arendt, the most dangerous hypocrisy is practiced by those political actors who loudly proclaim their total honesty and say they are only serving the universal good, a good that is revealed to them by truth procedures, but who in fact represent partial interests instead.

---

48   Ibid., p. 21.
49   Ibid., p. 24.

Perhaps the most fundamental distinction between the two positions concerns the location of a normative notion of politics, whether
it be called "the political" or in French "*le politique*" or mere politics or
"*la politique*." For Arendt, the critical arena is the subjective or intersubjective one, whether it be understood in terms of post facto judgment or creative action, in which the crucial distinction is between
truthfulness and mendacity. For Badiou, that level is mere ephemeral
surface, the level of opinion, judgment, interpretation, meaningful-
ness and the like. For him, the critical arena is the deeper level of truth,
whose opposite is error not lying. Thus, as we have seen, he is able to
mobilize the time-honored critique of psychologism, made by Frege,
Husserl and a host of others, which claims that the truths of logic or
mathematics are independent of the beliefs of those who may or may
not hold them. Thus $2+2=4$, no matter what anyone may think. Or, to
repeat Badiou's example of false beliefs that contradict ontological
truths, "If our knowledge of planetary motion relied solely on suffrage
as its protocol of legitimation, we would still inhabit a geocentric
universe." Politics is thus what he calls a "truth procedure," a difficult
concept to parse, but which involves a rupture with the status quo,
somehow contributing to an egalitarian, universal, just alternative. In
other words, to return to our initial point about Marx's dual notion of
truth, it is not adequation to what is, either on the level of appearance
or of essence, but of what can and should be, the true society of the
future.

Significantly, Badiou concedes that "we know that the overwhelming
majority of empirical instances of politics have nothing to do with truth.
They organize a mixture of power and opinions. The subjectivity that
animates them is that of demand and *ressentiment*, of the tribe and the
lobby, of electoral nihilism and the blind confrontation of communities."[50]
Badiou wants to purify politics of this messy realm of compromise and
mendacity, moving rapidly to those admittedly rare and exceptional
moments (or to use his terminology, "events"), in which a more redemptive version of politics as introducing truth into the world can manifest
itself. Although often proclaiming his allegiance to the Platonist philosophical tradition, which he juxtaposes to sophistry in any form, Badiou
does not to my knowledge affirm Plato's recommendation of "noble lies,"

---

50   Ibid., p. 97.

even told by well-intentioned rulers.[51] His idealized figure of the "militant" is thus far closer to the incorruptible Robespierre or Saint-Just than it is to Machiavelli. As in the case of the Marx of *The Communist Manifesto*, he revels in a politics of revelation, of unhiddenness, which in particular reveals the state as the repressive apparatus that he claims it always inherently is. Appropriately, he cites Marx's admiration in *The Manifesto* of capitalism's capacity to unveil what is hidden in previous socioeconomic systems.[52]

I am not going to try to spell out how politics as a truth procedure works for Badiou, as I am not sure I fully understand all of its complexities. Peter Hallward, in his patient and sympathetic account of Badiou's philosophy, points out that Badiou is aware of the dangers of seeking the whole truth or trying to say the truth about the totality, thus substantializing what should always remain unnamed. He cites Badiou's maxim "the ethics of a truth derive entire from a sort of restraint with respect to its powers."[53] Even Badiou's hostility to sophism does not lead to a plea for its ruthless eradication, although the main thrust of his argument is to distinguish radically between truth and mere opinion or judgment.

But what Hallward also acknowledges is that Badiou lacks any clear-cut mechanism for finding a way to produce the truth when there is disagreement among those asserting they have found it. Although he scolds Arendt for saying that arriving at the truth is always the result of deliberation, not the short-circuiting of it, Badiou's hostility to communication and compromise does not inspire much confidence in the nature of that deliberation, nor do his historical models, Saint-Just, Lenin and Mao. The history of Marxism in general and Leninism in particular is one in which discipline often outweighs open-endedness and enforced certainty trumps the preservation of diverse opinions. Once the expected practical confirmation of the truth of theory was no longer plausible with the withering away of the proletariat, the way was open for that coercive imposition of singular truths against which Arendt warned. It is perhaps here that the alternative acknowledgment

---

51 For a discussion of his debt to Platonism, which ignores the issue of "noble lies," see Peter Hallward, *Badiou: A Subject to Truth* (Minneapolis: University of Minnesota Press, 2003), pp. 5–6.

52 Badiou, "Politics and Philosophy," interview with Peter Hallward, *Angelaki* 3: 3 (1998), p. 120.

53 Hallward, *Badiou*, p. 265.

of the potentially positive role of mendacity in politics may be worth considering, especially if it is uncoupled from the Platonic tradition of the "noble lie."

To spell out all the ways in which this role might be played is beyond the compass of this essay, although curious readers can find a more substantial account in *The Virtues of Mendacity: On Lying in Politics*.[54] Let me focus here on just two of its arguments. The first concerns the role of hypocrisy in building coalitions. Even in a self-consciously pluralist polity that eschews the goal of homogeneity and valorizes agonism, there is often a fictional quality to more fragile coalitions of partners, whose interests and values may well clash, despite their protestations of unity. As the American political theorist Ruth Grant has noted, building solidarity requires a certain dissembling about the basis on which it is built. Machiavelli and Rousseau were correct in noting the inevitability in politics of dependency on creating coalitions of partners with different interests. "Politics," she argues, "is characterized by relationships of mutual need among parties with conflicting interests. To enlist the support of the other party requires flattery, manipulation, and a pretense of concern for his needs."[55] That is, because there is no fully homogenous majority in which a total congruence of values and interests creates complete solidarity, it is necessary to build coalitions on the basis, at least in part, of imagined, fictional commonalities. This involves inevitable hypocrisy, which means the public proclamation of shared values and interests combined with a private acknowledgment of their hollowness. Often this end requires the invocation of high-minded ideals. "Machiavelli and Rousseau," she explains, "appreciate the necessity of political hypocrisy, which is to say, they appreciate the importance of appeals to genuine public moral principles. Hypocrisy requires moral pretense, and that pretense is necessary because politics cannot be conducted solely through bargaining among competing particular interests."[56] Moral values, such as the proscription of lying, can therefore neither be abandoned, nor fully observed. For, as Rochefoucauld famously remarked, "Hypocrisy is the homage vice pays to virtue."

---

54   Martin Jay, *The Virtues of Mendacity: On Lying in Politics* (Charlottesville: University of Virginia Press, 2010).

55   Ruth W. Grant, *Hypocrisy and Integrity: Machiavelli and the Ethic of Politics* (Chicago: University of Chicago Press, 1997), p. 13.

56   Ibid., p. 14.

In democracies, in particular, where fragile coalitions need to be created to avoid coercive minority rule, the function of hypocrisy is especially important, despite the rationalist hope that the better argument can rally disparate factions around the common interest. That hope is not entirely misplaced, but it cannot be fully realized. The liberal faith in trust in a pluralist society is not enough to overcome the stubborn persistence of real differences in values, passions and interests. The wholesale moralistic condemnation of hypocrisy can in fact mask a partial interest that pretends to be a universal one, and therefore has the potential to employ violence to enforce its will on others. "Political relations," Grant argues tacitly against both Schmitt and Habermas, "are neither enmities nor friendships but friendly relations sustained among nonfriends."[57] As such, they require the fiction of greater common interest and values than is actually the case.

A parallel argument based on the often unacknowledged social underpinnings of political life is made by the political theorist Judith Shklar in her discussion of hypocrisy in *Ordinary Vices*: "The paradox of liberal democracy is that it encourages hypocrisy because the politics of persuasion require, as any reader of Aristotle's *Rhetoric* knows, a certain amount of dissimulation on the part of all speakers ... The democracy of everyday life, which is rightly admired by egalitarian visitors to America, does not arise from sincerity. It is based on the pretense that we must speak to each other as if social standings were a matter of indifference in our views of each other."[58] That is, we dutifully observe the fiction that egalitarian blindness to distinction is already a reality, rather than a desideratum to be sought, albeit never fully achieved. To the extent that democracy is always a condition to come rather than a state of being already realized, we cannot avoid a certain duplicity—and perhaps a necessary and even healthy one—in our claim that we live in one in the present.[59] Moreover, as David Runciman notes, "any politics founded on the idea of equality will produce politicians of a type with

---

57   Ibid., p. 175.

58   Judith N. Shklar, *Ordinary Vices* (Cambridge, MA: Harvard University Press, 1984), pp. 48 and 77.

59   It is, of course, no less the case that reality cannot lag too far behind the fiction without the situation deteriorating into a sham. As the case of the "democratic republics" of Communist Eastern Europe demonstrated, there has to be a popular belief in the approximation of the claim to the truth to avoid wholesale cynicism.

the people they rule, and yet recognizably different, given the fact that they also have to rule them. All political leaders in these circumstances will need to put on the appropriate mask that allows them to sustain this tricky double act."[60] In the place of the king's two bodies, we have the president's two faces, as brilliantly exemplified by the figure of George W. Bush, at once the privileged scion of a powerful eastern political dynasty and the "good-ole-boy" Texan with plebian tastes and the sensibility of a frat boy.

The second major argument for the political value of mendacity concerns the distinction between normal lying and what is often called the "Big Lie." The latter has, of course, come to be identified with totalitarianism and its attempt to create entirely imaginary worlds that defy any factual disruption, despite the irony that the term was initially used by Hitler in *Mein Kampf* to denounce those who had claimed Germany lost the First World War on the battlefield rather than being "stabbed in the back" at home. As early as the 1938 publication of *Au pays du grand mensonge* by the Croatian anti-Stalinist communist Ante (Anton) Ciliga, the Soviet Union was damned for its systematic distortion of the truth.[61] In his 1945 essay "The Political Function of the Modern Lie," Alexander Koyré, the Russian-born philosopher and historian of science then in American exile, contended that "modern man—*genus* totalitarian— bathes in the lie, breathes the lie, is in the thrall to the lie every moment of his existence . . . The totalitarian regime is founded on the *primacy of the lie.*"[62] Although one can, of course, distinguish between Stalinism and Marxism, that insistence on both truth and truthfulness, which we have seen in *The Communist Manifesto* and Marx's defense against the charge of mendacity leveled by Lujo Brentano, may have inadvertently abetted the connection. Politics as a "truth procedure," *pace* Alain Badiou, may be an oxymoron.

For, ironically, the mirror image of the "Big Lie" may well be the ideal of "Big Truth," the absolute, univocal truth, which silences those who disagree with it. Both are the enemy of the pluralism of opinions and the

---

60   David Runciman, *Political Hypocrisy: The Mask of Power, from Hobbes to Orwell and Beyond* (Princeton, NJ: Princeton University Press, 2008), p. 43.

61   The book appeared in English as *The Russian Enigma*, trans. Fernand G. Renier, Anne Cliff, Margaret and Hugo Dewar (London: Labour Book Service, 1940).

62   Alexander Koyré, "The Political Function of the Modern Lie," *Contemporary Jewish Record* 8: 3 (June 1945), p. 291 (italics in original).

unmuted clash of values and interests. Instead, it may be healthier to
foster lots of little countervailing lies, or at least half-truths, as well as the
ability to test and see through them, rather than hold out hope for
ending mendacity once and for all. It may well be wise to beware the
politician who loudly proclaims his own purity of intention and refusal
ever to lie, the paragon of authenticity who damns all his opponents as
opportunists or worse. This is not a brief for cynicism or immorality, nor
a justification of winning "by any means necessary," just a recognition
that politics will never be a fib-free zone of authenticity, integrity, transparency and righteousness. And maybe that is, ultimately, a good thing.

Acknowledgments

As in *Splinters in Your Eye,* a collection of my essays on the Frankfurt School Verso published in 2020, I find myself once again excusing the insufficiency of these acknowledgments by falling back on earlier opportunities to thank the myriad friends, colleagues, institutions, benefactors and family members who made them possible. For, truth be told, they would not have come into existence without the encouragement, support and criticism generously given to my more than half-century of efforts to recount and interpret the history and intellectual legacy of the Frankfurt School. In fact, to a certain extent, the essays in both collections may well seem to be attempts to revise the doctoral dissertation I completed in 1971, in the vain hope of finally getting it right. What makes this characterization inexact, however, is that they were all generated by kind invitations to think in new ways about the legacy of Critical Theory, which goes well beyond the types of questions that might have been posed a half century ago.

The first chapter, "1968 in an Expanded Field: The Frankfurt School and the Uneven Course of History," was written in response to an invitation by Rainer Forst to talk on the fiftieth anniversary of 1968 to the "Excellenzcluster" of the Goethe University in Frankfurt on the "Herausbildung der normativen Ordnung." It was then published, thanks to John Rundell, in *Critical Horizons* 21: 2 (May 2020). Chapter 2, "Adorno and the Role of Sublimation in Artistic Creativity and Cultural Redemption," resulted from an invitation by Peter E. Gordon, my former doctoral student at Berkeley, who has blossomed into one of the leading historians of Critical Theory in his own right. It was solicited for a volume dedicated to Adorno's *Aesthetic Theory* and marking its fiftieth anniversary. Appropriately, it appeared in *New German Critique* 143 (August 2021), the journal that has done more than any other to bring Adorno to an anglophone audience. The third chapter, "Blaming the Victim? Arendt, Adorno and Erikson on the Jewish Responsibility for Anti-Semitism," was prepared for a conference on "Arendt and Anti-Semitism" at the Yale Program for the Study of Anti-Semitism in 2018, at the invitation of Maurice Samuel and Adam Stern. This is its first publication. Chapter 4, "*The Authoritarian Personality* and the Problematic Pathologization of Politics," was generated by an invitation to another Yale Program for the Study of Anti-Semitism conference, this one on "The Relevance of *The Authoritarian Personality*," organized by Christina Gerhardt, Kirk Wetters, and Robyn Marasco in 2020. It was published in *Polity* 4: 1 (January 2022).

Chapter 5, "Trump, Scorsese, and the Frankfurt School," was a self-generated effort to apply a rarely recalled, never fully realized initiative in Critical Theory to make sense of the interface between popular culture and contemporary politics. A shortened version of it appeared in the *Los Angeles Review of Books*, April 5, 2020. The sixth chapter, "Go Figure: Fredric Jameson on Walter Benjamin," was a review essay solicited by Ethan Kleinberg for *History and Theory* 61: 1 (2022). Chapter 7, "*Leib, Körper* and the Body Politic," was written for a conference on somaesthetics organized by Richard Shusterman at Florida Atlantic University in 2021, and then published in Valentina Antoniol and Stefano Marino, eds., *Aesthetics of Existence or Somaesthetics?: Ethics, Politics, and the Art of Living in Foucault and Shusterman* (London: Bloomsbury, 2023). The eighth chapter, "Marx and Mendacity: Can There Be a Politics without Hypocrisy?," was prepared for a conference at the Universidad Diego Portales in Santiago, Chile, organized by Eduardo Sabrovsky in 2008 on "Marx a 160 Años del *Manifesto Communista*," and then published in *Analyse und Kritik: Zeitschrift für Sozialtheorie* 37: 1–2 (2015).

In addition to the cumulative guidance and support I've received over half a century of engagement with the Frankfurt School, these essays benefited from the critical advice of a number of interlocutors for whom special appreciation is merited. Among them are Paul Breines, Susan

Buck-Morss, Fabian Freyenhagen, Carl Gelderloos, Peter Gordon, Robert Hullot-Kentor, Anton Kaes, Rob Kaufmann, Hans-Peter Krüger, Philipp Lenhard, Michael Morgan, Elliot Neaman, Richard Shusterman, the late Paul Thomas and Meixi Zhuang. I appreciate as well the continued editorial support of Verso's Sebastian Budgen and Mark Martin, as well as the copy-editing of Steven Hiatt, and the indexing of Estalita Slivoskey.

And to reiterate expressions of heartfelt gratitude that never grow old (even if the one expressing it inexorably does), I want to thank my family for their unswerving love and support: my daughters, Shana and Rebecca, and their husbands, Ned and Grayson; my grandchildren, Frankie, Sammy, Ryeland and Sidney; my sister, Beth; and most of all, my ideal reader and no less ideal spouse, Catherine Gallagher, who always gets the first crack at everything I write and improves everything she reads.

Finally, I want to acknowledge my longstanding debt to the institution to whom I've dedicated this book: the Institut für Sozialforschung, which is celebrating its one-hundredth anniversary this year. I first entered its doors in January 1969, while I was researching my dissertation, and have returned on numerous occasions since. Although we have never had an official relationship, I have always been cognizant of the debt I owe it and have sought to tell its extraordinary story with the mixture of admiration and critical distance it deserves. May its second century be as productive and innovative as its first!

Index